THE
GERMAN ELEMENT
IN THE
NORTHEAST:

Pennsylvania, New York,
New Jersey & New England

By Gustav Koerner

Translated and edited by
Don Heinrich Tolzmann

D1127854

German-language edition
originally published
Cincinnati, 1880

Translation by Don Heinrich Tolzmann
Copyright © 2010
All Rights Reserved

Printed for
Clearfield Company by
Genealogical Publishing Company
Baltimore, Maryland 2010

ISBN 978-0-8063-5498-9

Made in the United States of America

Contents

Editor's Preface

In 1880, Gustav Koerner (1809-96), former Lieutenant-Governor of Illinois and confidant of Abraham Lincoln, published a comprehensive history of Germans in America: *Das deutsche Element in den Vereinigten Staaten von Nordamerika, 1818-48.* (1) In twenty-one chapters he provides an in-depth portrait of the German element throughout the country. Although his focus is on the first half of the nineteenth century up to the 1848 Revolution, Koerner does in fact often go beyond that date up to the time of the publication of his history, thereby providing coverage of the German element for the better part of the nineteenth century.

In the past, I have edited translations of chapters dealing with the Germans in Illinois and Missouri for works I have published on these topics. (2) I, therefore, decided to translate and edit those chapters dealing with the Germans of Pennsylvania, New York, New Jersey, and New England, and bring them together as a regionally focused volume entitled the *German Element in the Northeast.* Taken together, they document the German element in the nineteenth century, an extraordinarily interesting time period coming after the Colonial era and at the very onset of the period of mass migration from Europe. (3) As such, Koerner's writing sheds light on an important period in German-American history, and provides a wealth of historical and biographical information on the German element in the aforementioned states as well.

Don Heinrich Tolzmann

Editor's Introduction
The Author

Gustav Koerner (1809-96) was a *Dreissiger*, or Thirtyer, as members of the generation of German immigrants were called, who participated in the 1832/33 Revolution. (1) Born in Frankfurt am Main, he had studied at the University of Jena, where he became a member of the German student organization known as the *Burschenschaft*, which had branches across the German states. (2) The *Burschenschaftler* had visions of a united Germany under a republican form of government. After completing doctoral studies at the universities of Munich and Heidelberg, Koerner returned home to Frankfurt am Main, where he became involved in the uprising in 1833, causing him to flee to France. (3) Departing from LeHavre, he sailed to the U.S. and landed in New York, but moved on to St. Louis due to the glowing report of Missouri that had recently been published by Gottfried Duden. (4)

Disappointed with the fact that slavery existed in Missouri, Koerner moved across the Mississippi River to southern Illinois to the settlement of Belleville. This was widely known as the "Latin Settlement," as so many other well educated *Dreissiger* had settled there. (5) It was said that some of the farmers in the area read Latin classical texts while plowing the fields, and some poked fun at them as being more skilled at reading Latin than farming. Nevertheless, the Latin Settlement became a veritable German-American social, cultural, and political center that exerted its influence in Illinois, as well as in nearby Missouri. Koerner comments in his Foreword:

> After the author arrived in America in the summer of 1833, he selected Illinois as his place of residence and decided to practice law, which he had studied for four years at various universities in Germany, and which he had also practiced in his home town, Frankfurt am Main. After studying English, of which he already had some rudimentary knowledge, the next item on his agenda was studying the U.S. Constitution and commentaries about it, and then civil law, especially that of the

state of Illinois. By the age of twenty-three, he completed his studies of American law and commenced the practice of law in Illinois in summer 1835. (6)

Not surprisingly, Koerner quickly got involved in political affairs, and was elected to the Illinois state legislature in 1842, and in 1845 was appointed by the governor to a position on the appellate court and was confirmed in that position by the legislature in 1846. In 1852, he was elected lieutenant governor and was viewed as the leading German-American politician of the state. After joining the fledgling Republican Party, he campaigned for Lincoln, who visited with Koerner at his home in Belleville. (7) As a result of his support of Lincoln at the Republican convention in Chicago and the following campaign, Koerner was appointed U.S. ambassador to Spain. In the 1870s, he withdrew from active involvement in public affairs, and devoted himself to writing, completing his history of the German element, as well as a two volume autobiography. (8)

Julius Goebel, editor of *Deutsch-Amerikanische Geschichtsblätter* described Koerner's work a "valuable historical study" and the author as "a keen observer of men, a profound and sympathetic student of American institutions, politics, and life in general, and a man of calm judgment..." He felt that Koerner was "exceptionally well qualified to write the history of one of the great constituent parts of the composite American population during a period the great part of which he had followed as an eyewitness." (9)

The Book

Koerner emphasizes the goals and objectives of his history in a lengthy Foreword and Introduction that can be summarized as follows: He begins by comparing and contrasting his work to a history of German immigration to the state of New York by Friedrich Kapp. (10) He makes it quite clear that his work definitely is not a history of immigration, as he begins not in Europe, but in America and focuses on the Germans in America. He writes:

The author of the present work does not plan on writing a general history of German immigration. This would be adverse to his way of thinking, and be of no interest to him. I certainly make reference to immigration, but only as the foundation for a history of the German element in the U.S. The purpose of my work is to show if and to what extent the German element has influenced American society. (11)

He follows up by emphasizing: "I must reiterate that this is not a history of German immigration, but rather a history of the German element in the U.S., and one that focuses on a particular time period in the nineteenth century." (12) Koerner, therefore, is not interested in telling the story of German immigration and exploring its root causes in Europe. He wants to concentrate on the German element in the U.S. and explore how it has influenced American society, and he makes this crystal clear by comparison with Kapp's history.

Another point he wants to emphasize is that he views the component parts of the population as "elements" and that his particular focus is on the German element, a term that he uses to refer to German-speaking immigrants and their offspring. He notes in this regard:

The nations of the civilized world are few that do not consist of a mix of various peoples, some closely related, but also others that are not. These components of the population are frequently referred to as "elements." It has always been an interesting task to investigate the different influences these various elements have exerted on the life of a given nation, so as to ascertain and measure the extent of these influences. For those of us who live in America such a study has not only academic, but great practical implications as well. (13)

Here he makes it clear why he has written a history of the German element in the U.S. He obviously views the history of immigration as valuable; however a history of the German element in America would not only be something of academic interest, but would also be useful to demonstrate how the German element had influenced American society. Having experienced the anti-immigrant Know-Nothing Movement of the 1840s/50s, Koerner no doubt felt that German-American history would assist German-Americans as a means to demonstrate their significance for American society. He writes:

> A clear and correct picture of the role played by the German element in American society and the influence it has exerted and the ways it has been influenced by American society can only be advantageous for us. As this picture becomes clear, it will evidently form the foundation for an ongoing modus operandi of the German element in American society, and it is important that we do not deceive ourselves in being aware of this crucial fact. (14)

In this regard, it should be noted that Koerner states that his aim "is to do justice to the history of the German element." However, and this goes back to his legal training and background, he wants to do so in a judicious manner, stating the facts and not overemphasizing or overly praising the influences that he documents and records. Just as he compares his work to Kapp's German immigration history, so too does he distinguish his history from a history of Germans in America by Franz von Löher. Koerner critiques him as follows: "While on the one hand he is unjustly critical of Germans in America, on the other hand he overly praises them at times for contributions, some of which are either not theirs, or might not have been as great as he maintains." (15)

The two major points Koerner wants to emphasize at the outset are, first, that his work is not a history of German immigration to Pennsylvania, but a history of the German element of the state, and, second, that his aim is to explore the influence it has exerted in an objective and judicious manner.

Additionally, he has several other related points that he would like to emphasize. Most importantly, he would like to explain his views on the role of the German element in American society, and he does so in response to the question that was widely discussed in the 1830s-40s as to whether a German state might be founded in a western territory on the American frontier. Koerner makes it clear that he is adamantly opposed to such proposals, and that this would be adverse not only to Germans, but to Americans as well, and contribute to the anti-immigrant Know-Nothing Movement of the time. However, it should also be noted that Koerner himself was from the well-known German-American Latin Settlement in Belleville, Illinois and that throughout his work he does praise German settlements as they reflected the reality of German immigration history. He therefore supports the various kinds of German settlements, be they secular, religious, or communitarian, but opposes the notion of a German state as problematic. By means of his own example he demonstrated that members of German settlements could take an active part in American society, but stresses that a German state would be a move in the wrong direction that would isolate and separate the German element from the mainstream of American life. Here he indicates his agreement with Kapp, who wrote that:

> Therefore the goal of the German immigration lays not in separating itself off from the formative elements of the population, nor in fantastic dreams of forming a German state or utopia. It cannot prosper and thrive anywhere off track from mainstream America, but rather by working together with one's fellow citizens can obtain all the success and blessings that are possible here. A German nation within the American nation is impossible, but the richness of German life and the treasures of its cultural heritage can certainly be added onto the scale in terms of its contributions to America. Moreover, the German element's influence can only increase, and create for itself a greater degree of involvement in American life the less it presents itself as separatist. At the same time, it can hold on to all that is great and good that Germany has given to the world. (16)

Moreover, Koerner believes that the German cultural heritage can be preserved, and that it would be unnatural if it was not. Just as he opposes the extreme position of those advocating a German state on the American frontier, so too does he speak out in his history against advocates of total assimilation, who would deny their ethnic identity and heritage. He writes in this regard:

The love of German language and literature should of course be held sacred and transmitted to one's offspring. And, of course, the cherished German cultural heritage that we bear within us can never be lost. That would be ungrateful and foolish, since by preserving and defending this heritage, while at the same time declaring our loyalty to the land of our choice, we honor ourselves in the best way possible, as well as the people we are descended from and for whom our hearts beat with a never-ending love. (17)

This latter point relates to his views on Germany, which he separates from his love of the German cultural heritage. Here he praises the political freedoms of the U.S., noting that: "Once one has been here on freedom's ground with the American people, one will not wish to return to the old Fatherland, but will find one's own place as best one can, unfettered by memories of the past." Here he writes:

As noted, Kapp sees current conditions in Germany all too favorably. Germany is to be sure no longer the "cage" it once was, where free flight was impossible. And, yes, a colossal birdhouse has developed from this tiny cage, where one can now fly about modestly, so that one might almost believe that there are no boundaries to one's flight. But the soaring flight of an eagle will soon lead to a collision against the unavoidable bars that enclose the entire structure of its cage. (18)

His relation to German heritage therefore is cultural, relating to the ancestral homeland and to the background of Germans in America, rather than a political dimension relating to the new German Empire, which as a *Dreissiger* he still takes exception too, as did some of the Forty-Eighters. This is an important point to make, separating his German heritage off from any political associations to the Old Country, and making it an essential cultural component of his own identity, as well as that of Germans in America.

Contextually, Koerner does view the history of early nineteenth century immigrants as another chapter in the history of Germans in America, and as part of this ongoing continuum. He therefore begins his history with a discussion of the Pennsylvania Germans and highlights the ways in which Pennsylvania Germans and recent immigrants interrelate with one another. In stressing this sense of continuity of German-American history, he also emphasizes that more recent German immigration not only complements the early German immigration, but also builds on the foundations it laid. (19)

Although Koerner places his work within the framework of German-American history, he is most interested in concentrating on the German element of the early nineteenth century, especially those who came to America before 1848. A sub-text of his work is that like many of the *Dreissiger*, he felt that the contributions of his generation had been in a sense overshadowed by the more colorful, flamboyant, and vociferous Forty-Eighters. He diplomatically expresses this as follows:

> There are several reasons for closing this work off with the year 1848. To go further would have been a difficult and ambitious task. However, a major reason is that since the 1848 Revolution many individuals with writing abilities have found refuge in America, and there is absolutely no dearth of talent among them for those who want to take on the task of writing the history for the following years. (20)

He therefore assigns the task of writing German-American history after 1848 to the Fory-Eighters, while he takes on the task of telling the story of his own generation.

Finally, reference should be made to his approach to writing German-American history, which might best be described as "history as biography." He does not take a topical or chronological, but rather a biographical approach, focusing on individuals as his point of departure of discussing German influences. Here he notes that:

Although the following is not a history of German immigration and settlement, but rather a contribution to the history of German influence on America, it is not merely a chronological compilation of information relating to this topic. Rather it aims to present a series of biographies of those Germans, who in some way made contributions in this regard. These life histories at times naturally surpass the timeframe of the three decades covered here, especially as this relates to their previous life in Europe. However, I believe that this manner of presenting history will interest the reader, and will attain the goal I have in mind. (21)

The first part of this volume focuses on the German element in Pennsylvania, whereas the second covers the German element in New York, New Jersey. The third part of this work consists of the Editor's Conclusion, which contains statistical information regarding the size of the German element in the various states discussed here. The appendices of Koerner deal with the Germans in the colonial period, German immigration in the nineteenth century, as well as the Pittsburgh convention. They are followed by the original bibliography of primary and secondary source materials used by Koerner for the completion of his history. The notes provided by the editor provide references to more recent works dealing with the topics discussed by Koerner.

The German Element in the Northeast

I. **Pennsylvania**

Chapter One

The German Element of Pennsylvania

The Pennsylvania Germans – The German language and newspapers before 1818 – The German Society of Pennsylvania – Heinrich Bohlen – Other members of the Society – Social life – German farmers – Johann Georg Rapp
■■■

In the past, many have assumed that the descendants of Germans who immigrated to Pennsylvania in the eighteenth century were more or less assimilated, especially as a result of intermarriage with the English and Irish. (1) They continued to hold on to their Palatine dialect, which is mixed with English words and expressions, but only by means of their names, appearance and behavior, it was thought, could they be distinguished from the rest of the population. And, it was felt that they had basically become fully absorbed into the general population. However, I cannot go along with this characterization. It is generally well known that Americans, not only in Pennsylvania, but elsewhere as well, have learned much from the Pennsylvania Germans, especially as regards farming, fruit growing, cattle-breeding, not to mention their sound business practices and the value the place on diligence and hard work. So, in my view, the fact clearly stands forth that the Pennsylvania German has actually remained German to the core. (2)

Tenacity, perseverance, thrift, and stubbornness, and a certain naiveté combined with a knack for cleverness are but a few of the traits by which they are known, especially among those families not intermarried with other elements. In trade and commerce they stand on equal grounds with Yankees in terms of getting ahead, and could even give them a few pointers in this regard. A renewed sense of German identity emerged in the case of the American-born German population of Pennsylvania soon after the arrival of the German immigrants of the early nineteenth century. The Pennsylvania Germans often came into contact and associated with these recent arrivals, thereby improving their German, and taking a great interest in all things German. (3)

Many complain that Americans make fun of the Pennsylvania Germans on stage and that they are often the butt of jokes. This is only natural, but not as bad as it would appear at first glance. Do the Americans spare themselves at all? Isn't "Brother Johnathan" just as frequent a character as "John Bull" or "Dutch Fritz." And, how have the French dealt with the Alsatians, especially on the stage? And yet they have the highest regard for their reliable, stout-hearted, and persevering character. The highest positions (even if not the highest in the political realm) in banks, in administrative offices, in railway companies, even in the military and in management, were chiefly in the hands of the Alsatians, with whom the Pennsylvania Germans are closely related. And how much do the French now mourn this lost pearl, albeit with a degree of ostentation and affectation? And, in this regard, as has already been noted there has been a long series of governors and statesmen that derived from the Pennsylvania German element. (4)

The Pennsylvania German newspapers, in their uniquely humorous, often quite hilarious style, treated their fellow citizens of other backgrounds in like manner, with the New Englanders getting the worst of it. And, nothing can be said about the Pennsylvania Germans denying their heritage, especially those in the country. We recall that in the 1830s, Heinrich A. Mühlenberg, a descendant of the well-known family by the same name, which has given this country so many scholars, great generals, and articulate members of congress, and who at that time was a member of Congress, spoke the following words: "My German forefathers taught me the following saying: 'Do what is right and fear not even the Devil,' and I remain true to this position, even if it hurts my popularity or not." Mühlenberg, later on our ambassador to Austria, was held in high regard upon his return from Germany, and was nominated as the gubernatorial candidate of the Democratic Party in 1844. It is most likely that he would have been elected by an overwhelming majority had it not been for his untimely death shortly before the election, a loss that caused great sorrow among his supporters. (5)

Right at the beginning of the period with which we are concerned the German element of Pennsylvania found itself in what might best be called a crisis situation. (6) As noted earlier, the immigration from Germany had been nil for three decades. New York began to replace Philadelphia and Baltimore as the immigration port of entry in America. At the same time, trade and commerce were in bad shape due to the bankruptcy of many banks and the recent war with England, which business and industry in general to stagnate.

After a careful comparison of various sources, which all more or less agree, we believe we can safely estimate the number of the German-born and their American-born descendants at about 120,000 for the state of Pennsylvania. Already in the middle of the previous century, Franklin reported to the British Parliament that there were approximately 60,000, but added that this was only an estimate. Other sources place the number at 90,000, and even more. The well-known historian, Dr. Oswald Seidensticker, estimates the number at 75,000.

Of the many Pennsylvania German newspapers of earlier times, there were about twenty-five, mainly weekly publications, in 1818, as far as we have been able to ascertain. Dailies, even with the English-language press, were a rarity then, and their number in the 1820s was probably around six. All of these Pennsylvania German newspapers were more or less in the Pennsylvania German dialect, and where High German was cultivated, one can see at first glance that we are dealing with translations from English to German. The awkwardness of the language, the use of antiquated High German words together with the occasional use of dialect sentences made these older so-called High German newspapers very amusing items to read as compared to the truly authentic Pennsylvania German dialect papers. Most of these newspapers appeared in flourishing towns of Pennsylvania, such as Reading, Allentown, Lancaster, Doylestown, Easton, and Lebanon. (7)

At the same time, High German was maintained in the congregations of the Lutherans, the Reformed, the Moravians, and the Mennonites by means of the sermon and religious instruction. Ministers and teachers, in spite of all the hindrances to trade and commerce from 1776-1815, did manage to get to America and they helped preserve the use of High German in the churches they served. It should also be noted that the preservation and maintenance of the German language in America is really due to the work of the churches, a fact that is all too seldom taken into consideration. Even the Catholic Church, in spite of its inclination towards assimilating everyone it can, took care to preserve German, especially whenever Germans were found in great numbers. In the course of our research we met several Catholic priests and also many Protestant ministers and school teachers who have become quite popular in German circles because of their education, affability, and love of the old Fatherland. (8)

We should also mention that an active social life emerged well before 1830 in many towns and cities, especially Pittsburgh. And, further study might show that there were many well educated and successful Germans throughout Pennsylvania, who participated in social affairs. In Philadelphia, particularly in the first years of the nineteenth century and actually well before that, there were many prosperous and cultivated German businessmen also. Mention should also be made here of the German Society of Pennsylvania, whose history was written by the well known historian Oswald Seidensticker, who based it on the best of sources. We refer readers to it for further information, as we can here provide only a brief survey of its history.

The poverty of many German immigrants in the past century forced a great number of them to enter into service contracts with ship captains or companies, which required them to work for a given period of time to pay the expense of their travel to America. These were obligatory contracts of indenture insofar as the person involved was legally liable to fulfill the contract as well as any possible damages that might ensue. Such indentures were nothing new, and were common practice in the English colonies. In the case of minors, the parents or guardians could grant permission to their being bound into service, and they then would be in the service of their master who could hold them by law. (9)

The entire process was open to abuse in the colonies, especially in Pennsylvania, where immigrants could also bind themselves into service. On arrival of the ships, the work assignment would be agreed on to cover the cost of the passage to America. Parents were often separated from their parents and as a result many were no doubt taken advantage of, especially as they signed contracts which they could not even understand. Also, the laws of the land had done little to regulate overbooked ships, the neglect of passengers on board, and the oversight of ship captains and crews, who at times mistreated their passengers. The German princes, who had sold the services of their countrymen didn't care at all about providing the best of conditions for immigrants. Moreover, transportation was mainly in the hands of the Dutch, who for a long time had a bad reputation due to their overfilled ships, rough treatment of passengers, and the lack food and provisions for passengers. As a result of such conditions, horrible scenes had taken place at the harbors of Philadelphia and Baltimore. The older German press raised its voice powerfully, but in vain on behalf of its countrymen.

Such conditions cried out for help, and ultimately led to the founding of the German Society of Pennsylvania. On the second day of Christmas 1764 at 4PM, about sixty-five Germans met at the Lutheran schoolhouse on Cherry Street. Ludwig Weiss, a German legal scholar addressed the group, a constitution was then approved and officers elected. "The constitution, which the Society approved at this meeting, was approved as its basic guiding principles," and, according to Seidensticker, "have endured many changes as new circumstances created news tasks and these had to be brought into accord with the constitution. However, in spite of all additions and emendations that were found necessary from time to time, it remained essentially the same, as the oldest constitution readily demonstrates." (10)

The introduction of the constitutional document, which we unfortunately cannot reproduce in its entirety, is written in a style of antiquarian simplicity that, as Seidensticker reminds us, calls to mind the times in which it was written by our ancestors. It begins as follows:

In nomine Domini nostril Jesu Christi. Amen.

We, the German subjects of His Majesty, the King of Great Britain in
Pennsylvania, due to circumstances that are worthy of our sympathy on
behalf of our countrymen, who have arrived in the port of Philadelphia
most recently on ships from Europe, have thought of means of bringing
about some assistance to these immigrants and have by means of our
pronouncements and financial contributions come to the aid of many
newcomers to help them in their time of need.

This has brought us to the decision that we have joined together to
establish a society for the assistance and support of these poor immigrants
of the German nation and have formed its constitution, which this society
shall add to and expand as necessary. (11)

It should be noted that the manner of expression of this introduction, as well as
the entire nineteen paragraphs of this document cannot be distinguished from the
customary language then in use in Germany, and actually even surpasses the quality of
the chancellery style of the time. Also, it should be noted that these founders of the
German Society did not want to be British or American subjects, but rather German
subjects of His Majesty, the King of Great Britain.

One of the first accomplishments of the Society was the improvement of the
existing regulations regarding the transport of immigrants. By means of a law passed 18
May 1765 by the Pennsylvania state legislature, it was determined that more room be
provided for passengers and that every ship be provided with a physician and the
necessary medicine. The number of stoves and washing facilities was also prescribed, so
as to avoid problems with those in charge of provisions on board the ship. Ship inspectors
appointed by the state were now required to be accompanied by sworn translators to
inform passengers of the content of the laws that had been passed on their behalf. They
also assisted in monitoring the inspectors who often made dishonest deals with the ship
captains or companies. This initial law contained other relevant stipulations as well.

At the urging of the Society, the document of incorporation was obtained on 20 September 1781. This was signed by F.A. Mühlenberg as Speaker of the Pennsylvania state legislature. In the same document the original purpose of the society was expanded, so that the Society was permitted to make use of its funds not only to assist immigrants, but also for the maintenance and support of schools, for one or more libraries for the education of children and young people of German birth and descent, for schools and institutions serving these goals, as well as for school teachers.

As, has already been noted, German immigration came to a veritable halt as a result of the French Revolution, and the Society had no real field of activity in accordance with its original purpose of protecting immigrants and helping the poor. It is therefore understandable that in spite of its solid financial position that a degree of indifference set in, with few members now joining the organization. Since at that time, around 1818, most members consisted of American-born Germans, who were more fluent in English, it was decided to maintain records of meetings in the English language only. This last measure held true with occasional interruptions till 1859, even though, it should be noted that the German-born population of Philadelphia by mid-century was estimated at about 5,000. Aside from its assistance to the poor, only in 1847 did the Society again take an active interest again in immigration, and only then as a result of the formation of the German Immigration Society. It responded to this apparent competition by establishing an office for legal aid and assistance in providing referrals to possible places of employment.

In 1806 a hall was built and expanded with two additional wings in 1821, and the library increased as well. The further growth and development of the Society is beyond the scope of our history, but it now has about one thousand members, expends several thousand dollars annually to those in need, and in 1866 constructed a stately new building, whose library consists of some 18,000 volumes.

Johann Heinrich Keppele, a German businessman, served as president of the Society from 1764 to 1781. Between 1781 and 1818, the following served as presidents of the Society: Captain Ludwig Farmer, General Peter Mühlenberg and F. A. Mühlenberg, all veterans of the American Revolution. In the years 1791 to 1800 alone, the Society experienced a growth of 253 members. In the years 1818-48, the following served as presidents of the society: J. Wampole, 1818-33; Ludwig Krumbhaar, 1833-36; Samuel Keemle, 1836-42; and Friedrich Erringer, 1842-44. Among its officers we see such highly respected merchants and businessmen of Philadelphia as J.L. Lowber, J.R. Harmes, David Seeger, Heinrich Dühring, Tobias Bühler, Heinrich Tilpe, Gottfried Freitag, Karl Schaff and Heinrich Bohlen. The latter is of special interest, and it is regrettable that there is not more information available for a more lengthy biography of him. (12)

His father was Bohl-Bohlen, the founder of the famous business B. & J. Bohlen. It is improbable that Bohl-Bohlen is the same who found a special place in the heart of that seeker of love Rahel Levin. (13) Heinrich was born in October 1810 in Bremen. His parents lived in Philadelphia, but like other German businessmen spent part of their time in Germany, where Heinrich was educated. (14) He apparently attended a military school in Germany; but in any event had Lafayette's recommendation for a position as an adjutant on the staff of General Gerard, and in 1831 participated in the blockade of Antwerp. In 1833, we find him in Philadelphia, where he married the oldest daughter of J.J. Borie, a very well to do liquor and wine dealer of French descent, who later on became the minister of maritime affairs for a few weeks as a result of his friendship with General Grant.

Bohlen took charge of his father's company under the name of Henry Bohlen and Company, and managed it with great success, but his interest in military affairs never left him. He took an active interest in the formation of militia companies, and after a voluntary company was formed under the direction of E.L. Koseritz in Philadelphia in 1836, he decided to form a second company himself. (15) His wealth allowed him to fully outfit the company, including its fine musical corps. At the outbreak of war with Mexico he was irresistibly drawn to join the army. Due to friendship with an outstanding general by the name of Worth he became a member of his staff, participated in the battles of Cerro Gordo, Contreras, Chappultepec and Molinas del Rey, and entered the capital city of Mexico with General Scott. After peace was concluded, he returned home to his business.

His passion for military action remained so strong that at the time of the outbreak of the Crimean War, while he was visiting Europe with his family, he succeeded in obtaining a position in the French army and participated in battles as well as the occupation of Sebastopol. After returning to his family, which was still vacationing in Europe, he then heard news of the outbreak of the Civil War (April 1861) and sailed home, offering his service to the Union Army.

He quickly organized a German regiment in Philadelphia, the 75th Pennsylvania Vol. Regiment and covered all the necessary costs for recruitment and supplies out of his own pockets with his usual generosity. His regiment joined the army of the Potomac and he received the command of the 3rd Brigade in General Blenker's division. (16) In April 1862 he was appointed Brigadier General of the voluntary troops.

In the spring, General Fremont received orders regarding the campaign in the mountain region of Virginia, and Blenker's division was ordered by the army of the Potomac to move there. This caused it to enter a most difficult march, unfortunately poorly supplied with provisions, marching on winding roads through the grandiose mountains of the Shenandoah Valley of West Virginia. After uniting with Fremont's troops it came to the bloody battle of Cross Keys, 8 June 1862, where Fremont tried to cut off the retreat of the Confederates into the valley. Blenker, as well as Bohlen displayed bravery during this battle, which they saved from a total defeat.

Bohlen's division was next ordered back from the Potomac army and placed under the command of General Franz Sigel. (17) He then participated in a number of battles, beginning with the battle at Cedar Creek that preceded the second battle at Bull Run (28 August 1862) and in one of these battles at the Rappahannok (22 August 1862)

Bohlen, who had till this time survived all battles and skirmishes, was struck down by a bullet to the chest while leading his forces in an attack.

In that great conflict that embraced such great areas of the country and which was fought out on land and sea involving millions and costing hundreds of thousands of lives, there are countless names of the best of our nation. They sealed their love of country by means of their death. But the name of Bohlen should not be forgotten by his countrymen. Through his position, business connections and his bilingual fluency, it obviously would have been possible for him to have nothing at all to do with the German element, and this would have been natural, especially during his youth to have avoided such affiliations. But his true German nature brought him together with his countrymen, and he actively participated in German affairs and worked with anyone regardless of their station in life. From 1843-46, he served as vice-president of the German Society of Pennsylvania, and his loss in his home town of Philadelphia was deeply and sincerely felt wherever his name was known.

It should also be mentioned that many members of the German Society were elected at various times to the state legislature, as well as to other state and city offices. Information on other societies in Philadelphia is lacking for this work, but there no doubt were many, as there was an active German social life there.

In Philadelphia there were many well-to-do German businessmen, manufacturers, and tradesmen. Among them were the following: Wilhelm J. Horstmann, who had immigrated in 1824, established a large factory for lace making and golden lace together his son, which is now the largest in the U.S. Heinrich Dühring from Mecklenburg-Schwerin, Gottfried Freitag from Bremen, Friedrich Klein from Saxony, Ludwig Krumbhaar from Leipzig, Julius Leupold, Karl Vezin from Osnabrück (secretary of the German Society, 1818, 1821-23), Friedrich Lennig and Georg Rosengarten established large chemical factories, which greatly stimulated the regional industry of the area. Joseph Ripkow, a member of the German Society since 1827, established the textile factory of Monajunk, but was less successful than the aforementioned and faced financial problems in spite of hard work and careful management; the factories founded by him have been carried under the firm's new name of Patterson's Works.

With the growth and development of the German element in such early times there was no lack of social life, as has already been noted. Yes, there are travel reports of the time that refer to the exclusivity of the German upper classes, but when one thinks how little education there was among the mass of the immigrants in the 1820s and that there were many unusual personalities among the educated, then we can certainly excuse the exclusivity of some of the more well off classes, even if we can find no justification for their reserve in participating in social life. With the Moravian and Mennonite communities in rural areas, such as in Nazareth and Bethlehem, it is said that Germans were welcomed with great hospitality. (18)

In a country that offered so much seemingly endless room for agriculture and was still relatively unpopulated, one can readily understand that farming was not that advanced. The land was exploited with the certainty that one could always find fresh land at a cheap price in the West. It was not unusual for one to farm for only what needed for one's own family. One's other time was spent hunting, fishing and in other kinds of activities. The immigrants of earlier times probably had not established a true sense of homeland as yet, at least not strong enough to bind them to the place they first settled, especially if they thought there were more favorable prospects elsewhere. The stronger orientation of the Germans, on the other hand, and the tendency to hang on to their home place, which is a trait unique to Germans, was actually the reason that caused them to establish a firm and lasting home in not only in New York, New Jersey, but especially in Pennsylvania. They engaged in more rational kinds of farming and constructed more substantial barns and granaries than their American, especially Scotch-Irish neighbors.

Their example was imitated and there is no doubt that since the earliest times, German farmers have contributed to the advancement of agriculture in this country. In the area of farming and small industry there probably is hardly a German settlement that has accomplished more and provided a better example for others than the one established in

Pennsylvania by Johann Georg Rapp, a weaver and farmer. (19) He was born in 1770 in Maulbronn in Württemberg (some sources indicate 1757 as the year of his birth), but as the last twenty-seven years of Rapp's life fall within the time period of this work, we shall taken him into consideration here.

As a result of dissatisfaction with the religious orthodoxy of his time, Rapp came to reject all religious ceremonies and sacraments. He aimed to establish a community in accordance with his conception of the church of the first Christians. In his view, the only true way to salvation was by means of a direct relationship with God through Jesus Christ. He told the Prince Bernhard of Saxony-Weimar, who visited him in New Harmony, which was the second settlement that he established in Indiana, that: "According to the teachings of Christ we must view ourselves as an individual family, where all work to the best of their strengths and abilities for the common good of all." (20)

His settlements, however, showed how impractical and unworkable his entire plan for a community was: he never allowed his community to grow (it never surpassed more than 800 members), he forbade marriage, and expelled all those considered idle, disobedient or unfit. Such individuals received a settlement for money they had donated, or earned for work they had done. His ideas, when applied to a nation, become immediately untenable: Imagine a state with one individual, even if an enlightened prophet, who is empowered with the right of dividing people into groups, can assign their work, and then expels those considered undesirable! His concept of a community was only possible within the framework of a large state that offered the possibility of refuge for those who had left his community.

After Rapp and several friends purchased land in Pennsylvania in 1803 (6,000 acres), mostly woodland in the vicinity of Pittsburgh, he then brought over about three hundred members of his group to their new home in the following year. (21) These hardworking farmers transformed the wilderness into a prosperous settlement under the greatest of hardships. It consisted of the town of Harmony and several smaller villages.

They planted vineyards, cultivated fruit and raised livestock, especially sheep, developed machinery, and established weaving mills, dye-works, distilleries and other mills. They had stores with managers, enjoyed the greatest credit rating, as well as a reputation as a sound business enterprise, according to Franz von Löher. What motivated Rapp to sell this beautiful settlement for a pittance in1813 and move west to Indiana remains a mystery. Perhaps it was the result of a vision of his.

The land in Indiana (30,000 acres of woodland) was in a fertile region where corn thrived, but due to its location in the lowlands near the Wabash River was endangered by frequent flooding, and so was not considered the best of locations. (22)Apparently, Rapp had the idea of establishing a cotton plantation there, but did not consider that Indiana was in a free state, and that this kind of agriculture was not carried on very well by whites. Fortunately, he succeeded in selling New Harmony to another well known visionary, Dale Robert Owen, who definitely was not as methodical as Rapp, our sturdy Swabian farmer. He was greatly supported in all his undertakings by his son, Friedrich Rapp, who was a better administrator and also had a knack for working well together with Americans, so much so that he attained and held high offices in Indiana.

Rapp then moved back to Pennsylvania in 1825 to establish a new settlement known as Economy, located near the Ohio River. In a splendid location on a knoll, he created a veritable paradise that became an exemplary business enterprise. All work was done by means of the best machinery, and in addition to the aforementioned industries, cotton and silk weaving was also begun. How wealthy this smaller colony actually was at the time of Rapp's death (1847) can only be estimated. Some estimates runs as high as $20,000,000, but I am doubtful of this figure, and consider it an overestimation.

Rapp was generally not well regarded by Germans, who viewed him negatively, not only as clever, but also as a deceptive. However, there was no basis for such opinions. And, all those who visited him and saw him at work, had only the highest regard for him. This included a variety of well known travelers, including the American scholar Schoolcraft, the Scottish traveler Melish, the Englishman Cumming, as well as the Prince of Weimar, the latter of whom was repelled by Rapp's religious views and approached Rapp with a good bit of apprehension. (23)

Rapp might best be compared to another highly successful German immigrant: John Jacob Astor. (24) Both were farm boys, born not far from one another, who became well known for their hard work and have earned our respect. Talent and genius are but accidental gifts, but as Lessing comments: "Diligence is the only human attribute that one can truly celebrate." And it is this untiring diligence that is demands not only daily, but hourly sacrifices in the battle against the inborn human inclination to laziness. In the case of Astor and Rapp, it was their diligence that assured them the greatest possible success, and also contributed to their attaining great honor for the German name in this country.

Chapter Two
The German Press and Book Trade

The German-American press – **Johann Georg Wesselhöft** – *Alte und Neue Welt* – **Wilhelm L. J. Kiderlen** – **The German book trade** – **Friedrich Kapp's Observations on the German book trade** – **Later newspapers in Philadelphia and Pennsylvania.**
■■■i

Mention has already been made of the German press in Pennsylvania. In the early nineteenth century, there were only two German papers appearing before 1830 in Philadelphia and there were only a few newspapers of importance in the rural areas at that time. The major papers were: *Der Deutsche Courier*, published by Johann Georg Ritter, and *Der Wöchentliche Philadelphia Telegraph*, published by Herz, Ziegler and Billmeyer. (1) The American press itself was also only in its infancy at the time and daily papers could only be found in the larger cities of the East. German printing presses had existed in Pennsylvania for almost a century. In Philadelphia we find the press of Johann Georg Ritter, who also had a bookstore connected with his press. Its main stock in trade consisted of Bibles, religious works, sermon and school books, but one could occasionally find his announcements in the press for recently arrived books, including medical, technical and even the best of the German classics. (2)

However, it was not until the arrival of Johann Georg Wesselhöft in Philadelphia that the German press and book trade in America experienced a real upswing. (3) Wesselhöft came from a large family in northern Germany and Thuringia that gave rise to many important persons. In Meyendorf in the district of Hagen in Hannover, not far from Bremen, his father had a bakery, whose business had suffered greatly during the Napoleonic wars, so that Johann Georg, who was born 30 June 1805, had a difficult time as a youth. His father was an honorable man with the best intentions, but had a temper and made life miserable at home. As a boy Johann Georg had to help out in the bakery and the education he received from the local minister and elementary school was sporadic at best, but later on he did receive private instructions from a teacher. At the same time, the inquisitive youth made use of the family's substantial book collection, and memorized poems by Gellert, Bürger, and Schiller, and was given to reciting them with great pleasure at home. He was always known for his sense of fair play, which he ascribed to his reading of Gellert's poems, odes and letters, as well as his parents, as there was no lack of cultural life at home. Frequent visits from family friends and relatives, occasional trips, evening lectures, and musical programs were some of the high points of his otherwise difficult youth.

Wesselhöft's wish was to become a minister, and from all I have heard and been able to learn, he would have fulfilled this calling honorably and been quite successful in it as well. However, his father lacked the necessary means for such an education, so it was decided to send him to his uncles Frommann and Wesselhöft in Jena, where they operated the well known Frommann Bookstore and Printing Company, so that he could learn the book trade. So it came that he spent five years there (1819-1824) as an apprentice with his relatives. They treated him very well, but the apprenticeship was demanding and he worked exceptionally hard at it, something he did with regard to work throughout his entire career, and this was probably some kind of infirmity, which deprived him of truly enjoying life. In general it must be said that the youth of that time had demanding apprenticeships involving much hard work and little consideration was given the apprentices themselves.

Although he had no regular instruction in Jena, he managed to learn a great deal nevertheless. Frommann published scholarly works in German and other languages, and Wesselhöft set the type for them, learning much in the process of his work. Moreover, it was easy to meet educated people in this university town. Three of his cousins, Eduard, Wilhelm and Robert Wesselhöft studied there and became his friends. Frommann's home was also a very social one, and enjoyed many visits from scholars and authors. Goethe visited there as did Mina Herzlieb, the well known love of his later years. Moreover, she was even an adopted daughter of the family. Wesselhöft therefore met the old master himself, as well as Professors Gries, Oken, Luden, Fries, and also Johanna Schopenhauer and other notables of the time. (4) According to this autobiography, he often was "a silent listener of intellectual discussions of these highly educated men and women." And, the beautiful region itself also exerted a decidedly positive influence on him, stimulating his poetically inclined nature.

By 1824, he had completed his apprenticeship, which culminated with a very fine celebration. Thereafter, he reached to the wanderer's staff in good German tradition to complete his education. We cannot accompany him on all his subsequent journeys, but confine ourselves to the fact that he eventually gained employment at the Andraei Bookstore located in Frankfurt am Main, where he worked for three years, and later on worked in London and Brussels at various presses and in Paris as well. All in all he succeeded in acquiring a solid grounding in all aspects of the book trade. After extended travels in Switzerland and southern Germany, he then became manager of the Hänel Printing and Typography Company in Magdeburg. Here he visited his cousin Robert, who had been imprisoned due to his involvement in revolutionary activities. The work, however, proved too demanding for his health and also was not that rewarding. So after seventeen months, he quit the position and moved to Hannover to establish his own company, but found the situation ill-suited to the formation of new businesses. In spite of his best efforts his company soon failed.

He devoted himself at all times diligently to his work, but was at the same time driven by a thirst for knowledge to seek out and become acquainted with anything of interest or note in the places he lived. His diaries convey an intimate knowledge of these various localities, including art collections, theaters, and descriptions of his surroundings. He had an eye and appreciation for scenic landscapes, for example. He also had the ability to get to know people quickly and make lifelong friendships. Among them, we should definitely mention Heinrich Zschokke, who he came to know by means of friendship with his son, whom he often visited and corresponded with till his death (1848). (5)

Wesselhöft, who was an independent thinker at heart, like the rest of his family, decided to immigrate to America for several reasons: Starting a business in Germany had proven to be impossible and a reactionary atmosphere had set in after 1832. At the same time, good news was circulating about America, especially by means of the well-known book by Gottfried Duden. (6) Moreover, his friend and cousin, Dr. Wilhelm Wesselhöft had settled in Pennsylvania, where he sought refuge from the threat of having to face the wrath of a political investigatory commission in Mainz. Also, his parents had passed away while he lived in Frankfurt am Main. He had just gotten married to Johanna Monses, the daughter of a sailor. She was a very lovely, understanding, and courageous young woman, with whom he had been engaged with for several years, and together they came to the decision that it would be best to immigrate to America as soon as possible. On their journey they were accompanied by his brother and the well known Major Fahenrtheil, previously the second commandant at Erfurt, who had been imprisoned in Magdeburg due to involvement in revolutionary activities, and had escaped just in time to join Wesselhöft on the voyage to America. (7)

After a somewhat stormy trip lasting fifty-two days, he landed in New York on 31 October 1832, and traveled from there to Dr. Wilhelm Wesselhöft in Pennsylvania. The family moved to the vicinity of Nazareth, where his first son, Wilhelm, was born. Before settling down permanently, he wanted to get to know the country better. He visited Philadelphia, Baltimore, New York, and Boston, where he met Karl Follen, Dr. Beck, Frances Lieber, the latter of whom was then a professor of modern languages at Cambridge. (8) He also got to know the noteworthy professor of classical languages, Felton, and the author George Ticknor. Here he also met Franz Joseph Grund, who by this time was playing an important role in public affairs; Wesselhöft actually typeset Grund's work on astronomy that was published in Boston. (9)

Finally, he decided on settling down in Philadelphia (1833), because, as he wrote in his autobiography, the city formed "the center of German life in America, from whence he and other similarly minded persons could work to rejuvenate the cultural life of the German population of America." (10) He purchased Ritter's press, adding a bookstore to it, which he steadily increased in response to the interests of his customers. A great part of his customer base must have belonged to the educated ranks of the community. Already as early as 1834 we find his advertisements in the German press of

Philadelphia for a variety of excellent books, such as technical works, grammars, dictionaries and works dealing with homeopathy. We also find books, such as Rotteck's world history, Franklin's life and works, and the works of Jean Paul, Schiller, Goethe, Körner, Herder, Lessing, Jung Stilling, Zschokke, as well as Luden's German history, Bredow's general world history, etc.

In addition to his press and bookstore, Wesselhöft added an address information service. Most importantly, he also commenced publication on 1 January 1834 of the newspaper, the *Alte und Neue Welt*, which played such an important role in the history of the Germans in America. It continued publication till 1843, and was edited by E. L. Walz, Samuel Ludvigh, and Scheele de Viere, the latter of whom also published and wrote part of the content of the paper. (11) We shall return to this paper later on when we discuss the German press of the time. From now on, Wesselhöft devoted the best years of his life to the publication of his newspaper and the expansion of his bookstore business.

Branches of his bookstore opened up in the 1830s in New York (Wilhelm Radde), and later on in Cincinnati, Baltimore, and New Orleans. (12) A great deal of his time was spent traveling in the East, as well as to German settlements in the West and South. (13) He acquired an extensive knowledge of these settlements as a result of his frequent trips, which adds to our interest in his firsthand accounts of them. But he had other areas of interest as well. German beneficial, literary, and social organizations found their warmest possible supporter in him. And, he took great interest in plans for establishing German settlements in the West. In particular, he was interested in the German Settlement Society of Philadelphia, which established the German colony at Hermann, Missouri, and the Society counts him as one of its co-founders. (14) He was also dedicated to working for unity among the Germans in America, admonishing them to preserve the German language, and attain political influence as well. It cannot be denied that he often followed his heart rather than his head in dealing with people, and that he often set goals that were unattainable, especially during his first years in America.

Differences of opinion arose regarding the question as to the relationship of the German element to the rest of the population. In New York as well as in the West questions arose in the press and elsewhere as to the validity of the idea of establishing German settlements, and whether or not the idea was practical and feasible.(15) Philadelphia on the other hand remained the hotbed of these and other German ideals for many years. Wesselhöft was not entirely free of prejudice as it related to this particular question: He overestimated the nature of German character, while underestimating that of the Americans, probably because he knew so few of them in his early years here. However, he never aroused offense with anyone due to his mild-mannered nature, his moderation in taking a position, and his overall judiciousness, even though he nonetheless was resolute and determined in what he believed to be right. On the other hand, there was no lack of those who supported the idea of total assimilation, even going so far as to deny their ethnic ancestry. Some opposed Wesselhöft for no other reason than that they were jealous of his influence and others because they had a limited amount of education in Europe, and wanted to blend into the rest of American society. Men like Wesselhöft, therefore, provided a valuable counterweight and exerted a decidedly positive influence. Later, he modified his views somewhat on the question of German settlements, although he remained a stout-hearted German at heart to the very end.

He was well acquainted with the influential people of Philadelphia, such as the Keims, the Mühlenbergs, and was introduced to Van Buren, and met with him on several occasions and even corresponded with him. He also presented him with the plan for establishing a German consulate to represent all the German states, which would be charged with regulating German immigration, as well as informing immigrants about the U.S. The President approved the plan, but indicated that such a plan required Congressional approval. Nothing further ever came of the plan, which most likely was not even submitted to Congress, and it is moreover doubtful that the German states would ever have approved of it anyway.

In 1838, his nephew Dr. Wesselhöft, left Allentown, Pennsylvania, where he had been a professor of homeopathy and moved to Boston, where he was later joined by his other brother Robert, who had been released from prison in 1840 as a result of amnesty for his involvement in revolutionary activities. Robert later went on to establish the well known institute for the water cure at Brattleboro, Vermont.

The financial crisis that spread across the country in 1838, and lasted till 1844, had quite a negative impact on Philadelphia. Wesselhöft's health continually deteriorated, but he gave his undivided attention nevertheless to his business. However, he finally had to close it, as did many others at the time, due to the economic crisis. A brother of his had been in touch with a Mr. Franksen, who had a bookstore in St.Louis, Missouri and a married sister of his lived in nearby Hermann as did his daughter. (16) So as a result of these connections, he decided to move to St. Louis, where he became manager of Franksen's bookstore, which had opened in 1843, and his son, Wilhelm, as his assistant, even though he was only twelve years old. The bookstore also sold writing supplies and materials and remained in business till 1853.

Ill health and the disinterest of his son, who wanted to move to the country, caused the business to be closed, although it was doing quite well at the time. In St. Louis we also find that Wesselhöft strongly supported German cultural endeavors. He was the first president of the Polyhymnic Society, founded in 1845, whose musical director was W. Robyn, and was also the founder of the German Society for the Support of Immigrants. By retiring from business affairs, he hoped that his health would improve, and he was filled with the desire to visit his old Fatherland, which he loved so much. He therefore visited Germany in fall 1854. In spite of ill health along the way, he succeeded in visiting not only his friends and relatives in northern and southern Germany, but also made several new acquaintances and spent several weeks in Switzerland, where he was welcomed with open arms by the widow and sons of the author Heinrich Zschokke.

Wesselhöft returned to the U.S. in fall 1856, and spent the remaining two years of his life in Hermann with his sister and with his daughter Johanna in Mascoutah near Belleville, Illinois. His health continually declined and he finally passed away on 24 January 1859. He was buried in the cemetery at Hermann, Missouri, whose founding he had enthusiastically supported, and whose growth and development meant so much to him, and where many of his relatives and best friends had settled, and that had now become a town surrounded with vineyards and gardens.

His son Wilhelm, a well educated man, described his father's last days and sent me the following moving report about his father: "The entire population of Hermann participated in his funeral, but no monument adorns his grave. His memory lives on still, but only in the hearts of his children and the memories of his surviving relatives and friends. The great mass of Germans in America no longer knows the name of the man, whose entire life was dedicated to the advancement of the German element, but, as is said: 'He who has contributed to the best of his time, lives on forever.'" We can only endorse these words of his son, but believe that the memory of his father lives on to a much greater extent than he thinks. Historians of German immigration for this time period will of necessity come into contact with Wesselhöft, and no doubt will follow his life history with the greatest of interest and affection. (17)

The appearance of the *Alte und Neue Welt* on 4 January 1834 can be looked on as the beginning of a new era for Germans in America. The paper, which appeared in Royal Format and in its second year in larger Royal Format, was printed on good quality white paper with tastefully designed type, and contained more reading material in its very first issue than daily newspapers did in Germany, with the possible exception of the *Augsburger Allgemeine Zeitung*. (18)

As a rule, the first page contained such articles that now belong to the literary section of a paper, and consisted of novellas by recent German or French authors, biographical notices, essays on natural or cultural history, poems, among them many by German-American authors, the quality of whose work might be excused due to their noble poetic intentions. The selection was not always, but usually well done. The second page contained reports about European affairs, as complete as could be had at the time, and summaries of news from the larger English-language newspapers of the East, most of which had European correspondents. For several years the *Alte und Neue Welt* even had its own correspondent in Frankfurt am Main, whose articles, especially those dealing with European politics, were very good, leaving nothing important uncovered, and offering in-depth discussion of topics in a very concise manner. The same could be said of the paper's reports and discussions of American politics, as well as its analysis of the most important government documents and communications, such as messages from the presidents, the governor of Pennsylvania, excerpts of Congressional debates and speeches of other politicians. It aimed particularly, as did other German-American papers, at making American history, especially its political history, understandable to recently arrived immigrants. Page three of the paper contained general news from all parts of the country, focusing especially on events in Philadelphia and the surrounding area. And, the last page brought news from correspondents in this country, as well as several columns of advertisements.

At first, Wesselhöft and the early editors of the paper did not feel qualified to editorialize on American politics, and proceeded carefully in making judgments in this regard. But early on, it leaned towards the Democratic Party, rather than the Whig Party. From 1838 on, it came out more strongly for the Democrats, but without ever becoming an organ of the party. Of course, it sought a wide circulation for financial reasons, but its main goal was to strengthen the German element, and so it avoided contributing to any kind of political division. As Wilhelm Weber, editor of the St. Louis paper *Anzeiger des Westens*, observed, by 1836 the *Alte und Neue Welt* provided the most important news of the time together with a good selection of German literature. According to him, "It supports everything German, but in a judicious manner, and might well be viewed as the patron saint of German endeavors in America." (19) In its attempt to support "everything German," however, it at times went a bit too far. It at first enthusiastically supported the idea of creating German states in America, and then faced the strong opposition of the *Anzeiger des Westens* and the *New Yorker Staats-Zeitung*, the latter of which was quite vociferous in its opposition to the idea.

In its endeavor to fill the German element with pride and to increase its influence by engendering a greater sense of unity, it some times did not deal fairly with other ethnic elements, emphasizing more their negative than positive aspects. Yes, it was perhaps correct in pointing out and critiquing the fact that there are educated classes of the German element in urban areas like Philadelphia, especially among the merchants, that faced and succumbed to the usual societal temptations, and often identified with their American counterparts and denied their nationality. However, the paper often presented and advanced a view of German identify that was the exact opposite, which was as regrettable as it was too one-sided.

However, the editorial policy of the paper was generally moderate. It made no airs at being ingenious, but always took a respectable position, and was open-minded, especially in religious issues. Its involvement in religious debates emanated primarily from one of its editors, Samuel Ludvigh, the German-Hungarian known as "Torch-Ludwig." It was always above making use of coarse language as did some other papers, and on the whole its vocabulary was well chosen. Correspondence from well informed individuals in the East and West managed to stir things up a bit at times, however. It did devote more space than readers wanted to homeopathy and the water cure treatment, which were topics of great interest the publisher.

All in all, it was exactly the right kind of publication for the time, especially with regard to its judicious approach at passing judgment on its opponents, its moderation in politics, and its overall editorial stance. It communicated very well to the entire educational spectrum of its readership, which contributed to its large circulation across the country, which is something that distinguished it from other papers of the time. It was a most welcome weekly guest in cities of the East and South, as well as in settlements of the West and the influence it exerted on the German element throughout the country cannot be underestimated. For the history of the Germans in the years 1834-48 it remains a rich and indispensable source.

As noted earlier, a bookstore was soon added to the newspaper. What Friedrich Kapp wrote in an article that appeared in the January 1878 number of the *Deutsche Rundschau* about German-American reading habits was interesting and written in a lively and analytic manner, but only partly true for the period before 1830. (20) Moreover, it makes no reference to the period from 1830 to 1848. He refers to an obviously humorous communication from Wilhelm Radde dated 1877, and we can forgive Mr. Radde if he has forgotten what happened more than forty years ago. Perhaps he was only able to sell books in Pennsylvania (Reading) like the *Heilige Genovefa*, the *Eulenspiegel* and the *Vier Haimonskinder*. Also, his edition of selected German classics, which he put together in the 1830s, was unsuccessful, but such selections of German classics are questionable anyway, as those interested in certain authors would most likely prefer complete editions. For the same reason, a similar project failed in 1834 when S. Wagner brought out a German literature series at Lancaster, Pennsylvania. The first issue contained the first five parts of the Italian letters of Goethe. How many collectors in Germany would have taken interest in 1834 in such a series, especially if it came out of some small town in the country? It is also worth noting that almost no German family with some education ever immigrated without taking a small book collection along, mainly consisting of the major works of the German classics.

In the West one could find libraries of immigrants already as early as the 1830s, which consisted of several hundred volumes. Reference has already been made to the kinds of works by German authors that could be found in bookstores in Philadelphia in 1834. We must add the following works to demonstrate that German-Americans actually read more than the life of Johannes Bückler, known as *Schinderhannes* or *Des bairischen Hiesels*, as one was led to believe by Kapp's erroneous article mentioned earlier. We can mention the following, for example: Heine's *Pariser Reisebilder* and his *Salon*; Börne's *Pariser Briefe*; Thümmel's complete works; Schiller's correspondence with Goethe; Goethe's correspondence with a child; all of which were valuable books in the original edition, as there was no reprint editions available then. Also: *Spaziergänge eines Wiener Poeten*; Brockhaus' *Konverstionslexikon*; Grimms' tales; the German edition of Shakespeare translated by Schlegel and Tieck; and the works of Schopenhauer, Tieck, August and Friedrich Schlegel, Wilhelm Müller, Seume, Voss, and Oehlenschläger; Oken's natural history, etc.

In later years (1841), I was surprised to see not only these works in the bookstores
of Philadelphia, but also many illustrated works, some of them quite expensive, as well as
large collections of splendid lithographs from Munich, mostly depicting masterpieces
from the Royal Museum there. There was also no lack of copper engravings. Wesselhöft
himself (1841) had twenty original paintings for sale, among them works by Hannibal
Carrachi, Palamedes, Gerhard Dow, Van der Velde, Berghem Wouverman, Adrian von
Ostade, Peters, Tischbein and Brower.

The book trade must have been profitable, since a second bookstore was opened
by Kiderlen and Stollmeyer in 1836. They were lacking in neither experience nor
practical knowledge, and the former was especially a gifted individual. Wilhelm L. J.
Kiderlen was born in Ulm in 1813, attended school there, and then went on to become
fully trained in the book trade. (21) In Switzerland, he met Konrad Friedrich Stollmeyer,
who also was from Ulm, and together they decided to immigrate to America. They
founded a bookstore in Philadelphia that lasted for five years. Kiderlen actively
participated in German affairs, and was a co-founder of the German Settlement Society,
and later on devoted himself exclusively to writing, and published a geography and
history of the U.S. (1838).

The division of political parties into the Democrats and Whigs, the latter of which
was also called the Bank party due to its support of the U.S. Bank, took on full force in
the presidential election of 1836. Kiderlen decided to go with the Whigs, but the great
majority of Germans sided with the Democratic Party, and this led to great animosity
against him. In addition, his inclination to wit and sarcasm, his biting polemics in the
press, which was often directed at individuals, only served to increase the number of his
enemies accordingly. When the Whig Party succeeded in attaining power through the
election of Harrison in 1840, the successor of the soon deceased president, John Tyler,
appointed Kiderlen as American Consul to Stuttgart. But the appointment raised such
indignation with the German element of Philadelphia, that Tyler was forced to withdraw
his nomination. It is questionable that this was really the appropriate time for the German

element to demonstrate its political clout, especially as there was nothing at all to complain about with regard to the honorable nature of Kiderlen's character.

From 1846-48, Kiderlen edited the *Stadtpost* in the spirit of the Whig Party, advocating protective tariffs and supporting homeland industry. In editing this paper he gave free reign to his sharp polemics, and won a consular appointment to Zurich when Taylor and Fillmore were elected to office. After his return from there, he moved to Cincinnati where he married a well-to-do American lady and edited *Der Deutsche Republikaner*. (22) He returned to Philadelphia several years later and then became consul there for the states of Württemberg and Bavaria, a post he held till the unification of Germany. Kiderlen's colleague K.F. Stollmeyer, who is now the owner of an asphalt supply company and a coconut plantation in Trinidad, is quite well off today. In Philadelphia, he published a number of works at his own cost, among them an English translation of Rotteck's world history and an almanac for 1841 that was directed against slavery.

In 1844, the bookstore of Wesselhöft was taken over by L.L. Rademacher. In 1846, E. Schäfer opened a new bookstore that eventually became the Schäfer and Koradi Company. In the early 1840s, Friedrich Wilhelm Thomas, who passed away in 1878, opened a bookstore in Philadelphia. He became well known also for publishing the German classics, beginning in 1845. These were not selections, but rather complete edition of an author's works. Every year, his sales increased together with the ever increasing German immigration, and his company developed into a major publishing house. Here it should be noted that during the years 1820-30, German immigration stood at 20,000, but increased to 150,000 for the years 1831-40, and then to 435,000 for the years 1840-50.

Perhaps it is of interest to comment here with regard to misconceptions in Germany about the reading interests of German-Americans that the sale of the jubilee edition of Humboldt's *Kosmos*, which was published in a beautiful edition by Thomas in

1869, sold more copies in America, if we can trust newspaper reports, than the entire sale of the German edition published by Cotta did.

The German press in Philadelphia and Pennsylvania had a diverse history on the whole for the period we are talking about here. The so-called Pennsylvania German papers of earlier years, of which the *Readinger Adler*, the oldest of all existing German-American newspapers, is the best written and most substantial, had correspondents that included members of congress and the state legislature. Other papers included the following: the *Harrisburger Morgenröthe, Pennsylvanischer Beobachter. LEbanoner Morgenstern, Unabhängiger Republikaner* (Allentown), *Stimme des Volks* (Orwigsburg), *Bauernfreund* (Summytown, *Berks County Adler, Lebanon Demokrat, Freiheitswächter* (Norristown), *Vaterlandswächter* (Harrisburgh), and the *Bucks County Banner und Volksfreund*. They all flourished more or less to the extent that they supported the political parties of the time, and rose and fell accordingly.

In 1834, Wihelm Schmöle, who we mentioned earlier, purchased the *Susquehanna Democrat*, which was published in the beautiful Wyoming Valley and united it with a German newspaper, the *Allgemeine Staatszeitung*. (23) This was written in a German that did not go over the heads of its rural readership. Politically, it was successful, and supported Democratic candidates. For example, one of them was elected from the congressional district, to which Wilkes-Barre belonged, thereby defeating a candidate of the Whig and Free Mason party. It should be noted that it was Schmöle, who first proposed and discussed the idea in his paper of a national convention with German representatives from across the country to discuss topics of common interest to Germans in America.

Mention has already been made of the *Telegraph* and the *Courier*, which were both published in Philadelphia. At the same time the *Alte und Neue Welt* was being published, there were also a number of other papers that should be mentioned. Kiderlein and Stollmeyer published *Das Literarische Unterhaltungsblatt*; the *Demoratische Union*, later the *Philadelphia Demokrat*, which was founded in 1837 and acquired by L.A.

Wollenweber in 1838, appeared three times a week, but then daily from 1842 onwards (24); in 1836; A. Sage commenced publication of *Der Beobachter und tägliche Neuigkeitsbote am Delaware*, which was edited by Richtscheidt; the *Deutsche Nationalzeitung* was published from 1837 to 1839 by Stollmeyer; and the *Abendpost*, published by Botticher, appeared as daily beginning in 1839.

In 1840, Thomas published a monthly musical journal entitled *Popular Arts in Germany* with English and German text accompanied by piano accompaniments; I only subscribed to it for six months as a music store then opened, where I could acquire it. In 1842, Thomas founded a German daily newspaper *Allgemeiner Anzeiger der Deutschen*, which however closed down the next year. (25) Another publication of his was a journal entitled *Minerva*, which was directed against the anti-immigrant ovement which had recently reared its head again. It staunchly fought for the rights of immigrants who had recently become citizens of the U.S. The great Democratic victory in the Presidential election of 1844 brought a lamentable, but praiseworthy end to the publication, which had now fulfilled its mission. In 1848, Thomas commenced publication of the *Freie Presse*, which together with the *Demokrat*, were the main newspapers of the Germans in the city of brotherly love. It makes no sense to further discuss here the other attempts at publishing German newspapers in Philadelphia, as they were mostly of short duration.

In Pittsburgh a German weekly, the *Stern des Westens*, a political paper that began publication in 1826, supported the candidacy of Andrew Jackson against John Quincy Adams, but after Jackson's victory then closed down. In 1833, the *Beobachter*, which later absorbed the *Adler des Westens*, was published by Schmidt and Backofen in 1835. After its demise in 1840, Backofen then published the *Stadt und Landbote*, and later on the *Pittsburg Courier*. In 1836, the *Freiheitsfreund* was moved from nearby Chambersburg to Pittsburgh. This journal first appeared in the former city in 1834 and was edited by Victor Scriba for a long time. Scriba was a very capable editor and was of great service to the German element. (26) All three of the German papers of Pittsburgh tried with more and less success to present a good quality German, but often fought quite bitterly when it came to political matters. Also, in 1838, Backofen established a quite respectable bookstore.

The various German congregations all had their own churches and schools, as well as their own religious journals as well. While Pittsburg only had 7,000 people in 1820, it had grown to almost 50,000 by 1850. At that time, the German population was probably about one-fourth of the total population and here were many educated Germans among them. In 1807, the English travel author F. Cumming found a music society there, whose president was Friedrich Amelung of Osnabrück. Another German by the name of Gabler was described as an outstanding violinist.

C. Volz, who came there in 1820, had a large business there and an open door for all educated Germans who traveled through the Ohio Valley, according to Emil Klauprecht. (27) The German poet Lenau, for example, was received with great hospitality by Volz on his way to Ohio. Lenau had acquired land badly situated in a lowland region cut off from all traffic, so that he naturally left after a very short stay there, disappointed and sick of the country he had idealized and dreamt of. Volz's son later was twice elected as mayor of Pittsburgh.

At the same time, we find Major Karl von Bonnhorst, formerly of the Prussian army, and Mr. Passevant, a merchant from Frankfurt. The latter moved to the country in the vicinity of Rapp's colony and laid out a city there, naming it Zelinopolis in honor of his wife. Passevant belonged to one of the most respected families of Frankfurt and was a very educated man, only a bit too idealistic. One of his sons became a minister, who founded a hospital and orphanage for girls in Pittsburgh, as well as an orphanage for boys in Zelinopolis. Von Bonnhorst was likewise highly educated and a great connoisseur of music, even composing works of music himself and a splendid violinist as well. He was also very hospitable and social and served as justice of the peace, dying in 1838. (28)

These older settlers in Pittsburgh welcomed a considerable amount of newcomers in the 1830s, of which we can only mention here the names of Pastor Kämmerer, Dr.

Sachs, Eduard Hendrich, Braun and J.G. Backofen and Victor Scriba, the latter two of which have already been mentioned.

Discussion arose among the Germans of Pittsburgh as to how the German element could more effectively express and assert its influence. This came about as a result of the suggestion that had been made by Dr. Schmöle in the press that a national convention of German delegates from across the country be held to discuss questions of common interest. The topic was enthusiastically discussed in spring 1837 by many German-American newspapers, especially by the *Cincinnati Volksblatt*, the *Allgemeine Zeitung* of New York, the *Alte und Neue Welt* in Philadelphia, and the *Anzeiger des Westens* in St. Louis.

The following topics were suggested as agenda items for such meeting: First, the U.S. Congress should be requested to lower the price of public lands for settlers in the West, and, second, the Congress should also curtail the time necessary to attain citizenship. To accomplish these goals, it was suggested that German societies across the country be invited to send delegates to a national convention. Other items for discussion included a thorough discussion of the matter of establishing German settlements in the West, as well as consideration of the possibility of establishing a German university in America. (29)

Chapter Three

The Pittsburgh Convention

The idea of a German convention in Pittsburgh – The convention of the same on 18 October 1837 – The discussions there – Purchase of land for the seminary – Address of the school commission – Second convention on 18 October 1839 – An additional meeting on 17 August 1839 – Charter for the seminary in 1840 – Establishment of the school at Philippsburg – The failure of the seminary – General impact on the German element – Franz Joseph Grund
▪▪▪

On 3 June 1837, an invitation was sent out by an organizational committee in Pittsburg that was addressed to all Germans in America, inviting them to a convention to be held on 18 July 1837 at Pittsburgh. (1) German societies, regardless of what name they bore, were requested to send delegates to the meeting, which would be hosted by an arrangement committee organized by the Germans of Pittsburgh. However, on receipt of the invitation, it was widely recommended that the meeting be postponed to a later date. The Pittsburgh Germans quickly responded by means of a correspondence committee, which sent out an announcement moving the date of the convention to 18 October 1837, the anniversary of the Battle of Leipzig. (2)

The purpose of the convention was explained more specifically as follows: "It deals with issues relating to the preservation German language, customs and traditions from the possible threat of decline, and the maintenance their vitality, purity, and beauty, and the transmission of the best of German literature to America. It also aims to ensure and protect the rights and privileges of millions belonging to the ever-growing German element. This can only be accomplished by means of an all-encompassing and carefully planned out system of education that is fitting and proper for us citizens of a free couintry."

The announcement also rejected the view that the convention was an attempt to isolate the German element in any way from its English-speaking compatriots, stating "We do not seek any such separation. We solemnly protest any such plan, and consider this not only unfeasible, but also dangerous. However, much has to be done so that Germans begin to recognize their own importance for this country. They must begin to judge, think and act independently, without any political representatives and greedy office-seekers speaking on their behalf." The correspondence committee warmly and graciously called for a good attendance, stating:

> The success of the affair depends on the active and intelligent support of the German press and that of the Germans in America. Therefore, we call on you descendants of a heroic people, before whom the mighty Roman Empire fell and whose courage brought the French to their knees, to choose the most talented, honest, and respected delegates you can, without regard of political or religious affiliations, from your ranks, and the seed you sew will bear rich and noble fruits.

This circular was signed by the president and secretary of the correspondence committee: Nicolaus Vőgtly and Eduard Fendrich, and dated 20 July 1837. (2) Lively discussion soon followed in the German press about the proposed convention, its goals and the opportunities it provided. In the various German societies that had decided to send delegates there was a great deal of discussion about the meeting. All aspects of the convention's goals were discussed in detail. As is natural, opinions varied greatly on the topics the convention had set forth for discussion. While in New York and in the West, especially in Missouri and Illinois, Germans concentrated on concrete goals that were attainable, the Germans of Pennsylvania, with the benefit of a historically stronger and more influential foundation based on the older Pennsylvania German element, clearly went beyond the borders of what was actually possible.

A very highly regarded German in Philadelphia, for example, stated in the *Alte und Neue Welt* that the convention should focus not only on the preservation and advancement of the German language in schools and churches, the establishment of

German public schools, the support of the German press, and the founding of German teachers' seminaries, but also the recognition of the German language by state legislatures in states, where Germans formed a majority of the population, as in Pennsylvania, or where they were one-third of the population, as in Ohio, Illinois, and Missouri. Moreover, he advocated the introduction of German in the courts of districts, where Germans formed the majority ethnic element. This rested on a very significant overestimation of the size of the German element in the aforementioned western states, where they amounted to not much more than ten percent of the population, while the Germans in Pennsylvania, whose ancestors had immigrated hundreds of years ago, could only partly be considered as Germans in the same sense as they were being talked about at the Pittsburgh Convention. (3)

On 18 October 1837, the Convention began with a total of thirty-nine delegates, selected by already existing societies or at meetings held for the purpose of electing such representatives. Many delegates had excused themselves for not being able to attend the meeting. When one considers how poor the means of transportation were at the time and how great the demands on travel were, then it can readily be understood that many found neither the time nor funds to participate in the convention. (From Philadelphia on needed three full days, although one could take the train for one-third of the distance; from New York two days more; and six to eight days from Ohio and Indians even if one made use of the canals and riverboat steamers; and from St. Louis it would have been from eight to ten days by steamboat).

Franz Joseph Grund was elected president to chair the convention, and Fendrich and Dr. Schmöle were elected to serve as secretaries. From the state of New York there were only three delegates, including G. A Neumann, editor of the *New Yorker Staatszeitung*; one delegate from Virginia; two from Maryland; ten from Ohio; one for Missouri and Illinois; and the rest came from various parts of Pennsylvania. The most well known of all delegates was its president Franz Joseph Grund; Karl Speyrer from Beaver County, Pennsylvania; Neumann from New York; Wilhelm Weber from St. Louis; W.L. J. Kiderlen and W. Schmöle from Philadelphia; Victor Scriba from

Pittsburg; Peter Kaufmann from Canton, Ohio (4); and Wilhelm Steinmeier from Cleveland. Among those who became well known later on, mention should especially be made of Johann August Röbling from the settlement in Butler County, Pennsylvania, which had been established by immigrants from Mühlhausen. (5) The convention met till 25 October.

Convention participants displayed a sound knowledge of parliamentary procedure at the meeting and order was well maintained throughout the proceedings. The individual topics of discussion were referred to various committees for further study. These included committees for immigration questions; for the legal rights of immigrants; for the preservation and advancement of the German language; for the maintenance of German customs and traditions, especially music; military exercises for militia groups; social festivities; and for German-English schools and German teachers' seminaries. These committees met from early morning to late in the evening and worked very hard on their assignments. During the meetings many of the members demonstrated great talents at public speaking and, on the whole, debates were conducted calmly and moderately. Only once was there a real blowup and for a short time it was feared that the meeting could come to an end, and turn into a failure.

As noted earlier, many recommendations went too far and aimed at a separation of the German element from the rest of the population by means of the formation of German states in the west. In the heat of their opposition to this idea, several delegates, especially those from New York, countered by endorsing the idea of the rapid assimilation of the German element as being in the best interests of the nation, and some sharp words were said on the topic. However, the mediating voice of Schmöle, who had the trust of the entire convention, succeeding in bringing the meeting back on track. Fortunately, the magnanimity of the many educated gentlemen from Pittsburg and the festive banquets held by the hospitable citizens of Pittsburg contributed greatly to the delegates getting to know and understand one another better.

It was in the nature of the meeting that the convention's role was advisory, rather than administrative. Thereafter, no actual programmatic plan was adopted. Four standing committees were appointed: A central committee for business matters; a correspondence committee that was charged with publicizing announcements and publications of the various committees; a school committee charged with bringing about improvements in German schools and the establishment of a teachers' seminary; a welfare committee charged with oversight of the general welfare of the German element. The goal of the convention was defined as "Improving the Status of Germans in the U.S.," which was to be accomplished:

1. By improving their educational status; by establishing new schools and improving existing ones; by establishing one or more teachers' seminaries; creating, publishing and distributing good text books; by establishing German educational and cultural societies in all counties and cities; by disseminating German literature; and by contributing to civic education through various publications, such as journals, flyers, and almanacs.
2. By furthering the material well-being of the German element through the establishment of institutions for widows and orphans; by establishing a bureau to provide information to immigrants and assist them in finding employment.
3. By supporting the legal rights and social welfare of German immigrants.

Recommendations dealing with these topics were made, especially granting the school committee the authority to collect funds for a teachers' seminary and for the completion of a proclamation addressed to all Germans in America, requesting their support.

Recommendations as to legal rights and social welfare expressed the view that the existing laws pertaining to immigration were acceptable, and advised all immigrants to acquire citizenship accordingly as soon as possible. On the other hand, everything should be done to prevent a misuse of the immigration and citizenship laws. The transport of criminals from Europe to America should also be prevented and Germans should support the authorities at the port cities in this regard. But on the other hand, political refugees should be not be classified as criminals. The convention spoke out strongly against any changes in the naturalization laws that would work to the disadvantage of becoming a citizen as quickly as possible, and came out sharply against the Native American Party and its endeavors. (6) The convention noted that "It is the duty of Germans, as well as all open-minded Americans to give their vote to candidates at election time only to those who do not advocate negative changes in the immigration and naturalization laws.

Regarding the official use of the German language a motion made by Speyrer, which was too general, was finally amended and approved as follows:

The convention herewith fully supports the motion that German-English bilingual officials be appointed in courts and that all existing as well as new laws should be printed in both languages as well, and that this be done in all states and townships, with the general well-being in mind of these respective states and the country as a whole, whose welfare is of the utmost importance to us.

Moreover, it was decided to hold a second convention on 18 October 1838, and provisions were made for the number and election of delegates. Decisions were also made as to the collection of funds for the teachers' seminary, and the various committees were called upon to submit reports for the next convention. In accordance with a recommendation of the meeting, President Grund and Secretary Schmöle released a proclamation to the German-American press calling for support of the convention and asking the press to inform and instruct the public about its proceedings. A general proclamation addressed to all Germans in America was also to be released, but was not completed due to the untimely departure of Grund for Europe, as well as the illness of Wilhelm Weber, who was to have drafted the proclamation.

The reports of the meeting went to press late in May 1838 after interest in the convention had been pushed aside by other news in our seemingly fast paced society, and were no long newsworthy. However, at the time of the convention there was a great deal of interest in it on the part of Germans and Americans. The English-language papers of

Pittsburgh provided lengthy articles on the sessions and publicized their reports as well. American newspapers elsewhere took great interest in the convention, partly with a degree of skepticism and apprehension, which one can readily understand given the issues under discussion. A proclamation addressed to all Germans in America clearly would have been helpful in outlining the goals of the convention and should have been distributed in a timely fashion. This would have ensured greater interest in the establishment of a teachers' seminary, and had as a possible result, the realization of the only immediately attainable goal of the convention.

The school committee actively pursued its goal under the direction of its chairman, Steinmeier of Cleveland. With the consent of the central committee, a fine country home was acquired in the beautiful region of Phillipsburg, Pennsylvania, which was not far from Rapp's settlement. It had been built by a man whose name in Germany was Proli, but who was generally known here as Count Leon, and was widely considered a religious charlatan. This so-called Count Leon together with several well-to-do families from Frankfurt, had joined Rapp's community. Proli succeeded in forming his own following by means of which he hoped to take control of the settlement. But it came to schism, and a small group withdrew from the community after receiving a substantial monetary settlement. Leon then built a palace-like villa at Philippsburg, but could not afford it, and found it necessary to sell. His further activities are beyond the scope of this history, but according to von Löher, he and his followers moved to Red River in Louisiana, where he succumbed to the cholera at Natchitoches in 1832, thereby bringing the controversies surrounding his life to an end. (7) Funds had been raised as a result of the convention, so that Leon's property, including the home, which had been used as a hotel and the surrounding land that served as a park, were acquired for the relatively reasonable price of $3,000.

In April 1838, the school committee issued a general announcement addressed not only to Germans in America, but to the old country as well. In it the purchase of the property in Philippsburg was described, and all were called upon to support the establishment of a teachers' seminary there. Moreover, the underlying principals were explained that would serve as guidelines for the new institution. Denominational religious instruction would be excluded. However, the seminary would emphasize the importance of religion in directing the hearts and minds of mankind to that which is noble and beautiful and which provides the foundation for a moral life, as long as not perverted by deception or excess. Also, care would be taken to provide students with the opportunity of enriching their studies with general religious instruction so that they could form their own religious views for the purpose of educating others. It also stated:

> The teachers' seminary should be established so that all that is noble and good in the German character would not perish in our new homeland, and so that the language of our forefathers might gain recognition for its beauty and be preserved as the language of a people, which has such a praiseworthy history and which has historically advanced learning to such great heights. However, in order that our youth not remain strangers in the country they now belong to, and so that they are able to perform their duties and defend their rights as American citizens, they must also be fully conversant with the language and ways of the new homeland. In short, their teachers should provide youth with all the knowledge that might be expected of any American citizen.

Turning to Germans in Europe, the announcement closed with the following moving words, calling for support of the seminary:

> Even if we are divided by continents and oceans, let us nonetheless be united in spirit and cooperate together to accomplish something great and good, which will ring honor to the German name. Let us transmit our spirit to our descendants, so as to protect them from all harm and will truly preserve the virtues of our forefathers and be of honorable service to our new homeland.

In accordance with a decision of the first convention, a second one followed on 18 October 1838 in Pittsburgh. Peter Kaufmann of Stark County, Ohio was elected president, Dr. Hermann Gross its vice-president, and Eduard Mühl its secretary. (8) The main question at the meeting related to funding. The acquisition of the property in Philippsburg was approved, and arrangements were made to facilitate and speed up the collection of much needed funds. The meeting lasted four days, and a report of the convention stated, that it "was noted for its harmony, dignity and the hard work on behalf of a good cause." The hope was also expressed that the plan could be accomplished given the contributions that had been made thus far.

On 24 March 1839, the central committee of the convention, which consisted of president Kaufmann, vice-president Fendrich, and secretary Gross, released an announcement directed to all Germans in America. It called to mind how unanimous the first convention had been in deciding to establish the teachers' seminary as one of the main pillars for preserving and strengthening the German heritage and in like manner how the second convention had continued the task in spite of the initial shortage of funds as well as other minor hindrances. Finances eventually improved, especially as a result of the support of a considerable number of highly respected Germans. They emphasized the importance of Germans in world history and the importance of our ethnic element in American history and that we should not place our candle under a bushel basket.

A comprehensive report was issued of what had been accomplished thus far and which also called for another convention for 1 August 1839. This meeting consisted of only twenty-eight delegates, among whom we find many of the earlier representatives, as well as new ones, such as Wesselhöft of Philadelphia, Dr. Harz of Ohio, and Freytag from Baltimore. A board of directors for the seminary was elected. As a general guideline, it was decided that all instruction should be in German, but that English would also be taught and that students should receive a certificate upon graduation verifying the ability to teach in both languages. Moreover, it was decided that students should become acquainted with various churches, without favoring any denomination, that there be a comparative study of the various denominations, and that instruction regarding Christian morals be offered as well. Students wanting to become teachers would have their tuition covered, but were required to make a commitment to complete the program of study.

Other business was covered as well. A standing committee was appointed for the collection of statistical information that might be useful for those Germans interested in settling somewhere in America. And likewise, a committee was established to approach the federal government to establish a consulate that would represent the German states as a whole. Further decisions were also made regarding elections to future conventions, which, it was recommended, should take place every two years. Other general matters were also dealt with, and 10,000 copies of the deliberations of the convention were printed and distributed.

In 1840, the teachers' seminary was incorporated by the state legislature of Pennsylvania "as an institution to educate competent teachers, who could teach in English and German, and further the general welfare of Germans in America, especially with regard to education." Debts on the property were finally paid off ($3,000), and the fourth and last convention was then held at Philippsburg on 9 August 1841. At this meeting, it was decided to attach a school to the seminary, and a teacher, Mr. Winter, was hired for the former, and an advertisement published announcing the availability of two teaching positions at the seminary. A board of directors was installed, a list of contributors was assembled and the responsibility of further collections turned over to the treasurer of the corporation.

The school made progress, but few students applied to the seminary, and the funding for it was inadequate to support such an institution. The reasons for its ultimate failure were obvious. It could not count on much support from the American-born Germans, especially in Pennsylvania, New Jersey, New York, Maryland, and Virginia, nor from the recently arrived German immigrants scattered across the country, as they had their hands full with getting settled and established and in most cases did not even possess the necessary funds to support such a project. Another hindrance consisted of the fact that the teachers' seminary, which aimed to be an institution open to Germans of all faiths, had made its non-denominational status a guiding principle.

Obviously, the German Catholics, who were organized together in their own congregations and influenced by their parish priests with regard to educational matters, would not support such an institution. Members of the evangelical churches likewise were not interested in the teachers' seminary. Even though many recent German immigrants were open-minded regarding religious matters, many of them held their own religious services at home and wherever possible formed their own free-thought congregations with their own clergy. When one reads books about America, such as Büttner's *Die Vereinigten Staaten von Nordamerika*, one find that they are mainly concerned with religious affairs, and can only be amazed at how many German religious congregations had been formed by the early 1830s. (9) There were many that called themselves freethinkers, but most of them actually held to a religious faith, and if not, did so a result of the influence of the American religious environment. However, the members of mainline churches mistrusted an institution, whose founders were not only considered some of the most well-known German freethinkers, but were also rejected any kind of religious doctrine whatsoever. (10)

Also, there was no agreement during the first convention regarding the stance of the convention with regard to the question of whether the German element should separate itself off from the rest of the population by means of a separate state, or blend into American society. The majority opposed this notion, which was supported only by a minority, and feared more disadvantages than advantages would accrue to the German element by such a one-sided approach to this question, even if supporters of the idea had the best of intentions in mind. (11)

Even if the plan for the establishment of a German teachers' seminary and a German school had turned out to be a failure, the affect of such plans on the part of a group of highly educated Germans meeting together on several occasions from across the country nevertheless was nothing short of an important and influential undertaking. In every city or district, where there were German schools, they now actually increased in number. There also arose a number of well organized German school societies. Other German societies and organizations also arose where Germans had settled. They had now become aware of their presence and came to recognize their numerical strength. The convention's strong stance against nativism was well received and got more attention than any other recommendation of the conventions. Practical-thinking Americans got the message, recognizing the danger of voting for a nativist candidate at election time, instead paying attention to how Germans planned on voting.

A committee of the convention contacted President Van Buren to work for the creation of an ambassadorial position in the U.S. that would represent all of the German states instead of separate embassies for Prussia and Austria. The idea was well received by the President, but his defeat in the election of 1840, as well as that of the Democratic Party unfortunately snuffed out the plan, as there was no hope of support from the newly elected Whig Party, which was known to have nativist sympathies.

Reference has already been made to the president of the first of the Pittsburg conventions, Franz Joseph Grund, who played an important role in public affairs during his lifetime. Little is known of his early life in Europe, but he was born in 1803 in Austria, probably Vienna, where his surname is quite common. It must have been at the end of the 1820s or in the early 1830s that he came to America, and by 1833 he had obtained a position as professor of mathematics at Harvard University in Cambridge, Massachusetts. Another German, we might note, Franz Gräter, a rather eccentric man and professor of drawing and ancient languages, was also on the faculty at that time. In 1837, Grund had traveled throughout Europe, as Charles Sumner refers to him as just having returned from England at that time. Sumner says: "He is very capable and trustworthy. His conversation made a great impression on me. His talks sledgehammers. He would like to study law with me." (12)

In 1834, Grund took part in a German political meeting in New York, for which he drafted its decisions, and which were directed against the Democrats. However, in 1834 and 1836, he moved into the ranks of the Democratic Party and wrote a campaign biography of Martin Van Buren, who at that time was running against Harrison for the Presidency. (13) Such campaign biographies should be viewed as political documents that are naturally devoid of ant historical value, consisting merely of songs of praise designed to win votes for the candidate in question. But the one by Grund was actually not that bad, was written in a popular style, but of course was aimed at winning the sympathy of German voters. Great emphasis was placed on Van Buren's German ancestry, and it was not forgotten to mention that he raised the best cabbage on his estate. Van Buren was elected, and took office in March 1837, and Grund naturally applied for a consular position. His appearance in Philadelphia at this particular time, and his desire to become a delegate to the Pittsburg convention, as well as his candidacy for the presidency of the convention arose from his desire to present himself to the President as a man of great influence with the German element. He succeeded in winning an appointment to the consulate of Antwerp, but it appears that this position was not that promising, and he soon returned home, dissatisfied with his position there.

In the presidential campaigns of 1839-40, Grund underwent another political transformation, when Van Buren and Harrison were again the candidates. The success of his campaign biography of Van Buren encouraged him to continue on this course of writing, but this time around he supported Harrison. (14) And, now Van Buren with all his German ancestry and cabbage heads did not receive the same kind treatment as before. Harrison, who had been described in 1836 as a simple-minded, incompetent general, who earned nothing more than a warm red flannel blanket from the ladies of Chillicothe for his so-called military bravery, was now hailed as a second Wellington. At the same time, he edited the *Standard*, an English-language paper that supported the Whig Party, whose candidate was Harrison, and a German paper entitled *Der Pennsylvanisch-Deutsche*. From Harrison, who died only a month after taking office, he received an appointment in 1841 to the consulate in Bremen, but returned soon thereafter in 1842. Tyler, the vice-president, had in the meantime joined the Democrats and Grund, returning to his original political affiliation, came home with flying colors to the Democratic camp.

Traditionally, Germans do not respect such frequent party switching, and after 1840, Grund all but totally lost the influence he had once enjoyed among Germans.

However, his influence continued on in American circles. He was a quite well educated and intelligent man, and this served him well. He was not stupid, as Sumner once asserted, but rather a quite clever man, who practiced politics as a profession, or perhaps it would be more correct to say, as an art that eventually became his lifelong hobby. For many years, he attended congressional sessions in Washington, and wrote reports on them for various newspapers in the East. He was correspondent of the *Ledger* in Philadelphia, for example. It is not an overstatement if we call him the father of sensational journalism in America, a style that has become so customary everywhere now that we can only hope for its immediate demise. He stood behind the scenes; at least he liked to say that he did, even when this was not the case. His revelations were sensational, his stories based on the best firsthand sources, and his accounts of well known people excited the interest of readers, but on occasion brought him into some personally unpleasant situations.

He maintained that he was the force behind the candidacy of General Pierce. In this regard, his name was first mentioned in a newspaper article about Pierce's nomination at the convention at Baltimore in 1852, where Grund successfully offered his endorsement to Pierce. The election of Pierce appears not to have helped him at all, however. In the campaign of 1856, he then enthusiastically supported Buchanan, a fellow Pennsylvanian. The German element at that time had by and large become estranged from the Democratic Party and enthusiastically supported the banner of Fremont and the Republican Party. Grund, who most American politicians still considered as enjoying great influence among the Germans, was hotly pursued by the Democrats. They convinced him to campaign across the country on their behalf, especially in the western states in support of Stephen A. Douglas.

The election of Buchanan in 1856 won him an appointment to the consulate at Le Havre in France, which he held till 1861, when Lincoln was elected president. Even in the first years of the Civil War he remained loyal to the Democratic Party and edited a Democratic paper in Philadelphia, *The Age*. In September 1863, he experienced another metamorphosis, but we can only assume for the most laudable of reasons. At the end of

September, he appeared at the Union League and held a fiery speech, declaring himself a supporter of the Republican Party. (15) This courageous step on his part embittered his previous political allies, from whom he had received so many political favors and appointments, but the consequences of this move were also overestimated by Grund himself.

On 29 September, General McClellan had coincidentally come to Philadelphia. The Democrats demonstrated on his behalf and held a parade that moved down the street where Grund lived, making a great amount of noise. The procession stopped right in front of his home and the noise increased greatly. Grund did not know what the procession was about, but imagined that it was a demonstration against him and that the demonstrators planned to storm his home. Escaping through a back door, he hurried to the nearest police station, breathlessly seeking help, as he felt that his home was endangered. Hardly had he made this known to the police, when he collapsed and by the time a doctor arrived he had already succumbed to a heart attack.

Grund was a husky man inclined towards corpulence and was known to enjoy himself at the dinner table. He presented the image of a portly and worldly kind of priest. His conversational talents were quite impressive, and his wit and humor striking. On the stage or on the campaign stump, he reminded one of the lively Capuchin in Wallenstein's military camp and his eloquence was reminiscent of the famous Abraham a Santa Clara, especially as his dialect was immediately recognizable as that of an Austrian. (16)

For almost thirty years he was closely connected to and actively involved with the German press, and even longer with the English-language press, thereby exerting a great deal of influence in American political life. Journalists of his rank, with all their intelligence, analytical skills, and other diverse talents, often lack the scholarly background that Grund enjoyed. He had a solid education to his credit. And, in 1833, he had become a professor at Harvard, and published several textbooks, including: *Algebraic Problems, Elements of Astronomy, Natural Philosophy, Plain and Solid Geometry.*

With regard to American conditions he wrote *The Americans in their Moral, Social and Political Relations* (1837), which was published in Germany as *Die Amerikaner* ((1837); *Aristocracy in America* (1839), which appeared in Germany as *Die Aristokratie in Amerika: Aus dem Tagebuch eines deutschen Edelmannes* (1839); and, in 1843, he published a guide for immigrants in Germany entitled *Handbuch und Wegweiser für Auswanderer nach den Ver. Staaten.* In 1860, he published *Thoughts and Reflections on the Present Position of Europe and its Probable Consequences to the United States.*

His influence might have been greater, and his memory more long lasting had it not been for his frequent political transformations, which were done for his own personal aggrandizement, and they only served to arouse mistrust on the part of the German element. His exceptional talents and knowledge were therefore seemingly outweighed by this one character flaw, a trait for which he was frequently reproached.

Chapter Four

Social, Cultural and Political Life

German as an official language in Pennsylvania – Request to the state legislature of Pennsylvania – German-language printing of messages of governors in German in various states – German instruction in schools – Participation of Germans in politics – German militia societies – Ernst Ludwig Koseritz – Cultural and singing societies – The first German Sängerfest – The arts and sciences – Ferdinand Pettrich – Reinhold Friedländer – Homeopathy – Dr. Konstantin Hering – Societies for the establishment of German colonies – The founding of Hermann, Missouri – Other settlements and societies

Mention should be made here of the movement to have government documents printed in the German language, a movement that was already well underway before the Pittsburgh Convention. On 30 November 1836, a meeting of the Germans of Philadelphia and the surrounding county took place that was said to have attracted two thousand people. Tobias Bühler, who was active in public affairs, chaired the meeting. He has been described as a dignified, intelligent, and pragmatic-minded citizen, known as the "Swabian King" because of the great influence he enjoyed in the community. Dr. Wilhelm Schmöle served as secretary of the meeting. In the various speeches and in the letter sent to the state legislature of Pennsylvania it was emphasized that Pennsylvania had become one of the richest and most beautiful states of the U.S.A., and that this was due to the untiring perseverance and Germanic diligence of the Germans of the state, and that they were therefore entitled to complete equality before the law.

It was felt that the new state constitution as well as laws should therefore be printed in both languages (English and German) for two reasons. First, it would rejuvenate a truly vital civic spirit among the large German population of the state, and, second, it would contribute to a greater understanding of government on the part of the German element. Moreover, it would provide for an effective civic educational outreach program. There were also many similar meetings in the rural areas of the state during which German instruction in the public schools was also emphasized. The state legislature of Pennsylvania accordingly decided in 1837 to print the laws passed each session in the German language. (1)

These endeavors rested, however, on an incorrect understanding of the situation. Laws passed by the legislature are mainly of a private nature, more in the nature of administrative directives than laws of general interest, and what there are of the latter cannot be fully understood without a knowledge of previous laws, as well as the English common law, which can only be modified or eliminated by a single law. Officials and legal scholars create such statutes, and the average citizen wouldn't even think of acquiring such laws. Initially, there was interest due to the newness of the matter and this caused Germans to acquire such laws, but the interest gradually subsided, as did the printing in German as well.

Nevertheless, this agitation had as a consequence that in Pennsylvania as well as in other states, it soon became customary to have the messages of the governor printed in German. As a rule these documents contained quite a bit of interesting information about the financial affairs of the state, statistical data on the population, as well as information on mass communication, public institutions, and political questions under consideration in a given state, as well as the country as a whole. Since these gubernatorial messages were printed on order of the state legislature, Germans found it appropriate in those states where they formed a significant part of the population to request such translations in German. With the spread of the of the German press, the demand for the printing of public documents in German declined, since all significant documents were published in the German press as were the deliberations of Congress, the state legislatures, and the courts.

More important for the German element was the introduction of German instruction into the public schools that were supported by public taxation. This required a great deal of work to attain this goal in the various states of the country. As a result of the great pressure exerted by Germans, the state legislature passed a law in July 1837 that stipulated that in those areas where citizens requested a German school that such a school should be established and supported under the general law for schools in the same manner as were English-language schools. Moreover, schools could be established in accordance with this law, where German was the only language of instruction. In other states, laws did not go this far, confining themselves solely to the introduction of German instruction in the schools. (2)

The Pennsylvania Germans had long participated in politics. Indeed, their newspapers might best be classified as party publications. From 1836 on, we find an active participation in politics on the part of the recently arrived German immigrants as well. In newspapers we often find reports of political meetings held by Germans, for example. Candidates for office often printed their campaign literature in German, emphasizing especially their friendly relations with the German population. Here one sees that they were beginning to reckon with the German element as a political factor. Meanwhile, German candidates were rare and only in cities do we find an attempt on the part of Germans to obtain local office.

By 1840, the German vote had become a force not only in Pennsylvania, but also in other western states, especially Ohio and Illinois. Candidates for the office of president found it necessary to publish their views on the laws pertaining to naturalization. In the years 1844 and 1848, Germans made their presence known as delegates to the nominating conventions for president, governor, and other high offices, naturally more often than not in the Democratic than the Whig Party, as few Germans belonged to the latter. We generally tend to only find German merchants and manufacturers in the latter party.

Another expression of German involvement in public affairs came about with the formation of German militia units patterned after the American model for such companies. On paper every American citizen owed military service, but no such military organization existed in the various states. Only in the larger cities were there uniformed voluntary military companies and battalions, which enjoyed the distinct advantage of being recognized as military units by the state, which provided weaponry, equipment as well as the uniforms. The first of these German companies were formed in New York in early 1836. (3) It took on the name of the Jefferson Guard, and was first commanded by Captain Lassack, later a member of the state legislature.

In Philadelphia interest greatly increased in militia groups. Under Captain Koseritz a substantial German company was formed under the name of the Washington Guard. Other guard units soon affiliated with it, so that an entire battalion was then formed. The presentation of a flag to the Washington Guard in 1836 provided the occasion for a magnificent celebration, which brought the entire population of Philadelphia out on to the streets. American militia units also took part and it apparently was one of the greatest military parades that Philadelphia had ever seen. A banquet concluded the celebration, which was attended by the president of the supreme court of Pennsylvania, the well-known legal scholar Judge Gibson, several other judges and officials, as well as the mayor of the city and several military generals, including General Patterson, as well as many other noteworthy persons. The first toast was dedicated to Germany, and was accompanied by the music of "What is the Germans' Fatherland?" (4) The second was dedicated to the President of the United States, and the following to Washington and Lafayette. Other toasts followed that were dedicated to Poland, Kosciusko, De Kalb, von Steuben, Goethe, Schiller and Theodor Körner, as well as Franklin and Gutenberg. And, of course, there was no lack of speech-making. The Washington Guard was long the pride of the citizenry of Philadelphia, although Captain Koseritz, who acquired much praise for its military order and discipline, soon moved away from Philadelphia.

Ernst Ludwig Koseritz, born 1805 at Gaisburg near Stuttgart, had been First Lieutenant in the Sixth Württemberg Infantry Regiment that was stationed at Ludwigsburg in 1833. (5) He was a man of decisive character, great energy and was imbued with liberal ideas already as a youth. The July uprising and especially the Polish revolution had greatly interested him, so that after passage of the July 1832 decrees by the Bundestag he came to feel that a republican constitution for Germany could only be attained by revolutionary means. (6) Apparently, he exerted a great deal of influence due not only to his intellect, but also his dynamic personality. The official report of the 1832 uprising by the Bundestag provides the following information about him:

> At the same time the conspiracies took place in Frankfurt, Hessia, and other places, there arose elsewhere a more dangerous and consequential plot in Germany. This was the military conspiracy that began in the summer of 1832 in Wuerttemberg under the leadership of Ernst Ludwig Koseritz. He shared the views and aspirations of the faction that sought to bring about German unity under a republican form of government by means of revolution. At his garrison in Ludwigsburg he organized a club to bring together officers and citizens for this purpose. He selected Sergeant Lehr as his assistant. By means of the club he succeeded in attracting a number of competent officers, who promised that if the revolution broke out, they would hoist the banner of revolution and support the uprising. To facilitate the task he called on them to confidentially win over their comrades, so that their troops would support the revolution when it occurred. The place they should meet was told to them, with traitors of the cause being threatened with death. Koseritz went further by telling officers of the plot, encouraging them to assist in the plan in bringing over the entire regiment to the revolution, which would thereby violate their oath of allegiance. Some officers were led astray by him and abused their positions by influencing the non-commissioned officers in their ranks. Koseritz's failed in his attempt to accomplish the same plan in Stuttgart. In the meantime, Lehr informed him that the mutineers numbered between fifty and sixty, and that altogether they could count on the support of almost two hundred from various military units. (7)

Later on, Koseritz contacted the leaders of the movement in Frankfurt, Hessia, Baden, and the Rheinpfalz, who aimed at overthrowing the Bundestag and forming a provisional government that would call a parliament together, which would overthrow the existing regimes and establish a uniform government for Germany. One should not forget here that the idea had surfaced in the 1820s with the German Men's League and other revolutionary circles to raise the king of Württemberg to the throne as German emperor after overthrowing other rulers, and that this idea had not completely died out. It is therefore likely that Koseritz, who according to an unsubstantiated story was an illegitimate brother of the king, had this in mind, and that his eventual pardon from revolutionary activity was part of his plan.

The uprising in Frankfurt was planned to begin on 6 April, but due to fears of being discovered, was moved up to the 3rd. (8) Koseritz, who had promised to proceed with occupying Ludwigsburg on the first day of the uprising and then move on to Stuttgart, and unite with the garrison there and meet up with around five hundred Poles, who had already moved forth from depots at Besancon and Avignon and stood at the German border. They were to move forth towards Baden and the Rheinpfalz and were notified in a timely fashion of the change in plans. Exactly at 9:30 P.M. on 3 April, when the alarm bells rang in Frankfurt, a dispatch was delivered to Koseritz, signed by the leader of the Frankfurt uprising, the lawyer Karl Franz Gärth containing the following message: "Dear Koseritz, Hold fast to your word – strike now regardless of all else!"

But it was impossible for Koseritz to speed up the uprising. His plans were very complicated and was planned to begin on the 6th. According to the relevant documentation it can be assumed that he was definitely resolved to strike at the planned for time. But already on the 5th the news arrived of the failure of the Frankfurt uprising. Several days thereafter, Koseritz was arrested and after an investigation lasting two years, was sentenced to death along with Lehr. At the time of execution the command for the final shot was about to be given, with Kosertiz looking death squarely in the eye, when pardon from the king was suddenly announced. Lehr also was spared, but both were now forced to leave Europe.

It turned out that Kosertiz had voluntarily revealed plans to the king in order to obtain a lesser sentence. Some of the refugees here in America, therefore, reproached him for betraying the uprising. It is customary that there are disagreements in military companies, and he had similar problems in the past, but the continual allegations of treachery eventually made his position untenable and he decided to move to Florida to join the army fighting the Seminole Indians there. (9) He served there, and later on moved to New Orleans, where he apparently died, as nothing more was heard of him. It is possible that he was wounded there, or that he succumbed to the climate of the swampland areas, where the Indians had sought refuge.

Even if Koseritz voluntarily had admitted something, this does not necessarily make him a traitor. He was smart enough to know that after the failed assassination attempt and the arrest of so many participants that his plan was no longer a mystery to the authorities. An offer to testify for a grant of leniency for himself and his comrades was the best step to take at the time, and was reported accordingly in the press. And actually, the final judgments were in fact quite mild in comparison with the sentences meted out by other German states, as for example in the case of Prussia where more than thirty students, who had done nothing wrong at all but belong to the German student union known as the *Burschenschaft* and had not participated in any act of violence, were condemned to death, but then had their sentence commuted to life imprisonment. (10) Eleven non-commissioned officers were sent to prison, of which the shortest sentence was for five years.

In 1837, Captain F. Dithmar formed a *Jäger* company, and in 1841 was joined by a Uhlan and an artillery company. At the same time, the German presence in Philadelphia was making itself known in other ways as well. In 1835, an educational society was formed with J.G. Wesselhöft as president and Wilhelm Schmöle as secretary. Members consisted of merchants, doctors, and skilled workers. The group's purpose was cultural and consisted of lectures and discussions. It developed in typical German fashion, and soon spawned a German men's choir as well as a women's choir. Under the direction of an accomplished school teacher, Philipp Mathias Wolsieffer, the group rapidly. Its concerts were all well attended and received by the best circles in town and provided the model for similar concerts held elsewhere. In 1839, some very well attended concerts were presented of Haydn's *Creation* in Bethlehem, Nazareth, and Allentown. Soon similar groups were established by various American societies, most of which were directed by Wolsieffer. In Chambersburg and Pittsburgh singing societies also arose, as all as in many smaller towns of Pennsylvania, and which still exist to this very day under a variety of names and which have been joined by new ones as well. Naturally, it did not take long till German singing societies were formed in New York, Baltimore, Cincinnati, St. Louis and other towns and cities with German populations. And, in 1846, a well attended *Sängerfest* was held with great enthusiasm in Philadelphia. (11)

German cultural life was definitely beginning to emerge by this time. The bookstores of Kiderlen and Stollmeyer and Wesslehöft, the latter of whom had branches in Baltimore, New York, Cincinnati, New Orleans and Charleston, provided the public with the latest and best German-language publications. Moreover, an excellent lithographic institute blossomed in Philadelphia as well. Private institutions of learning were established by Germans, scholarly lectures were held, and even the creative arts found their most worthy representatives. Among the latter, Ferdinand Pettrich deserves to be mentioned. Born in Dresden, he specialized in sculpture, studied in Rome, and served as an assistant of Thorwaldsen. (12) His stay in Rome lasted eighteen years and he then became a professor of sculpture under King Otto of Greece at Athens, and thereafter settled down in Philadelphia in the 1830s.

Several monuments adorning the wonderful Laurel Hill Cemetery in Philadelphia contributed greatly to his reputation in Pennsylvania. A finely done sculpture of a girl fishing was probably completed earlier in Rome. This depicted a maiden half lying down and at whose feet Amor sits with his wings folded, and whose arrow lays broken at his feet. This was unfortunately done only in clay, but was nevertheless a beautiful work of art. In the Academy of Fine Arts in Philadelphia there was a marvelous *Mephistopholes* of his till the hall was destroyed by fire in 1844. He was then called to Washington, D.C. with a commission of doing the relief for the pedestal of the great Washington statue by Greenough, with would depict the various periods of American history; these were all done in clay, but never finalized. (13) The necessary permits had not been granted by Congress, and while work came to a halt on the project, an attempt was made on his life, apparently by an Italian rival, and almost cost him his life. President Tyler, whose love and respect Pettrich had won, took him into his home, where he received the best care from his family for several months. At the same time, his family lived in the bitterest of poverty in Philadelphia.

A society was formed in Washington, D.C. that had in mind to construct a colossal statue of Washington on horse and which was planned to be located on Independent Square. But the necessary funds ($50,000) failed to be raised. Pettrich then worked on a model for a less costly work, but the funds were lacking for this as well. Dissatisfied with this state of affairs, he is said to have gone to Brazil with the aid of friends in Philadelphia and have found a position as court sculptor, a position that suited his creative genius and artistic pride. According to reports, he then returned to Rome in 1847 to complete works of sculpture for the Papacy. But the passion that had fired his soul thus far was soon tempered realities there. Like Jansen in Heyse's *Im Paradies* he found that his kind of plans that emerged with his typical artistic enthusiasm, were more appropriate for massive works of sculpture than for the mere adornment of tiny crosses and statuettes in chapels and boudoirs. (14) In general, he could be very friendly, but additionally, he was known for his artistic passion and his true Saxon spirit. And, the author recalls with pleasure the many pleasant times he spent with him in his gallery.

Julius Reinhold Friedländer of Berlin also accomplished a great deal in Philadelphia. In Germany, he became involved with instruction for the blind, and opened the first such institution in Philadelphia in 1834 with four pupils. His excellent skills soon enabled him to expand his institute, which initially was supported by private funds, but then became a state institution. It proved to be exemplary for the whole country, and its success was due to his outstanding leadership skills. He was a man of great intelligence with a sound educational background, but his outstanding quality was his ability to win the love and respect of those working for him He enjoyed the greatest reputation among Americans, and when he died in 1840, hardly thirty-eight years old, his demise was greatly mourned by all who knew him.

At about the same time, Dr. Konstantin Hering settled down in Philadelphia. (15) Born on 1 January 1800 in Oschatz, he studied at Leipzig and Würzburg, obtaining a doctoral degree in 1826. Under the auspices of the Saxon government he was sent to Surinam for research in the natural sciences, spending six years there and sending quite valuable collections of plants and animals to the Academy of Science in Philadelphia, where he had become a member. In 1832, he settled down in Philadelphia. Hering always demonstrated the greatest interest in progressive politics, art and literature. Countless German artists and scholars were graciously received by him over the years, and he always had a warm place in his heart for his old Fatherland. In 1861, a small volume of his was published: *Die natürliche Grenze: Ein Gedanke für Deutschland*, in which he prophetically predicted the return of Alsace-Lorraine to Germany as an historical necessity.

Hering is considered the father of homeopathy in America.   A knowledgeable source noted: "the spread of this new teaching was rapid and he succeeded in establishing a homeopathic institute in Allentown in 1836 that flourished for a number of years." He was president of this institute and published writings on the topic in English and German that clearly paved the way for the acceptance of the teachings of Hahnemann. (16) His *Homöpathischer Hausartzt* appeared in several editions, as well as in English translation. Homeopathic schools were established in Philadelphia and other cities as well. Hering then returned to Philadelphia, where he carried on a successful practice. Dr. Joseph H. Pulte then brought homeopathy to the western states, while Drs. Hoffendahl and Wesselhöft did so for Boston and New England, and America soon came to be seen as a fruitful field for the new teaching. In the beginnings, some were skeptical of it as an exclusively German phenomenon, but it gradually even became more popular among Americans than Germans, especially in the East.

Dr. Hering was moreover a man who did not bury himself in scholarship, but was actively involved in public and political affairs, especially those dealing with the common good of the community at large. At a dinner sponsored by the Germans of Philadelphia in honor of the historian Friedrich von Raumer in 1844, Dr. Hering delivered the main address, which the honored guest heartily responded to. (17) With all the honors he had received in America, Dr. von Raumer took the opportunity to praise the progress of Germany, especially Prussia, but ascribed unfavorable conditions there, which differed from those in America, as being responsible for the lack of political freedoms. His somewhat conservative toast was as follows: "May the freedom grow and prosper in Germany and America, which always goes hand and hand with law and order, and which never contradicts true science, religion and morality." After the champagne got the circulation going, the toasts started flowing along much livelier, and the honored guest presented a toast in honor of the ladies of Pennsylvania, as they spoke "the beautiful German mother tongue."

The plans of founding German colonies in the U.S. had originated in Germany, but in the mid-1830s similar plans began to emerge here as well. Coming from New York first of all, such ideas found great resonance in Philadelphia. In a provisional meeting held on 9 August 1836 in the Penn Hotel that was presided over by Dr. Wilhelm Schmöle, a committee was charged with working out such a plan. At a later meeting, the idea was discussed further, a constitution was accepted and a board of trustees elected. Its president was Julius Leupold, a partner in the important mercantile firm of Hagedorn, Leupold & Co.; Wilhelm Schmöle was vice-president; and J.G. Wesselhöft and Friedrich Lüdeking served as secretaries; and Dr. Möhring as treasurer. The board consisted of nine members, among them: G.L. Viereck, A. Schmidt, Dr. Wohlien, W. Leupold, and W.L. Kiderlen. The best deputies were sought out, who would devote themselves to the planned for colony, including: L. von Fehrentheil, L.G. Ritter, and J.L.K. Gebhart. The society was organized as a stock company with shares, and its purpose was defined as the "unity of Germans in North America and the establishment of a new German homeland." One of the speakers at the meeting excitedly proclaimed: "Yes, indeed, German brothers, if something great and splendid is going to be accomplished for the German people in this country, then it will be by means of our society."

It was only natural that in spite of all the efforts, the hundreds of proclamations and announcements, the sound financial status of the undertaking (the shares were soon sold), and all the worthy individuals who had been involved with founding the society that only some of the hopes and dreams they shared were ultimately realized. One of the most enthusiastic and active supporters said: "The society, like many German societies, had many obstacles to overcome, but this one was greatly supported by most Germans." Later on, as is well known, about 12,000 acres were acquired in Gasconade County, Missouri and the town of Hermann founded along the Missouri River. The land outside the town was laid out as farmland and sold for a reasonable price that included surveying and other related costs, so that as far as is known, no more tillable land is to be had.

Germans transformed the wilderness into farmland and the area was almost exclusively settled by Germans. Several came in 1837, and then in greater number in 1838. The goals of the German Settlement Society have now been partly achieved. If not all plans were attained, then its founders, who worked so selflessly, nonetheless succeeded in establishing a very comfortable home in a beautiful area blessed with a good climate. They also have done much in terms of establishing schools and preserving German social life, according to Wesselhöft's autobiography.

In 1841, a social organization was formed by the free thought minister Heinrich Ginal that later developed into a communal society based on a moderate form of communism. Each member was to be paid according to work done and receive coverage for all basic needs. Soon the organization had three hundred members. A great strip of uncultivated land was purchased in McKean County, Pennsylvania, and the settlement of Teutonia, also known as Ginalsburg, was also laid out. Deposits of $200 were required of all adults and workers and $300 to $400 for older members. By 1842, $20,000 had been raised, and $6,500 was used as a partial payment to acquire the land (30,000 acres). (18) Heinrich Schweizer served as president, Joseph Rau as secretary, and Johann Lago as treasurer. Work assignments were decided upon by the membership and women and children became members based on their election to membership by the male members and, or fathers. The kitchen was communal and meals served twice daily. The community grew slowly in size and had four hundred members by 1842, but then dissolved sometime soon thereafter. In general, it could be said to have been formed on the model of Rapp's community, but it lacked the essential element of having a prophetic leader like Rapp. Faith can move mountains, but it was exactly this that was most lacking at the settlement of Teutonia.

A similar society, the German Culture and Trade Society, was also established in Pennsylvania, but aimed only to acquire land and then divide it up. The society purchased 36,000 acres of land in northern Virginia, or at least signed the contract for the land. The fate of the society, as well as that of two or three similar societies like it that were founded in Pennsylvania, remains unknown. We can only assume that most of them eventually dissolved, but often leaving German settlements in their wake here and there. (19)

On 20 July 1843, the German Immigration Society was founded in Philadelphia, which had as its primary purpose the assistance of recently arrived German immigrants, including legal aid, room and board. This society competed with the older German Society of Pennsylvania, and caused new life and zeal to return to it. The German Immigration Society organized a general information office with fulltime staff, like those in other cities, such as New York. The following gentlemen were particularly active here: Bühler, N. Kuhlenkamp, Franz J. Grund, L.A. Wollenweber, August Kraft, Dithmer, Schele de Vere, and Wiedersheim. The agent of the society was Lorenz Herbert, a man with his heart in the right place, who diligently worked for endeavors on behalf of the common good of the community, especially on behalf of German immigrants.

Aside from German societies in Philadelphia, Pittsburgh, Harrisburg and other cities of Pennsylvania there were countless other German social and cultural organizations that were established in the time period dealt with in this work. These included, for example, the Masons and Odd Fellow lodges, the singing and theatrical societies, etc., which all reflected the German penchant for sociability and the tendency to form societies. Wherever Germans settled in great number, they not only transformed social life, but all aspects of life in general as well, and which I have faithfully tried to evaluate as an observer of life here for the last several decades.

Chapter Five

The German Element at Mid-Century

Wilhelm Schmőle – Sympathy for Germany – Gutenberg Fest in 1840 – Dr. Georg Friedrich Seidensticker's arrival in the U.S. – His life – Reactions to the Revolution of 1848 – Hecker's arrival – Emanuel Leutze – Friedrich List – Heinrich Ginal – Dr. Philipp Schaff – Friedrich August Rauch – Isaak Leeser – Catholic Activities – Demetrius Augustin Gallitzin – Bishop Johann Nepomuk Neumann – German business and industry - Wilhelm Horstmann – Franz Martin Drexel – Dr. Owald Seidensticker

■■■

Among those who took an active role in public affairs mention definitely must be made of Wilhelm Schmőle, who exerted a great deal of influence in Philadelphia as well as throughout Pennsylvania. He was born in Westphalia and attended school in Plattenburg before moving to Arnsberg in 1825 at the age of fourteen. He continued his studies there and then attended the University of Marburg from 1831 to 1833. Thereafter, he immigrated to the U.S., although the exact reasons for his immigration are unknown. We then find him next in beautiful Wilkes-Barre, Pennsylvania as the editor and publisher of the *Susquehanna Democrat* and the *Allgemeine Staatszeitung*, both influential Democratic newspapers. (1)

In 1835, he moved to Philadelphia to engage in a medical practice based on a modified version of homeopathic methods. . His work as founder of the Educational Society, co-founder of the German Settlement Society, and as an enthusiastic member and secretary of the conventions held at Pittsburgh and Phillipsburg have already been mentioned. In 1843, he, his wife and children made a trip to Europe, where they stayed for three years, during which time he attended universities in Germany and Switzerland, as well as in Paris, studying medicine and the natural sciences. In 1846, they returned to Philadelphia, where he published several medical works, which earned him a doctoral degree from the medical and philosophical faculties at the University of Kőnigsberg.

In spite of an active medical practice he found time for involvement in community affairs, including the establishment of the first building and loan in Philadelphia under the name of "American Building and Loan Co.," which became the forerunner of countless others. In 1851, he advocated the establishment of parks in urban areas, and in particular was responsible for recommending the creation of the beautiful and now famous Fairmount Park in Philadelphia. Together with his brother and friend Wohlfsieffer he founded the German colony at Egg Harbor, New Jersey. In 1866, he published *Essay on the Causes, Diffusion, Localisation, Prevention and Cure of the Asiatic Cholera and other Epidemic Diseases.* He combined an unusual degree of idealism together with a pragmatic approach to public and business affairs. He created an altogether harmonious impression and his mild-mannered opinions of others were always marked by goodwill. A natural gift of eloquence in public speaking contributed to the influence he already enjoyed as a result of his kindly nature. Dr. Schmöle, now in Germany, recently published a medical work: *Makrobiotik und Eubanik.* (Bonn, 1879) dealing with the art and benefits of walking.

Germany was still in national slumber that lasted from the time of the Napoleonic wars to the revolution of 1832, and therefore could offer little of immediate interest to Germans in America. (2) Only by means of the new political life that was awakened in France, Belgium and Poland, as well as in Germany, which was stunted but never entirely suppressed by the ensuing reaction, did the attention of German immigrants again turn back to the old country. The many political refugees who came to America in the 1830s kept connections alive between America and the country that had forced them into exile. In spite of concerns for their own daily existence and the attentiveness they rightfully showed for their new homeland, we find that Germans from now on were actively involved in all kinds of German events. Moreover, they now endeavored to show they had not forgotten their old Fatherland and its many virtues. An opportunity to present these feeling was offered by the Gutenberg Fest, which was widely celebrated in Germany in commemoration of the discovery of printing on 24 June 1840.

In Philadelphia plans had long been underway for a fitting and proper celebration of this event. Wilhelm Schmöle served as president and Karl Schwarz as secretary of the planning committee for the Gutenberg Fest. Participants assembled at a meeting place and then proceeded in columns to Independence Square, where the organizers met them and then proceeded together to parade through the city. Major Daniel M. Keim, descended from an older German family, was the parade marshal, and was assisted with a dozen others who helped maintain parade order. It began with a company of German Uhlans, followed by an artillery company and a battalion of the German Washington Guard. A large choir marched on ahead of the planning committee, and was followed by printers and typesetters in a beautifully organized group bearing a magnificent flag, with the images of Gutenberg and his press on one side and the U.S. seal on the other. A German militia unit followed in civilian dress, and thereafter a wagon drawn by six white horses on which there was a press from which songs were printed in German and English and then distributed to the crowds. Next was the German Mens' Choir, which carried the black-red-gold German flag, followed by other German lodges and trade organizations, which closed up the parade. Many homes throughout the city were festively adorned for the occasion with wreathes and flags.

At a beautiful location just outside the city, by Gray's ferry on the Schuylkill, thousands had gathered around a stage that had been set up for a program. The first toast was dedicated to the noble art of printing, the second to Johannes Gutenberg, and the third to "Germany, the homeland of the greatest discoveries in history that have contributed greatly to the civilization of the world, to the incubator of the arts and sciences, and the homeland of domestic virtue." One can therefore readily see that there was no lack of German pride at the time. Another toast was made to "the press of the United States, the only free press in the world." The editor of the *Saturday News* responded with a toast, followed by an excellent address on the topic.

At this very time, we should note that the circulation of the *Alte und Neue Welt* was forbidden by the police in most of the German states. (3) Other German newspapers from New York had also been banned there for several years as well. Also, we might note that in 1836, a society had been established in Philadelphia to support German political refugees, who had been expelled from Switzerland due to political pressure, and had landed destitute in London, and now sought assistance for immigrating to America. Wollenweber served as president of this society and Kiderlen as its secretary.

In 1841, a large assembly of Germans took place to express and convey their sympathy on the death of Karl von Rotteck, and a letter in this regard was sent to the family. (4) This gathering included: J.G. Wesselhöft, Gustav Remack (a well-known attorney), Dr. Wittig, Karl Minnigerode, K.F. Stollmeyer, Dr. C. Brodbeck, and W. Langenheim.

In 1842, a committee was formed to collect funds for the support of those in need as a result of the fire in Hamburg. Collections for the same purpose took place in other cities of the U.S. where Germans had settled as well. In Pittsburgh (1842) the birthday of Schiller was celebrated. As in other cities, meetings were held in Philadelphia by friends of Professor Jordan, who was imprisoned in Marburg, for the benefit of his family, and a total of $150,000 collected. (5)

A very impressive ovation greeted political martyr Dr. Georg Friedrich Seidensticker, when he arrived in America and landed at Philadelphia in spring 1846. (6) Born 16 Feburary 1797 in Göttingen as the son of a chancellery official, his studies came to an end at age fourteen with his voluntary entrance into the army of the Kingdom of Westphalia. This came about with the special permission of minister of war Simeon, so that his later studies at the university would not be interrupted by military conscription. Already fairly well grown up by age fourteen with a large and well-built frame, he had no problem in so doing. As a member of the Westphalian Hussar Regiment he survived the terrible campaign of 1812 in Russia, and then fought on Napoleon's side in May 1813 as a lieutenant of the Westphalian Guard Cheaveaux-leger Regiment in Saxony. In the decisive battle at Kulm he and the entire French army corps under Bandamme were taken captive. Thereafter, he joined the Austrian army, following his feelings of German patriotism, and participated in the campaigns of 1813 and 1814 against Napoleon.

After the war, the returned to Göttingen, completed his studies, and then went on to the university in 1816. Not following the wish of his family to study theology, Seidensticker focused his studies primarily on mathematics, and then after several years concentrated on the study of law, and took his exam at Celle in 1824. In the following year, he set up a law practice in Göttingen and married. Due to his abilities, devotion to his profession, his unshakable sense of justice, and his impeccable honesty, he succeeded in winning the trust of many and in building up a large practice. In court documents it was said: "With regard to his character, it should be noted that he is possessed of a sincere feeling of justice and honor, which he has effectively combined with a powerful intellect."

The following description provides the best information about him: "Dr. Seidensticker had a robust build, was more than six feet tall and had a military stature about him that probably came from his days as a soldier and which remained with him in spite of his long imprisonment. He combined an inborn kindliness with an iron-like will that could become somewhat brusque when it came to conflict, as well as an unbendable determination when it came to duty and honor. All of these characteristics won him the goodwill of people of all ranks and made him the most pleasant kind of friend."

The revolutionary movements that took place in January 1832 in Hannover and particularly in Göttingen, and which were disastrous for Dr. Seidensticker, came about as a result of the July 1830 revolution in France. They were among the most moderate of all that took place, however. The uprisings in Hessia, Braunschweig and other small states, which preceded those in Göttingen, were more tumultuous and dangerous, but did win a number of important concessions from the governments there. In no other German state was the overthrow of a government more justifiable than in the kingdom of Hannover with all its antiquated feudal rights, especially as regards civil and criminal law, and its absolutist system of court justice. Without the consultation of local magistrates provisional councils had been formed in Göttingen and other cities, and civilian militia units had been formed to maintain order. Petitions were submitted to the ruling cabinet urgently expressing the desire of the people for a representative form of government. The council in Göttingen was composed of some of the city's most respected citizens, including lawyers, teachers from the university, and other well-known individuals. And. Dr. Seidensticker was elected commander of the militia.

All directives issued by these councils were moderate in tone and requested a legal solution to the problems at hand. Naturally, a number of proclamations were issued by other parties calling for more revolutionary steps, and served as the convenient pretext for the authorities to hold the aforementioned honorable individuals as responsible for them. In a few days, the entire movement had been suppressed by the military. As usual the guilty parties escaped. Dr. Seidensticker, who had first left town, decided to return, feeling that he was innocent of any wrong-doing. But as a result of recent events the government had become all that more vengefull, and sought to take its wrath out on the leaders of this bloodless revolution. As usual, the governments of the German states struck at those involved, including Weidig in Hessen-Darmstadt, Jordan in Hessen-Kassel, Eisenmann and Behr in Bavaria, all of whom were among the best and noblest of their generation. (7)

Only those who know firsthand, as does the author, the secret inquisitional style of justice of that time, which as noted earlier, was under the thumb of the court, or has studied criminal cases, can have an idea of the physical and psychological torture that Seidensticker was subjected to. He faced his inquisitors with manly courage and steadfastness in the course of two trials. This only contributed to making matters worse as regards the treatment he received. In 1836, the first verdict was issued against him, sentencing him to life imprisonment, a judgment confirmed by an appellate court in 1838.

His incarceration in Celle was initially very hard, but was gradually alleviated somewhat, as friends were allowed to bring him books and he was permitted to spend his time writing. He excerpted and commented on everything that he read and found significant. He also completed several of his own works at the time. He was especially preoccupied with studying the philosophy of Krause, who had a small group of quite enthusiastic followers in Germany, and who later enjoyed greater recognition, especially in Italy and Spain. (8) All attempts to seek amnesty by means of an act of mercy were rejected by the mailed fist of the House of Hannover. Although some were let free at times when there was a change of court officials, or as a result of some joyful event in the family of the ruling house, the doors remained closed for Seidensticker. Only with the birth of a now exiled grandson, Ernst August the elder in 1845 (the nemesis affected the dynasty only much later) was it decided that an amnesty might be granted, but only under the condition of exile from Europe, and this after a prison term of fifteen years. Seidensticker's release was greeted with great joy across Germany. Accompanied by a squad of dragoons, Seidensticker was transported to Bremerhaven in November 1845 and placed on the ship *Argonaut*. However, it had to remain in harbor for six weeks due to adverse wind conditions. Finally, it arrived in New York on 12 March 1846.

According to reports, "he was met with jubilant crowds here and in other places in the U.S." Banquets were held in his honor and presents were bestowed on him, demonstrating the warm feelings his countrymen had for him. It was almost too much light after such a long period of darkness." In New York, a formal public reception was held in his honor that was even attended by local authorities as well as a number of prominent Americans. On his arrival in Philadelphia he was welcomed by great festivities and given a magnificent banquet as a pioneer fighter in the campaign for constitutional freedom in Germany. Dr. Schmöle presented an emotional address in which he also made mention of Seidensticker's oldest son, Dr. Oswald Seidensticker. He referred to him as a highly educated young man filled with enthusiasm for all that was good and noble, and who would make an ideal citizen of his new homeland. Kiderlen and others also delivered fine addresses as well. In his response, Dr. Seidensticker emphasized how he had been heartened during his many years of imprisonment by the many letters from America, and that numerous petitions had been sent from America on his behalf, not only seeking his amnesty, but also offering financial assistance on his behalf.

In a letter published in the *New York Schnellpost* on 17 March 1846, Seidensticker eloquently expressed his heartfelt gratitude for the many honorable receptions that he had received. In August 1846, he was finally joined by his family of wife and five children. After some hesitancy he settled down in Philadelphia, where he was heartily and hospitably welcomed by Wilhelm Schmöle. At first he found work, editing the *Philadelphia Demokrat* for about a year, and then established his own newspaper, *Der Bürgerfreund*. However, a quite serious illness caused him to give this up before the end of the year. He opened a currency exchange office for immigrants and then later on became the accountant of a respected import company, a position that he devoted himself to with "indefatigable zeal and conscientious loyalty" till 1861 when he obtained a position at the toll house in Philadelphia.

His business affairs did not hinder him at all from participating in progressive movements, however. He was one of the founders of the *Freie Gemeinde* and one of its most active and reliable members. As natural as it was for a man like Seidensticker to be a Democrat, he was nevertheless one of the first German Democrats to bolt the party after the demise of the Missouri Compromise and he also spoke out against the spread of slavery and later on for the preservation of the Union. He also did so with all the seriousness, decisiveness, and strength at his disposal till the last day of his life. On 27 December 1862, he was buried in a most impressive funeral ceremony attended by a countless number of his friends.

News of the February Revolution of 1848 and the uprising that followed in March in Germany was joyfully received in America. (9) As in all larger cities, a number of public demonstrations were held in Philadelphia to express sympathy for the various revolutions in Europe. Mostly organized by Germans, these meetings were also attended by Americans of other nationalities. The German element came out to show its strong support for Friedrich Hecker and his companions Tiedemann and Schöninger when they arrived in New York in early October 1848. (10) Hecker was received with huge celebrations not only by thousands of Germans, but also by almost as many Americans, and even the authorities participated in these events. In Philadelphia similar welcome celebrations were held. Here he was also received by the citizenry and authorities. His all too brief visits in Baltimore and Louisville were also met by large celebrations. In

Cincinnati and St. Louis there were festive and enthusiastic receptions for these foremost
representatives of the 1848 Revolution. (11) They were simply overwhelmed by the
receptions they received from German-Americans, and by the fact that they also received
such a hearty welcome from Americans, who actively participated in these German
festivities and celebrations. This can only be ascribed to the fact that the German element
had by this time attained a firm and respected place in American society.

There are still a number of other persons relevant to the time period under
consideration here, and who contributed in some way to the advancement of the German
element. With the exception of Benjamin West, a born Pennsylvanian and later president
of the Royal Academy in London, and John Trumbull, American painting, which
excelled in portraits (Copley, Peal, Sullivan, and Elliot) and landscapes (Brown, Church,
Durand, Gifford, Cole and others) had not done as well in the area of historical
representation. It was none other than Emanuel Leutze who paved the way in this branch
of American painting. (12) He was born 24 March 1826 at Schwäbisch-Gmünd and came
to America at an early age with his parents, who were not very well off, and settled in
Philadelphia. He soon lost his father and his school education thereafter was sporadic at
best. However, his artistic talent surfaced and he began painting portraits at age fourteen,
becoming his own teacher, and then earning a living by doing decorative painting. At age
seventeen, he entered an art school. Later on, he concentrated on portrait painting, finding
employment especially in the South. He soon became well known as a portrait painter
and found sponsors, so that in 1841 he had the necessary funds to enable him to study at
the Art Academy at Düsseldorf. His first painting "Columbus, Explaining his Travel Plan
to the High Council of Salamantha" attracted considerable attention at the exhibit there
and was purchased by an art society. He also received the gold medal at an exhibit held in
Brussels for his painting "Columbus in Chains." In 1842, we find him in Munich, then in
Rome and Venice, where he studied Titian and Paul Veronese, all the recognized masters
of color.

The "Landing of the Normans in America" was completed in Rome and
represents a romantic and legendary, rather than realistic depiction of the topic, but is

nevertheless quite attractively done. In 1845, he returned to Düsseldorf and entered the most productive period of his life as a mature master of his art. He was now happily married to the daughter of Captain Lottner. It was at this time, that he created some of his best works, including "Washington crossing the Delaware." The roughly constructed boat carries the General and his companions through the icy waves and rushing currents of the river by means of its sturdy rudders, with the painting emphasizing Washington's determined stance and countenance, seemingly creating the impression that victory is at hand. The winter landscape is vividly presented, and the coloring of the scenery and the groupings of those in the boat are so well done that the painting cannot fail to make a powerful impression on the onlooker, expert and layman alike. It has been reproduced a thousand times as a lithograph and photograph and is no doubt the most popular work of art in America, with the exception of Trumbull's painting of the Declaration of Independence. Leutze was awarded the Prussian Medal for the Arts and Sciences for this particular work of art of his.

In 1851, Leutze was in America, but by now Düsseldorf had become his second home, as he had acquired such great recognition there as an artist. Nevertheless, as a successful artist he did have his share of critics, and so in 1859, he decided to return to the U.S. to complete a series of wall murals for new buildings at the Capitol in Washington, D.C. He undertook several trips to the West for the purpose of completing his great tableau in the corridor of the U.S. House of Representatives entitled "Westwards the Star of Empire Takes its Way," which was completed in 1862. It is a magnificent painting that is more reminiscent of the Munich historical school than that of Düsseldorf. It was stereo-chromatically produced and depicts a procession of life-size immigrants, equipped with all the necessary tools for mining and agriculture but also toting their trusty rifles, even the boy as well. The procession reaches a high point in the mountains and then joyfully gazes forth at the lands stretching forth before them to the silent ocean. It is well nigh impossible to enumerate all his works, but some of his central themes were drawn from the life of Columbus, from English history, especially the Reformation period, from the early history of New England, and the American Revolution.

The great number of portraits of prominent individuals from the U.S. and elsewhere, landscapes studies, and genre paintings bear witness to his tremendous output of his creative energy. On 18 July 1868, he succumbed to a heat stroke as a result of overexposure to the sun. One might say that having completed more than a hundred paintings that he had probably taken on too many projects altogether. He was highly regarded in Europe, but frequently underrated in the U.S., especially as he had no rivals here in the area of historical painting. It goes without saying that all of his works were not of the same high quality and his coloration is probably not in accord with newer trends in painting, which view coloration as the greatest challenge to the artist, although it might be said that Leutze clearly surpassed many of the German masters in this regard. According to the *Deutsch-Amerikanisches Konversations-Lexikon*, "Leutze is by all means the most important and intelligent historical painter that America can count as its own, and no other artist can portray American history as he could." (13)

Friedrich List settled down in Pennsylvania in 1825, and by that time had already had experienced a quite eventful life. (14) Born in Reutlingen 6 August 1789, he had studied economics and administration before taking a position as professor of economics in 1817 at Tübingen. However, he resigned the position shortly thereafter in 1819 to assume his responsibilities as an elected representative to the chamber of deputies in Württemberg. However, due to his liberal-minded critique of conditions there he was held in ill favor by the government, and was, therefore, excluded from the chamber and placed under investigation, resulting in a ten month jail sentence. Fortunately, he escaped, but returned several years later, only to be re-arrested and imprisoned at Asperg. He was then released in 1825 on the condition that he would immigrate to America.

At first he concentrated on economic studies. An unconditional opponent of Adam Smith, he advocated the concept of a national economy with great vigor and skill against the theories of free trade and unlimited competition industry. Here he wrote his *Outlines of a New System of Political Economy*. (Phildelphia, 1827). His teachings fell on fruitful ground in Pennsylvania. The railway system, which was still in the cradle at the time, became the object of a comprehensive study of his, as he sought to have its administration placed under governmental control. All of his plans were conceived of on a national scale. For a time he was quite fortunate in private speculation, such as in coal mining and in investing in newly established towns. His speaking engagements and many publications brought him into contact with influential individuals and in 1830 he was offered the consulate at Hamburg, but never accepted the position. After a short visit in Europe devoted to attracting interest in his theories and plans, especially in Germany and France, he returned to the U.S. Thereafter, he accepted a consular position at Leipzig. From now on his direct contacts with the U.S. had come to an end. He actively proposed and advocated his views in Germany, France, and England, and could be viewed as a devoted follower of John Bright. He advocated the view that: "every nation would have to exploit its own resources to attain the highest level of independence and harmonious development, protect its new industries as necessary, and favor the national goal of ongoing expansion of its productive powers rather than those of the individual." His rich and interesting life, which came to a voluntary end in 1846, might be said to belong more to German than American history, and has fortunately found a biographer with Professor Häussler, who published List's collected works in three volumes in Stuttgart in 1850/51. (15)

Heinrich Ginal was mentioned earlier as founder of the freethinking, socialist settlement of Teutonia. He was born in 1802 in Augsburg and came to America after theological studies. He served as a Lutheran minister for seven years in York County, Pennsylvania, and in 1836 moved to Philadelphia, where he established a freethinking congregation. In 1845, we find him next in Milwaukee, where he also established a similar congregation. His rationalist way of thinking was like that of Paulus, Neander and Schwarz. His views were always presented with great passion, intellect and wit. He left Milwaukee in 1846, and returned to the East, and the freethinking congregation he established in Philadelphia lasted into the 1850s. During the Civil War, he served as a minister in a Philadelphia regiment, earning the love and respect of officers and soldiers alike. In old age, he devoted himself to writing, and also offered private instruction in Latin, German, and English as well. On 20 January 1879, he celebrated the fiftieth anniversary of his arrival in America. (16)

The exact opposite of Ginal is seen in the example of another German, a doctor of theology, who became well known in religious, theological, and scholarly circles in the U.S.: Philipp Schaff. Although born in Chur in Switzerland on 1 Janaury 1819, Schaff studied in Tübingen, Halle and Berlin, so we may well consider him a German for our purposes. After extensive travels, he established himself as a private docent in Berlin and held lectures (1842/43) noted for their orthodoxy and inclination towards the pietism then prevalent in Prussia. In 1844, we next find him as a Lutheran minister in Mercersburg, Pennsylvania, a position he held till 1862. From 1863 to 1867, he lectured on church history at the theological seminary at Andover, Massachusetts, and from 1868 to 1870, he held similar lectures at the theological seminary at Hartford, Connecticut. In 1871, he accepted a professorship at Union Theological Seminary in New York.

Schaff was one of the most scholarly theologians of his generation in America and enjoyed the greatest respect and was moreover a prolific author. (17) Only the most important of his works can be listed here as follows: *The Principles of Protestantism* (1845); *Geschichte der christlichen Kirche* (1851 and 1861); *St. Augustin, His Life and Labors* ((1853); *America, its Political, Social and Religious Character* (1855); *Germany, its Universities and Divines* (1857); *History of Ancient Christianity*, 2 vols. (1860-61); *Slavery and the Bible* (1861); *The Christ of the Gospel* (1864); *The Person of Christ and the Miracle of History* (1861); *Lectures on the Civil War in America* ((1865); and *Christ in Song* (1869).

He also published a German hymnal that included an introduction by him. Most of his works appeared in German and English, and several were translated into Dutch. His contributions to American and foreign journals were extensive. From 1848 to 1850, he published a religious monthly *Der Deutsche Kirchenfreund: Organ für die gemeinsamen Interessen der deutschen protestantischen Kirchen des Landes* by means of which he hoped to affect a greater sense of unity among the German Protestant churches in America. He was largely responsible for the meeting of evangelical Christians that took place in New York in 1873, which was attended by clergy representing numerous countries. In 1871, he was a member of the deputation attending the international evangelical alliance that met in Germany. The Russian emperor attended this meeting during his visit in Germany for the purpose of better understanding the German Lutheran officers serving in the Russian Army in the eastern ocean provinces of Russia.

When Dr. Schaff arrived in America, he found most religious denominations estranged from one another. Freethinking, or so-called rationalist congregations and the secular German press campaigned against orthodoxy, particularly against the various German denominations. Our young professor, fresh from the University of Berlin, still under the influence of the romantic and mystical King of Prussia Friedrich Wilhelm IV, felt that not all church members were as firm and resolved in their convictions as they should be. A second Savonarola, he went on the attack against what he perceived as a lack of faith among his countrymen, as well as what he considered the frivolous and immoral behavior rampant in American society. He did so by means of public addresses and articles in various journals. His campaign aroused the enmity of many, since it was in 1844/45 that the ugly specter of nativism began to rear its head. The diatribes of a German against other Germans could only pour water on the millwheel, and Germans now angrily struck back at him. In 1846, a large meeting was held in Milwaukee to express indignation against Schaff and resolutions were drafted describing Schaff (naturally written as "Schaf," which means sheep in English) as an "unconscionable slanderer that no German could consider a countryman." Similar protests were held elsewhere against Schaff, who was described as an impetuous zealot. And, the secular German press bitterly refused to publish his response to such attacks.

Since he was accused of heresy by the Lutheran Synod of Pennsylvania several years later, and was only found innocent after a spirited and hard-fought defense, it might be the case that he was actually more of a freethinker than one was led to believe at the time. In any case, the point should be made here that Germans by now would not tolerate any kind of insults directed against them, not even from the learned professor from Berlin, and that they now had a shared sense of pride. Nevertheless, it should be said that Schaff was first class in his field, and that he exerted great deal of influence, and actually did bring honor to the German name as a noteworthy scholar and theologian. The French call such a gifted member of their nation, regardless of love or hate, a "glory" to their nation, and we Germans also do so. (18)

A predecessor of Schaff's, who was almost of greater significant, was Friedrich August Rauch. (19) Born 27 July 1806 at Kirchbracht near Salmünster in Electoral Hessia, Rauch's parents were simple farm folk, who sent him to school in Hanau on the recommendation of the local minister, as he had shown promise as a youth. He came one of the most dedicated and industrious students and then attended the University of Marburg, receiving his doctorate in 1823. Thereafter, he went on to further studies of theology at Giessen. In 1829, he served as an assistant teacher at a literary institute in Frankfurt am Main, and then as a docent in Heidelberg. At the age of twenty-four he received a call to a professorship at Giessen, and in 1831 an offer to another professorial position at the University of Heidelberg. However, before he could take on this position, he was charged with conspiracy for speaking out in behalf of the imprisonment of Weidig and other political dissidents, and immediately fell into disfavor with the powerful university chancellor, Franz Joseph von Ahrens. Facing the more than likely possibility of arrest, he decided to flee to America. He first stayed at Easton, Pennsylvania, where he concentrated on studying the English language. In 1832, he was ordained a minister in the Reformed Church, and received a call to York, Pennsylvania to head a classical school connected with a theological seminary.

When the Marshall College at Mercersburg was opened in 1835, Dr. Rauch was called as its president, combining this with a professorship of Biblical literature at the theological seminary, which had moved there from York. Rauch held both offices till his death 2 March 1841. Additionally, he also served as minister of the Reformed Church at Mercersburg. In 1840, he published a philosophical work *Psychology: or a View of the Human Soul, Including Anthropology*, which appeared in numerous editions and was also used as a textbook. At the time of his death, he was working on a work entitled *Christian Ethics* that remains uncompleted. A volume of his sermons, edited by Dr. Gerhard, appeared in 1856 under the title *The Inner Life of the Christian*.

Among the Germans in America who have made a name for themselves by means of their writings in English, the name of Isaak Leeser certainly should be mentioned. (20) He was born 12 December 1806 in Neukirchen near Bochum in Westphalia, and came to America in 1824, settling down in Richmond, Virginia, where he worked in various stores. However, he felt driven to study literature and history whenever he found the necessary time. He became an active member of the Jewish congregation in Richmond, later serving as its rabbi, and eventually acquired the reputation as a Talmudic scholar as well as an accomplished preacher. In 1829, he was called as rabbi to the leading synagogue of Philadelphia, a position he held till 1850. From 1857 till his death 1 February 1868, he served as rabbi of the congregation Beth-el-emeth in Philadelphia.

His scholarship was not confined to the German and English languages, the latter of which he was considered a master, but was also well versed in other modern and classical languages. In 1843, he established the second oldest Jewish periodical in the U.S. *The Occident*, which he edited for several years. Among his many works, the following should be mentioned: *The Jews and the Mosaic Law* (1833); *Discourses, Argumentative and Devotional* (1836-41); *Portuguese Form of Prayers* (1837); *Descriptive Geography of Palestine* (1845); and an English translation of the Bible according to Jewish authorities (1856).

A gentleman, who began his literary career under the direction of Leeser, notes: "It is astonishing that he mastered several languages to the degree he had." He was not only conversant and fluent in English, German and the Romance languages, but also in several Slavic and Asiatic languages, as well as Hebrew, all of which he handled with a rare degree of proficiency. He wrote English exceptionally well with a truly classical style, earning him a place of honor as an American prose writer.

Reference might be made here to several settlements founded by German Catholics, especially St. Mary's in Elk County, located along the Philadelphia and Erie Railway. This settlement has blossomed forth into a thriving town. It was established and organized by Schröder and Eschbach as a German Catholic utopian settlement, with the assistance of Mathias Benziger. In the first year, the latter gave every settler twenty-five acres of land and a building-lot in town. Ignatius Garner was appointed general agent by Benziger, and charged with attracting German settlers to the area. In 1844, he succeeded in bringing a sizable number of settlers to the colony, many of whom came from Philadelphia as a result of the violence against Catholic churches in 1844. The growth and development of this German Catholic settlement led to a bitter controversy between Benziger and the editor of the *Auswandererzeitung*, Georg M. von Ross. His concern was that St. Mary's would engender hostilities between Germans and Americans, but since that time, this has proven to be completely unfounded. Moreover, there is now even a protestant church there, located between two Catholic churches and the Benedictine cloister.

More important than the settlement of St. Mary's was that of the colony of Loretto in Cambria County, which was established by Catholics from Maryland, and from which the following settlements emerged: Münster, St. Augustin, and Gallitzin. In the course of time, they were settled mainly by Germans. In this area of settlement we come upon a fascinating and extraordinary person: Prince Demetrius Augustin Gallitzin, who was more generally known as Father Schmidt during his more than forty years of service to the region. (21)

Born at his family's castle Vischeringen in Münster in Westphalia on 22 December 1770, he was raised among the highest levels of Europe's aristocracy. His father was a well-known Russian diplomat of the eighteenth century, who had served as the Russian ambassador at the Hague. His mother was the daughter of the Prussian Field Marshal Samuel, Count von Schmettau, and a sister of Count Karl Friedrich von Schmettau, Lieutenant of the Prussian Infantry, who had been killed at Auerstädt in 1806. The father of young Gallitzin, who from 1783 on served as Russian ambassador, was an enthusiastic supporter of Voltaire and Diderot. His mother was a friend of Countess von Droste-Vischeringen and although born a protestant joined the Catholic Church in 1787, as did her son, with the approval of the father.

In 1790, he served as adjutant of General Van Lilien in Brabant, who had occupied Belgium with the imperial army in November of that year. The outbreak of the French Revolution motivated the young price to reject military service and turn to religious piety and quit the army and the conflict that now enveloped all of Europe. Together with a Catholic priest, Father Brosius, he sailed for America, landing in Baltimore in August 1792. There he entered a Catholic seminary, and was ordained a priest in 1795 by Bishop Carroll. He then served at Connewango, Pennsylvania, and then in Maryland and Virginia till he established the Catholic mission of Loretto in Cambria County, Pennsylvania. Here he purchased a great amount of land consisting of dense woodland. "After untold hardships and deprivations," writes Robert Johnson in Egle's *History of the Commonwealth of Pennsylvania*, and after having spent a princely fortune, Gallitzin succeeded in transforming this uninhabited wilderness area into a veritable rose garden. (22) His untiring energy made it possible for the German Catholic colony to gradually grow and develop to a population that has now reached three to four thousand in number. He died 6 May 1840 in Cambria after ministering to the area for forty-two years. He was buried at the cemetery in Loretto, and a monument was erected in his honor in 1848.

Aside from his untiring efforts as a priest, Gallitzin wrote under the name of "Father Schmidt." Among his various works, the following might be mentioned here: *Verteidigung katholischer Prinzipien*; *Briefe an einen protestantischen Freund*; and his *Aufforderung an das protestantische Volk*, which also appeared in English-language editions, and were widely read. A biography of Prince Gallitzin in German was prepared shortly after his demise by his successor Peter Heinrich Lemke, and an English translation was published by Rev. Thomas Heyden of Bedford. An extensive biography by Sarah M. Brownson appeared in New York in 1873. (23)

Johann Nepomuk Neumann, Dr. of Theology and Catholic bishop of Philadelphia (1852-60), was born at Leitmeritz on the Elbe in 1811. (24) He studied at the University of Prague, receiving his doctorate there in 1834. The story of an uncle who had gone to

South America as a Jesuit missionary and published several works about life, so inspired the youth that he decided also to go to America as a missionary. He did not, however, come as a missionary to the Indians, as he had hoped to. In New York, he was ordained as a priest in 1836 and joined the Redemptory Order there, and established the first monastery of that order in the U.S., whose superintendent he then became. In 1852, he was appointed bishop of Philadelphia, and lived the rest of his life there quietly and modestly till his death 5 January 1860. Dr. Neumann was the author of several theological works, as well a number of treatises on botany (which he avidly devoted his free time to), including *The Ferns of the Alleghenies and Rhododendrons of the Pennsylvania and Virginia Mountains.*

All these individuals accomplished a great deal in their particular fields of endeavor and did great honor to the German name in America. Another name worthy of note is that of Franz Martin Drexel, who founded the banking house of Drexel & Sons in Philadelphia. (25) His life story borders on romantic legend. Born at Dornbirn in the Tyrol in 1792, he escaped the invasion of the French and conscription by the Bavarians (1809) by fleeing to Italy via Switzerland. He then began a career of portrait painting, carrying on a successful life there. He immigrated to America in 1817, although the exact reasons for his immigration are unknown. After arrival here, he continued his art work successfully, got married in Philadelphia, and took many trips, especially to South America, where he visited Chile, Ecuador, and Brazil, and came to know many interesting people, such as Simon Bolivar. He also found work in South America as an artist, and added knowledge of Spanish to his knowledge of French and Italian. These linguistic skills together with his social talents, especially his musical skills, won many friends and acquaintances.

Aside from earning a good income, he also acquired a valuable collection of interesting items that were on exhibit for a time at Peale's Museum. Another trip took him to Mexico and Central America, from where he returned to Philadelphia in 1836. He tried his hand in the banking business in Louisville but was not successful. However, by means of cleverness, perseverance, and personal energy he worked his way up the ladder

of success in the critical years of 1837 to 1840, when banks failed across the country.
Together with his sons he established one of the major banking houses that survived
financial crisis after crisis, when others could not. In 1850, he established a bank in San
Francisco in partnership with others and remained with it for ten years. Until the time of
his death, which came about quite unexpectedly (5 June 1865), he lived a life devoted
completely to his business. His kindly and open-minded nature contributed to the great
respect he enjoyed, and his passing aroused great sorrow among all levels of the
community. His funeral was one of the most impressive that ever took place in
Philadelphia and reflected how widely he was respected in private and public life. He was
survived by three sons and three daughters, of whom one married John B. Lackmann, the
current president of the German Hospital Society.

Dr. Oswald Seidensticker, the son of Dr. Seidensticker, whose life story has
already been told, was born 3 May 1825 in Göttingen. (26) He entered the university
there in 1843, studying until 1846, when he accompanied his mother and his four
surviving siblings to Philadelphia to join his father there. In Philadelphia, he studied
medicine till 1848, when he received his doctoral diploma. He decided not to practice
medicine, but instead accepted a position as a teacher of classical languages and
mathematics at Jamaica Plain, Massachusetts. Thereafter, he opened a school in
Brooklyn, which he directed until 1858. From then until 1867, he directed a private
school in Philadelphia, and since that time has been a professor of German language and
literature at the University of Pennsylvania.

Dr. Seidensticker's connection with the German Society of Pennsylvania and its
Library led him to write the history of the German population of Pennsylvania, and
compile German-American bibliographies as well. His writings covered various topics,
including Franz Daniel Pastorius and Germantown, and many were published in the
historical journal published in Cincinnati *Der Deutsche Pionier*. His history of the
German Society of Pennsylvania deserves particular mention. All of his works bear
witness to a thorough knowledge, exacting critique and research of the topic under
consideration. The simplicity, clarity, and elegance of his style provide his writing with a

unique quality of its own. Dr. Seidensticker is a member of the board of directors of the German Society of Pennsylvania, the German Hospital and the Historical Society, and a member of the Philosophical Society of America. His communications, references, and explanations have been invaluable to the author for this completion of this work.

The German Element in the Northeast

II. New York, New Jersey, and New England

Chapter Six
Germans in New York City

New York – Founding of the German Society of New York – Johann Jakob Astor – Charles Sealsfield – German newspapers – Wilhelm von Eichthal – German bookstores – Political Life – Societies – Religious Life – Friedrich Wilhelm Geissenhainer – K.F. Eyler – Opposition against the Know-Nothing Movement – Annual Celebration of the German Society of New York – August Belmont

German immigration to New York, which was substantial in the late seventeenth and early eighteenth century, increased considerably again towards the end of the latter century, and concentrated mainly in the western part of the state. (1) The German population of New York City was insignificant at the time, as the Census for 1800 registers a total German population for the state of only some 60,000. Nevertheless, a German Society was formed in 1784 to support recently arrived German immigrants. (2)

Its first president was Captain Heinrich Lutterloh and its first vice-president was Friedrich von Weissenfels. (3) While the German Society had no trouble in obtaining its charter from the state legislature of Pennsylvania, the New York society, strangely enough, was not able to obtain one until 1825 in spite of the fact that several petitions had been made in this regard and even though several highly respected New Yorkers belonged to the Society.

No less that General von Steuben succeeded Captain Lutterloh as its president on 21 January 1804; Philip and Georg Arcularius, Jakob Lorillard and other highly respected men served as president before 1825. (4) The charter itself listed the following members: Georg Arcularius, Martin Hoffmann, Friedrich C. Schäffer, Theodor Meyer, S.W. Schmidt, Jakob, Lorillard, J.P. Groschen, Anton Steinbach, F.W. Geissenhainer, Georg Meyer, and Philip Hone and others. Later presidents were: Jakob Lorillard, 1837-41; John Jakob Astor, 1841-45; and L.W. Faber, 1845-47. (5)

The purposes of the German Society of New York were similar to those of the German Society of Pennsylvania, and it also blossomed like its predecessor from quite modest beginnings to become an influential and successful institution. By 1854, it already had more than a thousand members, and the most prominent German businessmen of the city belonged to it. In the time period under consideration, the name of one individual clearly stands forth, namely, the prince of trade and commerce, John Jakob Astor. (6)

Astor, born on 17 July 1763 in Walldorf near Heidelberg, came to the U.S. in 1783, and his life certainly falls into the time period under consideration here, as he died in 1848. The excellent and exhaustive description of him by Friedrich Kapp in his history of the Germans of New York goes well beyond the objective of this work and prohibits us from following his life story in the detailed treatment he surely deserves. (7)

In recent time, common folk in Germany, who did not have the good fortune of an education and grew up in rough and needy circumstances, eventually working their way to a position of wealth and social and political influence have frequently been underestimated. Without distinguishing one from another, they are thrown together with house servants, etc. who have attained wealth in life. It is quite true that in the mix some are given to an ostentatious display of their newly found status, something equaled only by their basic lack of education. Nevertheless there is always something instructive about such people, as no one rises to a moderate degree of wealth, and even fewer become millionaires, especially those who arrive as immigrants not knowing the language or customs, if not as a direct result of meritorious achievement, be it as a result of extraordinary work, will power, level-headed thinking, or perseverance. Nothing can be said to come from nothing, and fortune is not as blind as we would like to think.

The son of a good for nothing butcher given to drink, Astor was born in a small town. Early on, he had to help out in his father's business, but did not receive the best of bed and board at home, something he keenly felt, because he lost his mother at an early age, and his step-mother ran the household. But from what we know, the village school had a very good teacher from whom our Hans Jakob learned to read, write, and figure. He also became thoroughly acquainted with the *Heidelberg Catechism,* and the teacher was said to have remarked that he had no concern about Astor's future, and that he would make his way in the world, as he not only had an open mind, but more importantly some brains between his ears. (8) His older brothers all left their meager home as soon as they could. Georg, the oldest, moved to London, where he established a store that sold musical instruments. The second, Heinrich, had made it to New York, and when Astor arrived there, he found him married and in relatively good circumstances, although we do not know for sure what kind of business he was in.

After leaving Walldorf, Astor apparently traveled down the Rhine to Holland as a rudder boy and from there went to England, although we are not exactly sure of what date this was. It is assumed that due to the poverty of his family that his brother in London provided him with the funds necessary to purchase a ticket for the journey to America. When he arrived in the U.S. in 1784, he was conversant in English, so that it can be assumed that he spent three to four years in London with his brother. Therefore, we can probably assume that he left the Palatinate in 1780 at age seventeen.

What funds he saved in London, he invested in musical instruments, which he had brought with him. On arrival in New York, where he had gone to live with his other brother, Astor sold the instruments for a nice profit. Due to conversations with a German travel companion he became interested in the fur trade, and was encouraged by his brother to learn the trade from an accomplished fur trader and furrier. He soon acquired such in-depth knowledge that his master sent him to upstate New York and Canada to purchase furs, which he did to the latter's satisfaction of his boss.

After the death of the master tradesman in 1786, Astor started his own business and began exporting furs to England, while also importing wares for trade in America, soon acquiring for himself a solid reputation as a shrewd businessman in London and New York. His word alone was considered as good as cash. By the end of the century he had acquired a fortune of several hundred thousand dollars. In his wife, who he married in 1790, he found a life companion, who was unpretentious, loyal, and intelligent.

Although she brought no wealth to the marriage, she was quite perceptive and brought great insight into Astor's growing business.

From 1800 on, he carried on an extensive business, shipping entire shiploads of the best furs to England and China, making gigantic profits in the process. At the same time, he came to recognize the future possible importance of New York much earlier than anyone else. At the time of his arrival in America, there were only about 25,000 inhabitants in New York City, in number and importance as a commercial center it was therefore much behind Boston, Philadelphia, Baltimore, and other cities. In view of the geographical location of the city and in the certainty that the town would flourish some day, Astor began investing great sums in real estate, including land beyond the city limits. These acquisitions became the foundation of his later colossal wealth and helped him survive the extraordinary losses that he later incurred. In the last years of his life, he was still making large land purchases throughout the state of New York, as well as in states out West.

Due to the acquisition of great wealth Astor's goals and objectives expanded accordingly. English fur trade companies in Canada and in other British regions in North America had taken control of the fur trade, and as they possessed a great deal of capital, they could overcome all competition from the U.S. Astor therefore decided to challenge these powerful monopolies – the Hudson Bay, the Northwest and the Mackinaw companies. He contacted the federal government, and presented his plan to President Jefferson (1807), and was greatly encouraged by him to proceed. However, he was told that due to constitutional limitations and financial concerns that there could be no direct governmental support of his work.

By means of the 1804 Lewis and Clark Expedition, which had been given a government subsidy, the way to the Pacific Ocean from west of the Mississippi had been explored – from along the Missouri River on through the mountains to the Columbia River to the coast. Astor came up with a plan of establishing stations along this path for his fur trade business. He would establish a station at the mouth of the Columbia and annually send a ship around South America to this station, which would provide the basic necessities to colonists and inhabitants of Russian settlement of Sitka (Alaska) and at the same time purchase furs, and then send them off to market in China, and bring back goods for sale in New York.

According to Kapp, "Astor saw himself as the founder of a new international system based on the Pacific Ocean that would form a trade network embracing the world. He saw in his colony out West and the stations leading to it the seeds of a civilization that would blossom and conquer the wilderness and he welcomed an equally industrious and western-minded American population on the coast that seemed to grow daily before his eyes." (9)

In 1810, he received the charter for his Pacific Fur Company from the state legislature of New York. Naturally, he was its director and the soul of the company, in which he invested millions of dollars. It was the genius of Astor that was responsible for the plans and detailed instructions for his agents. He also lent his impressive name to the endeavor. It would go beyond the purpose of this work to focus on Astoria and its subsequent history; this has already been covered by the fascinating work entitled *Astoria*, which appeared under the aegis of Washington Irving, and is as exhaustively written as it is interesting. (10) Astoria, the stations and the forts on the Columbia of course came to an end, mainly as a result of the War of 1812 with Great Britain. One of the ships was taken by disloyal Indians at Vancouver Island after the crew had been murdered, but was then blown up by one of those mortally wounded. Another ship crashed and sank somewhere in the Sandwich Islands, and the war itself prevented sending more ships.

The expedition there had been led by the energetic Wilson P. Hunt, who passed away several years ago. Several forts and trading places had been established and a lively and profitable fur trade was begun, and one which Astor was again involved with in later years. One can say therefore that the plan succeeded only in so far as the fur trade with Asia was opened up and that the U.S. secured land holdings in the Far West, otherwise the undertaking was a failure. On the other hand, it did mark the beginning of the opening and organization of the fur trade in the Northwest, and contributed to our knowledge of the region. Astor bore the financial losses caused by the failure of the plan with a sense of equanimity. And so great was his fur trade business that it continued on as usual. His real estate possessions certainly came to his assistance at this time, bringing in great sums of money into his coffers. When he died on 29 March 1848, his wealth was estimated at $30,000,000.

Such a success story presupposes the following character traits: natural talent, an unusual intelligence, thriftiness, investment skills, punctuality, cold-blooded perseverance, and above all a sense of fairness. Astor possessed all of these traits in the highest degree. He was often reproached for being miserly and petty, and to be sure with some justification, as his donations for charitable causes were in no means commensurate with his tremendous wealth. His gifts included, for example, of $100,000 and a piece of property valued at $400,000 for the construction of a public library, which now has 200,000 volumes; $50,000 for a home for the poor children in his home town of Walldorf; and, $20,000 for the German Society of New York to help German immigrants. All of these might be considered great contributions from someone a millionaire ten times over, but perhaps not from someone thirty times over and hence could be seen as modest contributions. His son William A. Astor in the meantime has donated $200,000 to the library for the acquisition of some additional real estate nearby. (11)

That a man like Astor often had to reject many requests for contributions is obvious. He was therefore frequently and unjustly accused of being narrow-minded and stingy, and this was only to be expected given his wealth. Everyone in some kind of need turned to him and flooded him with requests for support. He usually only gave when he himself was convinced of the need and the merit of the individual request. Moreover, he is said to have done much good that was never reported on, so he made the mistake here of not publicizing his good deeds. He also did not heed the admonition that he, who happily gives, gives twice as much. But, on the other hand, to expect chivalry and generosity from one who had experienced a youth in such unfavorable circumstances would be unwarranted and would demonstrate a misunderstanding of human nature.

As a poor village boy he often had to eat his "bread in tears" due to the drunken altercations of his father, spending many a night sleeping in the hayloft of a neighbor's barn, eventually earning and saving every penny he made far from home by means of the strictest of deprivations. This enabled him to eventually to lay the foundations for a great business enterprise, one that he built and expanded by sticking to his well known thriftiness and punctuality. One thing is certain, and this says a lot in itself, his wealth did not make him arrogant at all, and he remained a simple and modest man devoid of any and all passion for luxury.

Although in an American environment, he always considered himself a German at heart. For many years he was not only a member of the German Society of New York, but was also an active member of its board and various committees. (12) His son William C. Astor was sent to Germany for an education at a time when this was not often done. He also enjoyed social life and the theater, which he visited as often as possible, and these traits further testify to his German inclinations. His wealth brought him a great deal of influence and as weak as the German element was in the early decades of the nineteenth century, it could not fail but to bask in his reflected glory, something that contributed to their status in American society.

There is no doubt, although sources on this are few that he sought to educate himself whenever possible. He must have read and written a lot. So much is certain, that the well known popular author Washington Irving undertook an expedition on land and water to the Pacific Ocean to put together the story of the rise and fall of Astoria and that made use of the well organized correspondence of Astor, his detailed instructions to agents, and his reports, all of which were supplemented by interviews with Astor. Irving said of Astor: "Astor is a man of great understanding from whose conversations one can learn a great deal." His nephew, who was the actual author of *Astoria*, and to which

Irving himself contributed, wrote as follows: "Astor can help you. He has organized all of his papers and documents."

Irving visited Astor frequently, especially at his estate at Hellgate, and even spent several days with him; Astor's house guest, author Fritz Green Halleck, spent several years there as well. Irving also spent time with Astor in his villa on the Hudson, and was actually named the executor of his estate. Astor did not take part in politics, but did know many politicians, such as Henry Clay, Webster, and others. He corresponded with one of the most important statesman of the day, Albert Gallatin, who valued his friendship. His letters to Gallatin remind us of the style of Addison, but are very well written, and reflect the intelligence of the author, who knew how to judge political affairs accurately. (13) As noted, funds were often requested from him for charitable causes, and he often presided at public affairs on their behalf.

For the years from 1820 to the early 1830s there are few sources regarding the German element. There is no lack of travel reports from Germany that describe New York, but they are of little use, as they are sketchy and unreliable. Also, they either have the tendency of painting an all too rosy picture so as to encourage immigration, or tend to stress the negative aspects of New York so as to discourage it. We can only assume that what Prince Bernhard von Sachsen-Weimar, who visited the U.S. in the 1830s, said about Baltimore, Philadelphia, and Washington also holds true for New York. (14) Everywhere he traveled, he found German societies for the support of German immigrants, as well as many well-to-do educated Germans, even scholars and engineers, and among their offspring many lawyers and elected officials. Almost all of the German states had consuls in New York, and they usually belonged to the merchant class, and German sociability and hospitality reigned supreme in their homes, which served as veritable centers of German social life.

It was in 1823 when the mysterious man landed in New York, who has gone into the annals of literature as Charles Sealsfield. (15) His real name was Karl Postl and who was born 3 March 1793 near Seefeld by Znaim in Lower Austria. His father was a judge in Seefeld, and provided for a good education for his son. After elementary education in Znaim, he entered the Knights of the Cross with the Red Star in Prague to become a priest, and later became secretary of the order. In fall 1822, he secretly left the monastery to come to the U.S., but the reasons for his leaving are unknown to this day. Just as little do we actually know of his first stay in New York, which lasted till 1826. He was next in Germany for a short time, and in England in 1827-28, where he anonymously published a work in English entitled: *Austria As It Is*, which attracted a great deal of attention due to its harsh critique of conditions in Austria, and which also rendered a return trip there an impossibility. (16)

In 1828, Sealsfield was back in New York, and traveled widely in the South, and served for a time as editor of the *Courrier de Etats Unis*, and then traveled to Paris in 1830 as correspondent of the *Morning Courier and Enquirer* and then was in London till 1832. From there he moved on to Switzerland, which he chose as his permanent place of residence, although he continued to visit the U.S. on several occasions. He died on his estate at Solothurn on 26 May 1864. Sealsfield never participated in public affairs in the U.S., and we only learned that he had become a U.S. citizen by means of his last will and testament. However, hardly any American understood American life as well as this foreign-born author. His writings exerted a great deal of influence on the educated classes of Germany, and also made quite a considerable impression here in the U.S., as his works were either written or translated in English and sold very well. Although he did not ignore the negative aspects of American life, he was obviously animated by a glowing love of America and its institutions.

If we knew more about the mysteries of monastery life, we could probably better understand the psychology of his mind, but there is no doubt that the ten years he spent in the monastery were quite a bit different than the rest of his life. In him we find not only an outstanding talent, but real genius. Familiar with classical languages, he was also fluent in modern languages as well. His German style is to be sure not what you could call exemplary. He created his own unique style and made use of it masterfully. His works reflect a rich and glowing imagination, an incomparable gift for inventiveness, an

incisive dialectic, and deep insight into the innermost recesses of the human heart. These
together with his gift for swiftly and accurately sizing up a situation provide his works
with an appeal that is as absorbing as it is lasting. To speak with the words of the poet
Platen:

> His spirit, the equal of Proteus, was tuned a thousand fold,
> His words are jewels, and astonish the world. (17)

It is too frequently the case that the best authors, who write novels that take place
abroad with foreigners as the main characters, attain but limited success. Mistakes about
the local setting, the customs, and national character are unavoidable in such works. But
Sealsfield is completely at home, be it in Puritan England, among the Dutch of old New
York, or among recently arrived immigrants. He is on intimate terms with plantation
owners in Louisiana, treacherous gamblers on the Mississippi, woodsmen in Texas, light-
hearted Frenchmen, a dim-witted Pennsylvania German, and the Creoles, all of whom
vividly come to life in his works. And he who knows the Spanish and Mexicans can only
admire his descriptions in his *Virey*. (18) Just as realistic are his descriptions of nature,
be they of Saratoga, the Green Mountains of Vermont, the Ohio or Mississippi River
banks, the prairie in Texas or the volcanic regions of Mexico. And, social and political
conditions are portrayed by him with great accuracy. Moreover, one can read between the
lines to ascertain how he foresees the seeds of the downfall of our way of life.

His most important works are: *Tokeah, or the White Rose* (1828), which appeared
in German as: *Der Legitime und die Republikaner* (1833); *Transatlantische Reiseskizzen*
(1833); *Der Virey und die Aristokraten* (1834); *Lebensbilder in beiden Hemisphären*
(1834); *Ralph Doughby's Brautschaft, Pflanzerleben und die Farbigen, Nathan der
Squatter Regulator* (1834); and *Deutsch-Amerikanische Wahlverwandtschaften* (1842-
43). (19)

As elsewhere, German life had begun to develop in the city and state of New
York by the 1830s. Not only after the appearance of the *Alte und Neue Welt* in

Philadelphia (24 December 1834), a stock company came together in New York City to establish the *New Yorker Staats-Zeitung* under the editorship of G.A. Neumann, who became sole owner of the paper in 1837. In 1845, ownership transferred to Jakob Uhl. Initially, the paper appeared twice weekly, and then became a daily. It developed into the most important German paper of the country under the capable and circumspect direction of Oswald Ottendorfer (1859), and compared favorably with the leading newspapers of Germany, even surpassing many of them in terms of quality. (20)

In February 1836, the *Herold* made its appearance, and was published twice weekly. It was edited by a German political refugee by the name of Zerlaut, who was from Baden. He focused mainly on European affairs, representing the most radical of views, as is often the case with exiles. In 1838, the rationalist preacher Fŏrsch founded the *Vernunftsgläubige*, and in 1838, Samuel Ludvigh commenced publication of the *Wahrheitssucher*. The first issue of the *Deutsche Schnellpost* appeared on 3 Janaury 1843 under the editorship of Wilhelm von Eichthal. The goal of this paper was to provide German-Americans with the most important political, scientific, and literary news from Germany, and it accomplished this task very well. (21)

Von Eichthal assembled an excellent selection of articles from the best journals from Germany, France, and England and provided his readers with the most recent and up-to-date news from Europe (news that had not been mixed up or mangled by cable dispatches). Several European correspondents wrote just for this paper, but he was not happy with all of them, especially when viewed from a higher intellectual standard than is usually the case with newspapers. However, for such a journal it was probably good business to have the more piquant than reliable, the more sensational than well informed kinds of news stories that it published. The still existing *New York Demokrat* was established by Wilhelm Schlŭter in 1846. (22)

The first German bookstore in New York was established by Wilhelm Radde, who had learned the book trade in Germany, and arrived in New York in 1833 after having stayed in Philadelphia with his friend, the book dealer and newspaper publisher,

J.G. Wesselhöft. In 1834, he opened a branch of the latter's bookstore in New York, which he took over some time later on his own account. His book stock consisted of the same kind of materials as at the Philadelphia bookstore. He also published several editions of selections of the German classics, but these proved to be unsuccessful. What stood in the way of the German book trade was the high price of German books. The best English works, which were all reprinted in the U.S., could be purchased quite cheaply, and so many an educated German who could understand English would become immersed in English literature due to the availability of cheap books in English. Only in later years, when local book dealers began to reprint German popular German works were the publishers in Germany forced to bring out cheaper editions. (23)

Julius Helmich from Bielefeld arrived in New York in 1846, and established a bookstore, Helmich & Co. His business blossomed, as he was a most enterprising and gentlemanly kind of person. By 1848, he was selling more than a thousand copies of *Fliegende Blätter*, which was quite good in terms of the German market here. He also created a great market for the writings of Otto Wiegand, and the works of liberal and radical authors. He left New York after several years, but his store was taken over and continued by L.W. Schmidt. The well known Braunschweig bookstore of Georg Westermann established a branch in New York in 1848, which was run by B. Westermann & Co., which was separate from the main firm. It soon became the best general bookstore in America, and thrives to this day.

In 1834, we find the first evidence of Germans appearing on the political stage in New York City. Gideon Lee, then mayor of New York, had spoken in a communication to the city council about the lamentable moral conditions of the city, and ascribed the main responsibility for them to the presence of German criminals. (24) The German papers protested this apparent slander, and a committee was organized to address the mayor with this issue. The latter gave the most placating kind of explanation and published a letter in which he rejected any kind of insult, stating that: "it is exactly the German immigrants, who are the most hard-working citizens." He also indicated that he counted Germans as his best personal and political friends. He had often been honored to have been invited to the annual festivities of the German Society of New York, and had spoken warmly and enthusiastically of the great value he placed on the German people.

In defense of the mayor it might be said that the governments of several German states as well as several Swiss cantons secretly had indeed exported their poor and criminals to America. To be sure, the total number did not amount to much on the overall scale of the immigration to America, and this element could not really teach the native American criminals anything new, but rather learned much from them. However, Germans everywhere protested vociferously against this disgusting policy on the part of the aforementioned governments.

Thereafter, we begin to hear of German political meetings. It appears that in the summer of 1834 that a German political meeting took place at Tammany Hall, the headquarters of the Democratic Party, which endorsed the principles of the Democrats. On 3 August, a meeting of Germans was held at the Free Masons Hall, and was chaired by Franz Joseph Grund. (25) It protested the earlier meeting at Tammany Hall, stating that it had been a one-sided meeting that had endorsed principles not in the best interests of the country and moreover that the meeting had consisted of people, who had not been in the country long enough to understand the political questions of the day. Although the term "Whig" was not used, it was clear that it was not a gathering of Democrats, and that it aimed to form a counterweight to the German Democrats. The whole affair was well orchestrated, as can readily be understood, especially when one considers that Grund chaired the meeting. Nevertheless, the entire affair served to effectively awaken the Germans politically.

On 27 October, more than 3,000 Germans assembled at Tammany Hall. Among the officials there were German politicians, such as J. Georg Rohr; Jakob Biedernagel, the lawyers John M. Stemmler and Friedrich W. Lassack (he was later elected to the state legislature, but did not remain a Democrat); R. Plant, and John J. Ricker. In an address by Stemmler Germans were called on to unite and make their presence known, and were advised to endorse the Democratic Party. Buchberger, Lassack, and others also delivered speeches, calling for the support of the Democrats with all available means. At the same time, committees were appointed to organize Germans in all quarters of the city.

The proceedings of the meeting were widely publicized in the Democratic papers of New York, and the German Democratic Party can be said to have had its origins at this time. The group met shortly before election time, when the Democrats of the city succeeded in winning by a slim majority at the city and state level, were Gov. Marcy won election. Germans ascribed the victory, especially in the city, as the result of their support, as the vote had been won there only by a margin of 1,800 votes and the majority of the Germans had voted for the Democratic ticket. Thereafter, a feeling of unity and of success at asserting their rights began to take hold among the Germans of New York City.

The Germania Society, which was founded 24 January 1835, owes its origin to this time period. Its purposes were as follows:

To unite Germans in America for the preservation and advancement of German identity, customs and instruction; to support the principles of true democracy in the new homeland; to nourish the love of the old country; to work for the improvement of conditions in Germany; and to support German political refugees in any way possible.

It can be assumed that the founders of this society were mainly exiles, who wanted to publicize their platform here as well as in Germany. Unfortunately, the constitution does not contain any names, and, we have no record that, as was suggested in the statutes, other branches were formed elsewhere in the U.S. The Germania Society first took part in public affairs at the celebration of the 4th of July 1835 and attracted a good deal of attention at the time.

On 23 September 1835, the first German militia company, the Jefferson Guard was formed under the direction of Captain Lassack, and was soon followed by many others. In 1839, one was also formed in Albany.

Germans had settled in the Schoharie Valley in the second decades of the eighteenth century, and actually were the founders of Protestant worship services in the state of New York. Their preacher, Wilhelm Christopher Bodenteich, should be viewed as the pioneer of the same, even if Justus Falckner had preached before him. (26) In the city of New York Johann Christopher Hartwig founded the first German congregation in 1748, which later on was led by the preacher Johann Christopher Kunze, D.D. (1784-1807). (27) After Kunze's death, Dr. Friedrich Wilhelm Geissenhainer was called to New York, and preached in German with various short interruptions to the end of his life (1838) at the old "Swamp" Church and in the Matthäus Church.

Geissenhainer was mentioned earlier as one of the prominent members of the German Society of New York and always occupied an influential position among the Germans of the city. Born 26 June 1771 at Mühlheim on the Ruhr in Thüringen, he lost his parents at an early age, but received an education in the home of his grandfather, who was a well known Lutheran theologian of his day. He also attended the universities of Giessen and Göttingen, and was a private docent for a short time in Giessen. In 1793, he came to the U.S., and served as a minister of a Lutheran congregation in Montgomery County, Pennsylvania till he was called to New York in 1808. Dr. Geissenhainer was a man who exerted a great deal of influence among the Germans of New York City. Small in stature, he had an extraordinarily expressive physiognomy, and when he spoke, he did so not only with his mouth, but with his entire face. He always gave the impression of being an energetic, fair-minded and scholarly person. He tenaciously clung to the German language, and as long as he was alive, his congregation remained a German church.

Geissenhainer was also a strong defender of the Old Lutherans and opposed the newly formed Evangelical Church in Germany. (28) However, it was to be expected and did so transpire that this new church also came to America. In 1837, a German

Evangelical congregation was formed in New York City, whose first minister was F.K. Eylert, the son of a Prussian bishop. Born in 1805 in Hamm, he was raised in Schulporta, and studied theology at Berlin and Halle. At Erlangen he wrote his doctoral dissertation on Clemens of Alexandria as a philosopher and author. He also published a collection of addresses and songs for military congregations (1830). What motivated him to come to America remains unknown to the author. Apparently, problems soon developed in his New York church, and there were reports of a negative campaign of letters, but the further fate of this scholar are of no further interest here, other than noting that Eylert was the founding father of the German Evangelical church in New York City.

Nothing did more to unite Germans than the activities of the "Nativists," who organized in the larger cities in 1836 and 1837, and embittered Germans by their explosive manifestos, causing them to pull together in self-defense. (29) The actions of the Nativists had already led to several clashes. In 1839, for example, a German society had held a ball that was attacked and roughed up by a bunch of rowdies, as frequently was the case at that time in other cities. Several men came to the defense, and the leader of the gang was killed and three others wounded. This bloody lesson exerted its influence for only a short time, because in August 1840, friends of German music and art were serenading the famous dancer Fanny Eisler in front of her hotel, and were then driven off by a bunch of ruffians. As a result, Germans held a meeting on 12 August that attracted many, and at which time the following statement was approved:

> We take note with deep displeasure of the rowdy and murderous behavior of a certain segment of the population, which conspires against us and we regret the failure of the authorities to put a stop to the same. We Germans, who were attracted to America as the land of freedom, did not come here to place ourselves at the mercy of such a criminal gang. We demand that the laws of the land be enforced and should our requests not be heeded, then we shall take the necessary steps to protect ourselves, our families, and our property.

Moreover, a committee consisting of Neumann, Bayer, Johannsen, and Bissing was appointed to publish the proceedings of the meeting in all of the leading English-language newspapers.

At this time, other German societies emerged alongside the already existing German Society of New York, such as the German General Beneficial Society (10 September 1840). Its goals and objectives were stated in its constitution:

> To provide an active, united and decisive opposition against the principles of the so-called Know-Nothing Movement (regardless if in an organized party or among individuals), so as to ensure the rights guaranteed by the Constitution; to create respect for German immigrants who have become citizens; and to confront and control the violent outbursts of an unjustifiable ethnic bias.

> These goals and objectives should be viewed as above and beyond all politics and political parties regardless of their origin.

> Further: We call for the establishment and maintenance of German schools in general and for the creation of the aforementioned as public schools in particular.

> Finally, the Society aims to awaken an active interest in everything literary and artistic that might be advantageous to German cultural life in New York.

It should be noted that it was around this time that an active agitation began for the introduction of German instruction in the public schools. On 12 March 1844, the annual celebration of the German Society of New York took place, and this splendid event was held at Astor's home. Consul K.W. Faber presided over the affair. A might black-red-gold flag flattered majestically from atop the dome of Astor's home. A toast was presented to "a free and united Germany!" Another, which reflected the Nativist atmosphere, was presented to "Our rights as American citizens. What the constitution grants us, we will never allow to be stolen from us!"

That Germans now as in earlier times did not place their candle under a bushel basket (but could also often be misunderstood) is shown plain and clearly by the following excerpt from the speech presented by Franz Joseph Grund:

> In education we stand at the head of all civilized nations. Schools and educational institutions follow our lead. The Americans, English, and the French have also been greatly enriched by the treasures of our literature. What would we Germans be if not for the blessings of our own nationality and the influence we enjoy as a united people, both of which strengthen the intrinsic value of our cultural heritage?

It was only natural that participation in the political process would reflect the rising tide of German immigration. Germans had already actively participated in the presidential election of 1840 between Van Buren and Harrison. Large meetings were held and there was no lack of skilled speakers. The Democratic defeat of 1840 did not discourage Germans, as it has always been their characteristic trait to pay less attention to a victory as compared with other elements of the population. And in the election of 1844 between Polk and Clay, they worked all that more diligently. And so in October 1844, a magnificent torch lit parade of the Democrats took place, which attracted more than ten thousand in spite of inclement weather. The banners and posters carried political slogans such as "Equal rights for all citizens, regardless of place of birth" or "We are not citizens by accident, but by choice."

The election of 1844 resulted in the defeat of the Know Nothing party, and removed it from the scene as a political factor for more than a decade. It was in this year that a man stepped forth, who exerted long-lasting influence in the political arena: August Belmont. Many immigrants assimilate so much into American life that they seem to forget their origins. Many of their countrymen are then surprised that this or that person is of the same origin as them. This is especially true when the name of the person does not specially relate to the person's country of origin. The name of August Belmont has certainly been heard of by hundreds of thousands of Germans, and has often been in the German press without many even realizing that he was one of them.

Nevertheless, August Belmont was a son of the Palatinate, and in spite of everything if we are not mistaken, a German to the core. Belmont was born 6 December 1816 in Alzei in Rheinhessen, and enjoyed a good education as a result of having a well-to-do father. (30) He spent a great deal of time as a youth on his family's country estate, and ascribed his love of horse and wagon riding to this background. At age fourteen, he became an apprentice in the banking company of the Rothschild brothers in Frankfurt am Main, and was then appointed to a position in a branch of the firm in Naples. He was so highly regarded that at age twenty-one (1837) he was sent to New York to open a bank there as a representative of the House of Rothschild. It soon became one of the leading banks of New York, and this was due to his energy, talent and zeal for success.

His stay in Italy awakened a love of art and his previous positions in Frankfurt and Naples provided him with the social graces that made his home in New York one of the most attractive among the upper classes of the city. In 1844, he was appointed Consul General for Austria, but he resigned in 1849, as the position did not suit his political views of the time, especially as he had become an enthusiastic American citizen. In 1844, he had joined the Democratic Party, and had cast his vote for Polk and Dallas. His impulsive nature did not allow for him to do anything halfway, and so he was as active in politics as he was in his business affairs. His marriage to a daughter of Commodore Perry, the famous naval hero, in November 1849 contributed to his increased social status. Four sons and a daughter survive to this day. He used his wealth particularly to collect valuable paintings, which still adorn the city of New York. His later stay in life in Holland drew his attention to the more recent French and Flemish schools of painting, and so we find works in his gallery by Knaus, Meissionier, Rosa, Tryon, Brion, and Galoit.

He actively took part in the presidential election of 1852, and after the Democratic candidate, General Pierce, had won election, was then appointed ambassador to Holland, a position he held till 1857 to the great satisfaction of the State Department. Due to his ongoing efforts the Dutch government allowed the U.S. to appoint consuls in its various colonies, which it hitherto had not permitted. During his stay in the Hague, Belmont became acquainted with diplomats from England and France, partly in Holland, but also party during his frequent visits to London and Paris, connections that proved to be valuable during the Civil War.

The leadership role he played in American politics actually began during the presidential election of 1860. He had often chaired political meetings in New York, and had done so with great skill and tact. He saw in Stephen A. Douglas a man that was neither a southern secessionist, nor a fanatic abolitionist and therefore as the best person to maintain the peace of the country. Belmont felt that the best hopes of preserving the Union lay in Douglas's popularity in the northern and border states. He therefore opposed the machinations of President Buchanan with all the influence at his disposal and worked very hard to get Douglas nominated as the Democratic candidate for president. In 1860 in Baltimore, he was appointed Chairman of the Democratic National Committee (of the northern wing of the Party). In spite of all his efforts and those of his party, the election went to Lincoln as a result of the division in the Democratic Party.

Belmont remained Chairman of the Democratic National Committee till 1872, when the Democrats nominated Greeley as their presidential candidate, who was also endorsed by the Liberal Republicans meeting in Cincinnati. One can imagine how difficult the political situation was for Belmont after the Civil War had broken out .His position, if not his principles, made it impossible for him to join the Republican Party, and yet he condemned the secession as strongly as anyone, and saw in the Union the best hope and salvation for the nation. There was no lack of opponents in his own party, while at the same time ruling Republican Party made a number of mistakes that could not be ignored. When southern states hesitated as to what do after the secession of South Carolina, Belmont exerted all of his influence to encourage the moderate politicians in the south to not follow the example of secession. The letter he wrote to John Forsyth in Alabama; Governor Johnson of Georgia (who had been a candidate for vice-president); to

Governor Aiken of South Carolina; and many like-minded politicians breath with life for their great love of the Union and contain the strongest arguments against secession. On 30 November 1860, he wrote, for example, to William Martin in South Carolina:

> The secession of South Carolina means civil war, which will result in the dissolution in our entire structure of state, and will mean the loss of life and treasure. If love of country and the Union are not strong enough to prevent the South from its insane plan, then I can only hope it does not lose its basic instinct for survival.

He also contacted the most moderate of the leading members of the Republican Party (Thurow, Weed, Governor Sprague of Rhode Island, and William H. Seward) to try to keep the peace right up the very end. Once war broke out, he was strongly supported the vigorous execution of the same. He corresponded with Lincoln and Seward, both of whom valued Belmont's influence in England and France. He was actively involved in raising the First German Vol. Regiment in New York (Blenker), and presented the same with a flag (15 May 1861), at which time he presented an outstandingly patriotic address. (31)

His greatest service was provided by means of his clear and penetrating reports of the conditions in our nation, which he sent to influential friends in England and France. In form and content these letters are nothing less than excellent. The few that have been published were sent to Lionel Rothschild, a member of Parliament; Lord Dunfermline; Nathaniel Rothschild in London; James Rothschild in Paris; and to Lore Rokeby. He clearly set forth and explained the reasons of how unjust it would be for the leading powers of Europe to recognize the Confederacy as an independent nation. Moreover, he stressed the strength of the North and the weakness of the South and the dangers that would ensure from a division of the Union. All of these correspondents of Belmont then contacted Russel, Palmerston, and Thouvenel. In July 1861, he himself traveled to London, and had a long discussion with Palmerston, and then sent Seward a repot on the meeting. When Belmont expressed his surprise that England, which had long led the battle against slavery, would now support the South, Palmerston responded "We do not like slavery, but wee need cotton, and we hate your protective tariff."

In 1863, we find Belmont in Paris, where he sought to exert his influence. He correctly saw that the chief danger of the time lay in Louis Napoleon's attempt to bring about England's recognition of the Confederacy. He wrote to Seward: "Now, as already during my first stay in Paris, I am convinced that the Emperor is the main person we have cause to fear. The secessionists are legion and are confident that the recognition of the Confederacy is forthcoming due to the support of France."

During the war he often had occasion to express his ideas in his speaking engagements. As Chairman of the Democratic National Committee he opened the Democratic convention in Chicago in 1864 with a speech in which he of course criticized the Republican administration, but at the same time re-iterated his support of the Union. In like manner, he opened the Democratic convention in New York in 1868, which selected Seymour and Blair as candidates for president and vice president.

Even if not as active as earlier, he still took the greatest interest in politics. However, he was never concerned with personal gain in the matter. His brilliantly independent position, his love of art, and interest in sports prevented him from ever being just a "politician" filled with nothing but power plans and intrigues. If we did not have a collection of his letters and speeches before us, which were only printed for small circles of friends and was never available in the book trade, then one would be led to presume that he dabbled in politics as a hobby. But in his book he showed that he was not only a real statesman, but a serious, devoted and enthusiastic friend of his country. A glance at his collection of writings full supports this view. Even his political enemies had to admit that his abilities were extraordinary and his character impeccable.

In New York perhaps more than anywhere Germans remained held the warmest of sympathies for Germany. Several papers were even devoted to exerting political influence on the status quo in Germany. Karl Heinzen's arrival in New York in 1846 was viewed as an event with political implications. (32) After the death of Eichthal, he took over the editorship of the *Schnellpost*, and changed its character so completely that it had to find a new readership. The arrival of the first steamboat, the *Washington* (1847) was jubilantly greeted, and the Germans of New York City presented it with a beautiful black-red-gold German flag. Two thousand dollars were collected for the widows and orphans of those who perished on the barricades of Berlin in March 1848. Hecker and his friends received a tremendous welcome from Germans and Americans of the kind that the princes of Europe only rarely receive. (33)

Chapter Seven
Germans in Literature, Science & the Arts

Scholars and Authors – Dr. Georg G. Adler – The Tellkampfs – Karl Göpp – Karl Nordhofff – Hermann E. Ludewig – Hermann Kriege – Anton Eickhoff – Magnus Gross – Max Oertel – Therese Albertine Louise Robertson – Albert Bierstadt – Thomas Nast

■■

As in the political realm, so too do we also find some outstanding German representatives in the fields of literature, science, and the arts in New York. Karl Follen was only active in New York as a preacher and lecturer for a short time, and Dr. Beck moved from New York to Boston, but others soon arrived in their stead. Elias Peissner was a professor of modern languages at Union College at Schenectady, New York, from 1832 to 1840. He published a grammar of the German language, based on a comparison with English. Students are shown the similarity of both languages from the outset, and were greatly assisted by this approach.

Isaac Nordheimer served as a professor of Hebrew and German at Union Theological Seminary (1836) and later at the University of the City of New York. He hat studied in München and received his doctoral degree there. Nordheimer was an important scholar and published: *Hebrew Grammar*, 2 vols. (New York 1838); *Chrestomathy* (New York 1838); *History of Florence* (1840); and, together with Professor Turner: *Hebrew and Chaldee Concordance* (1842). Nordheimer passed away in 1842. (1) His successor was Dr. Georg J. Adler, who was born in Leipzig in 1821, and came to America in 1833. (22) He served as professor at the University of the City of New York till 1860, and died at the Bloomingdale insane asylum in a mentally unstable condition. He was the author of many works, mostly dealing with philological topics, including the following: *German Grammar* (1846); *German-English Dictionary* (1848); *Manual of German Literature* (1853); *Latin Grammar* (1858); a translation of Goethe's *Iphigenie* (1860); *History of Provencal Poetry*, translated from the French of C.C. Fauriel (1860); *Notes on Agamemnon of Aeschylus* (1861); and his last work was a review of Lessing's *Nathan the Wise* in *Putnam's Magazine* (1868). Adler gave lectures in New York on Roman literature in 1862 and in 1864 on Goethe's *Faust*. His *Letters of a Madman* appeared in 1854.

A long and fruitful career was also established by Dr. Johann L. Tellkampf, who was born 28 January 1804 in Bückeberg and received an education in Hannover on the estate of his father. (3) After attending school in Braunschweig and Hannover, he studied law at Göttingen, where he received a doctorate. He then practices law for a time in Hannover and published a work on the improvement of the legal system in the German states. In 1835, he became a private docent at the University of Göttingen, but left the university along with seven other professors when the constitution was dissolved by King Ernst Ludwig, as they did not want to break their oath to it. Although the Prussian government invited to teach at one of its universities, Tellkampf preferred to travel abroad for research purposes.

On 4 July 1838, he landed in New York, and proceeded to Cambridge, and while he was there he received a call to a position as professor of political science at Union College in Schenectady, New York. He remained there till 1843, enjoying great success in that position. Many students as well as professors studied German literature with him, and he spoke enthusiastically of their diligence in studying German language and literature. In 1844, he was called to a position as professor at Columbia College in New York City, where Franz Lieber later on also held a position. Before Tellkampf took on this position, he traveled to Germany and English, and in the latter country engaged in extensive studies of the social, political, and economic conditions there. After returning to New York, he took up his position, and focused his studies on American business and industry, and wrote numerous works dealing with political and economic topics. . He also became a contributor to the journal *Hunt's Merchants Magazine*. He also worked for the establishment of steamship connections between New York and Bremen.

Earlier, while still a professor at Union College, he actively worked for the improvement of education in the state of New York together with Secretary of State J.C.

Spencer and Professor Potter. With the latter he published a work entitled *Political Economy* (1840). He was one of the founders of the Prison Association, whose task it was to work for the improvement of prisons and the reformation of prisoners. He was also a member of the German Society of New York and of another German society that aimed to provide for the poor. He studied the American judicial system and published a study of it in *The American Jurist*, and was influential in causing the state legislature to appoint a commission for the completion of a new legal code for the state of New York. This was chaired by David Dudley Field, who sent parts he had worked on to Tellkampf for his review.

By means of his numerous trips he came to know most of the leading statesmen and scholars of the time, and enjoyed their esteem and respect. A work he co-authored with his brother, Dr. Theodor Tellkampf, *Über die Besserungsgefängnisse in Nordamerika und England* (Berlin 1844), attracted the attention of German statesmen, and was followed by a call to the University of Breslau to a position as professor of political science, which he accepted to the dismay of many of his friends here in 1846. However, it was mainly due to the desire of his beloved and widowed mother that her son be near her that he gave up such a highly regard position here.

The further exceptional career of Tellkampf in Germany is beyond the scope of our work here. Suffice it to say that he commenced lecturing in Breslau in 1848, and was elected to represent two districts at the Frankfurt Parliament, but declined to run for a position there again. On recommendation of the University of Breslau he was appointed by the King to lifelong membership in the upper chamber of the Kingdom of Prussia, where he was a member of the liberal minority. In March 1871, he was elected to the German Reichstag, serving as a member of the National Liberal Party. After his return to Germany, he wrote a series of significant works in the fields of political science and economics, finally passing away on 16 February 1876. It is doubtful that he would have enjoyed a better future here. In any case it is regrettable that our country lost such an outstandingly knowledgeable man, who took such great interest in the public welfare, and was moreover a person of such a noble and impeccable character.

Dr. med. Theodor A. Tellkampf, came to America in 1839 for scholarly research, as had his brother, Johann Ludwig earlier. (4) Born 27 April 1812, he attended school and then proceeded to study natural sciences and medicine at the universities of Göttingen and Berlin. Although he graduated in 1838, he decided to continue his studies in Vienna. He then decided to travel abroad to study the topic of the geographical spread of diseases, and moved to Cincinnati, Ohio, where he established a highly successful medical practice, and then decided to continue his travels. From here he traveled widely, especially to Pennsylvania, New Jersey, Maryland, Virginia, and New York. He visited hospitals and asylums, especially those at state and local prisons, for the purpose of ascertaining the impact of group and solitary confinement on the inmates.

With the same intention, he then returned to Europe, visiting similar institution in England (1843). His exact observations made him an enemy of solitary confinement and he published widely on this topic. In Prussia, on the recommendation of Alexander von Humboldt, he was invited to discuss this matter with governmental officials in the hopes of eliminating this kind of imprisonment. He also visited Paris for several months to visit the hospitals there. He was offered, but rejected an offer of a professorship in Berlin. After publishing several more scholarly works, he then returned to the U.S., settling down in New York, where he opened a medical practice.

In New York, he took part in founding several societies, especially those devoted to medicine and the natural sciences. He helped found the Prison Society and served on the board of the German Society of New York. By means of his efforts a commission established regulations for the protection of German immigrants, including the provision that German doctors be hired in public health facilities. In 1849, he was appointed by this commission to a position as chief physician of the immigrant hospital on Ward's Island, but then resigned in 1850 after he and his assistants had survived a serious fever even as they continued to carry out their duties. He refused appointment on two occasions to the position of Coroner of the City of New York, as he explained that he had no interest in a political office.

In September 1861, he received a telegram from General Fremont asking if he would accept the position of chief staff physician in the Western Army. On accepting the offer, he received orders to go to St. Louis, and from there to the main headquarters in Jefferson City, and then on further to Springfield. After the recall of Fremont (20 November 1861), his staff, in so far as it involved those appointed by him, were dismissed, and Tellkampf returned to New York. He resided there with only a short interruption in 1867, when he brought his son to Germany to attend school there. In New York he enjoyed a great reputation due to his expertise in his field, his great intelligence, and his various endeavors. Aside from his many scholarly contributions to German and American medical journals, he published with his brother the aforementioned work, as well as *Tracts on Generation* by Bischoff, translated from the German by E.A. Gilman and T.A. Tellkampf.

Among Germans, who especially made a name for themselves in later years, mention should be made of Karl Göpp, who was born 4 September 1827 in Gnadenfeld, Silesia. (5) His father was a teacher there at a Moravian seminary, and in 1833, he received his first schooling at Herrnhuth in Saxony, where his parents had moved to. In 1834, his parents immigrated to America, landing in New York in September of that year, where they stayed as guests of Van Vleck, preacher of the Moravian congregation there. They then moved to Bethlehem, Pennsylvania, where his father served for many years as the administrator of the properties of the Moravians there.

In Bethlehem, he attended a private school from 1837 on, receiving an excellent education, and only German books being read at home. In 1841-42, he attended the theological preparatory school of his congregation. Classical studies, even Hebrew, were taught there, but what most interested him was English literature. At the wish of his father, who had been a teacher at the same school, Göpp entered the theological seminary of the Moravians at Nieskey in Lausitz, but which did not appeal to the Pennsylvanian youth, who had grown up in the atmosphere of American freedom, due to its rigid discipline as well as its mystical and pietistic orientation, which were then prevalent.

Instruction in the classical languages, as well as in history, however, was done very well and conscientiously.

Two years later he returned to Pennsylvania, and turned to law, with in-depth studies at Easton. In 1848, he got active in politics, and campaigned for Van Buren and Adams, the candidates of the so-called Free Soilers, in opposition against Cass, the candidates of the regular Democratic Party. Both Democratic wings were defeated by the election of General Taylor, the Whig candidate. In 1851, he opened a law office in Philadelphia in partnership with Joseph Minor, a kind and splendid man. This association came to an end two years later by means of the untimely death of Minor.

Although had left Germany in his early youth and had later spent two years there at a reactionary, pietistic Prussian Moravian seminary it might seem that he might be positively disposed to Germany, but this was not the case. He followed the German Catholic movement in Germany with the greatest interest, and viewed it was the herald of a new political rebirth. He strongly supported the political agitation of Heinzen in Germany, and considered the *New Yorker Schnellpost* like Gospel with regard to its news on Germany and European politics. His youthful heart burned with enthusiasm for Hungary and the heroic struggle of the Magyars. He shared the feelings of the majority of Americans, who saw in the Hungarian uprising a repetition of their own revolution against its mother country and found it fully justified with regard to basic constitutional rights.

It may have been the catastrophe in Hungary that awakened the thought in him that the U.S. should not only be an asylum for political refugees, but also the cauldron of new revolutions. At the time, he wrote a pamphlet entitled *E Pluribus Unum*, which advanced this particular view. America should become the point of departure of a political reformation of all nations and eventually the center around which all European powers would gravitate. He had in mind a kind of republic of nations, whose centrifugal point would become the United States. If we consider that Göpp was only a little over twenty at the time and was by nature poetically and romantically inclined, as was clearly demonstrated by the poetry he had written by that time, so then we can really not reproach him for such an all-embracing system that he proposed here. The world has rejected it, and always will, but the youth, who was filled with such ideas, deserves our recognition, rather than our scorn. There was no lack of this after the well-known German Congress at Wheeling (September 1852), which included the ideas proclaimed in *E Pluribus Unum* in its program and publicized them. (6) Göpp took an active part in raising funds in support of the 1848 Revolution, which had been set in motion by Gottfried Kinkel's arrival after Kossuth, and served as a member of the fund raising executive committee.

At the same time, he translated and edited a work published by Theodor Pösche entitled *Das neue Rom*, which also supported the ideas advanced in *E Pluribus Unum*. (7) Later, he translated Auerbach's *Dorgeschichten* for Thomas' publishing house in Philadlephia, a literary undertaking that enjoyed a great success.

His association with Thomas led to his assisting the famous attorney Brewster in defense of Thomas in a case brought against him by the publisher of Stowe's *Uncle Tom's Cabin*. Thomas hat brought out a good translation by Adolph Strodtmann of the work that had the whole country in an uproar. (8) The publisher of *Uncle Tom's Cabin* considered this a reprint and as damaging their book. However, the district court decided that the translation was a literary work in itself and did not infringe on the original, and moreover was a product of original literary work and as such entitled to protection.

That a man like him, who had always belonged to the most independent-minded wing of the Democratic Party, joined the Republican Party in 1854 like most of the leading Germans of the country, and actively supported the election of Fremont (1856), was only to be expected. In like manner, he fought for the election of Lincoln (1860). At the same time, he was a contributor till 1867 of Alexander Cumings's *Evening Bulletin* and wrote for other newspapers and journals. A younger brother of his, Max, had opened a law practice in Easton and done good business there. Karl Göpp joined him as a partner and both carried the practice on till 1863.

In 1861, he entered service as a Lieutenant of the Easton Infantry, became Captain, and later on Adjutant of the 9th Vol. Regiment of Pennsylvania, which his company had joined. Under General Patterson, the Regiment occupied Virginia, but its troops did not come into battle as a result of the incompetence of the General, who failed to pin Jackson down, and which led to the loss of the first battle of Bull Run. The Regiment was mustered out then, as the first call of the President had been for three months service, and G returned to civilian life.

In 1863, he became a partner of Friedrich Kapp, who at that time carried on a successful law practice in New York. This association was advantageous for him. In the meantime, he was actively engaged with literary work, translated Kapp's *Leben des General Kalb* into English, edited the article on the U.S. for a new edition of the Brockhaus encyclopedia, and wrote an interesting article on Canada for Kaspar Butz's *Monatshefte.* (9)

In 1868, he was nominated as candidate of the Republican Party for the office of judge of the Superior Court of the City of New York, but was defeated at election time by a strong Democratic majority. This was particularly unpleasant for him, as his business association with Kapp came to an end in 1869, when the latter returned to Germany. At this time, he wrote his *Leitfaden für parlamentarische Praxis.*

After having the misfortune of losing his wife in 1870, he then traveled to Europe to bring some of his children to his sister for their care with her. At this time, he visited Switzerland and a great part of Italy and England. His main occupation since 1869 consisted of literary work und translating materials from German and French.

In 1874, the attempt was made to close down instruction in the German language in the public schools, as also was the case in many other places, with the claim that the bad economic times made such cutbacks necessary. A large demonstration of Germans and other citizens took place (May 1875) at the Cooper Institute that protested vociferously against this movement. Göpp appeared as a speaker and his address was received with great approval. This first public appearance for some time brought him back to mind among the citizens of New York and probably contributed to his election by a significant majority to the office of judge of the Marine Court in fall 1875 as a candidate of the Reform Party, which consisted of Democrats, Republicans and independent voters. He served in this office to the great satisfaction of legal scholars and the general public.

As he had spent the greatest part of his life and especially his childhood and youth here, he was fully part of American life. However, his ongoing interest in German literature; his inborn inclination towards the land of his birth, which gave him an active concern for events in Germany; his need to publicly discussed the issues of the time; his fluency in both languages; his legal and political knowledge made him perfectly suited as mediator between Americans and Germans and to one of the more important representatives of the German element.

In the English-language literature of America there has hardly been any German as productive as Karl Nordhoff, who was born 31 August 1830 at Erwitte, Westphalia. (10) He is the son of a Prussian official, who participated in the War of Liberation (1813-15) and had independent political views. His father believed that a better future could be found in America under its republican institutions and therefore immigrated to the U.S. in 1835. The elder Nordhoff spent his first years after his arrival in Beaver, Pennsylvania, where he became interested in Rapp's colony, but then moved on further west, to St. Louis, and from there made trips further west, much beyond the borders of Missouri. He also visited northern Illinois and the Great Lakes. In the meantime, he spent a great deal of time in Arkansas, occupying himself with the fur trade. In 1839, he moved to Cincinnati, where he became acquainted with Dr. Pulte and Pastor Wilhem Nast, but then passed away in 1842, leaving his son over to the care and patronage of Nast. (11) He then attended preparatory classes at Woodward College in Cincinnati. However, he was thankful to his father for a strict German education, for he often accompanied him in spite of his father's travels. After several years at the College, he then learned the book printing trade at the Methodist Book Concern in Cincinnati.

From his youth on, he had an irresistible desire for the life at sea. As soon as he had acquired the necessary means, he fled the print shop for Philadelphia, where in spite of the fact that he was almost a boy, he spent three years on a war ship, honorably doing his proscribed length of service. After his apprenticeship had run its course and after having sailed around the world, he continued on with his life as a sailor on commercial ships till 1855, an indication of how much he loved this adventurous life. On return to Philadelphia, he worked for a newspaper, and then he moved to Indiana, where he taught German for a while at Asbury College in Geencastle. He also worked on the staff of the *Indianapolis Sentinel*, but then moved to Cincinnati, where he stayed with friends, where he published his first books about life at sea. From there he went to New York and worked for four years with the world famous firm of the Harper Brothers.

Thereafter, he worked on the staff of the highly regarded *New York Evening Post* for a period of ten years. During this time, he published several of his major works, such as his work on Califonria, *Die kommunistischen Gemeinden in den Vereinigten Staaten*, *Politik für junge Amerikaner*, etc. Since 1874, he has belonged to the editorial staff of the *New York Herald* and serves as a correspondent for the well known journal during the sessions of Congress. His book, *The Cotton States*. (New York: Appleton & Co., 1876) attracted the greatest attention and gave rise to vigorous controversies. As a dedicated Republican he expressed he spoke on the basis of a six month long tour of these states, expressing the opinion that the still terrible conditions there were for the most part due to the Republicans from the North who had gone there. Moreover, the book was dedicated to President Grant and to be sure in the following forthright manner:

To the President of the United States:

Dear Sir,

I respectfully submit to you a report on the political and industrial situation of several southern states, the results of a research trip that I made in the spring and summer of this year in the commission of Mr. James Gordon Bennet for the *New York Herald*. The facts that I have collected will perhaps be of interest to you. I respectfully believe that you have not succeeded in satisfying the needs of the people of the south, especially because you in your position have unfortunately found it difficulty to ascertain the true condition in these states, a condition that has changed so quickly and constantly during your administration. If you had tried to personally visit the same in 1874-75, as you did in 1865, then I doubt that your policy towards the South would have been different in many aspects from the course you have taken, since it is your duty, as it is certainly y our desire as well, to secure the freedom of all your fellow citizens, as well as to increase their welfare and happiness.

The independence of his judgment, which clearly came through in his report, however, brought him into opposition with the radical wing of his party, although Nordhoff, as he said, had learned to hate slavery at the knees of his father and had always supported the candidates of the Republican Party for federal office. Moreover, this disagreement brought no remuneration to his literary efforts. It might be noted that Grant had made a report on conditions in the South soon after peace had been made that was so rosy one that it aroused the deepest displeasure with Republicans, such as Sumner, Schurz and others.

A review of the life of Karl Nordhoff brings us irrevocably to a comparison with Bayard Taylor, whose recent death was so deeply mourned. Germany was the homeland of Nordhoff, for Taylor it became a second home from an intellectual point of view. Germans regarded him at least as half belonging to them. Both began their careers in the dark rooms of printing presses, both were driven as youth to far off lands, both were not blessed with wealth and made their first great trips under the most unfavorable circumstances, and both became writers and journalists with the largest newspapers of the American press. The richer imagination of Taylor led him to the field of poetry and novel writing, while Nordhoff tilled the field of practical politics, statistics, and national economics. If Taylor ended with a splendid diplomatic position, then so did such a position not lay beyond the reach of Nordhoff. At the time of Taylor's death, there were many important persons saying that Nordhoff should be appointed to replace him. As a very important force in the American press, which is not only called a great power here, but actually is one, German-Americans have just cause to give to tender their highest regard to Nordhoff.

Hermann Ernst Ludewig has an honorable place among German-American scholars. (12) He was born in 1809 in Dresden, and had devoted himself to jurisprudence in the old country and we find him in New York in 1842, where he established an extensive law practice. In Germany he already had published a work entitled *Livre des Ana, Essay de Catalogue Manuel* and a *Bibliotheque economique*. He also published a bibliographical work here, *Literature of American Local History*, which was greatly valued, as well as several other smaller works for the purpose of building libraries and catalogs. He was a path breaker for this field that is now actively being cultivated, and for which there is an association, which sponsors its own very interesting annual meetings.

The work, however, to which he devoted the best ten years of his life with all his strength, that is as far as he had time from his extensive law practice, is *The Literature of American Aboriginal Languages*. It remained in manuscript form at the time of his death. He regarded this valuable work as only as a first draft, but turned it over to the famous German book dealer in London, Nikolaus Trübner for publication when he visited New York as he had heard of the work. Ludewig died in 1856 and the work appeared in London in 1857, with additions and improvements of Professor W.W. Turner of Washington. It consists of an alphabetically arranged bibliography of the literature dealing with the Indians of North America. For every tribe, of which 1,030 were listed, it is exactly indicated in which works and on which pages there is information on their history, language, religions, etc. The well known German-American author Karl Knortz noted with regard to this book:

It contains references to works on more than six hundred tribes, and to be sure references that are not only in English and French sources, but also to books in all the European languages. One can only imagine what an astonishing amount of scholarship, what industry and what stamina and perseverance must go into such a work by glancing at a page of this book and then you will know that the author has based it on works much less significant than his. (13)

In 1845, Hermann Kriege landed in New York, a young man of great talent, filled with a love of freedom and the improvement of the conditions of the downtrodden. (14) He was born on 20 June 1820 in Westphalia, first studied in Leipzig, then did his military year of service in Bielefeld as a volunteer, and then continued his studies in Berlin. There he formed a socialist literary circle, but then came under investigation and so fled to Belgium, then to London, finally finding a place of freedom here. In New York, he founded the *Volks-Tribűne* and was one of the first to call for a social democratic movement among the working class.

With the enthusiasm that was inborn with him he agitated actively against slavery. He did a great service by his advocacy of granting public land to those who would settle it. His deepest wish in this regard, however, was only fulfilled by the Homestead Act of 1862, whose greatest advocate in Congress was Andrew Johnson, who later fell into disrepute. In like manner he was deeply interested in elevating the political status of Germans, as well as their political education. For this purpose he wrote a series of life stories of the heroes of the American Revolution as examples for his German compatriots. This series of booklets appeared under the title *Die Väter der Republik*, which contained biographies of Thomas Paine, George Washington, Benjamin Franklin and Thomas Jefferson. He presented them, as to be expected, less critically than in a positive and gripping manner.

The stormy year of 1848 brought him of necessity back to Germany. (15) He sought to agitate as a social democrat, attended the workers' congress in Berlin, but soon became disenchanted. "The proletariat for which we fought does not exist," he wrote to a friend.

He returned deeply disappointed in 1849, trying his hand at literary efforts in Chicago and elsewhere, but then due to his health returned to New York, where he died 31 December 1850 in dissolute spirit. He had succeeded herein acquiring a group of friends who loved him with great adoration. And even those who considered his views as to extreme and overboard regarded him as talented and honorable man as he was honest and true to his convictions.

Later arrivals in the U.S., who made New York their permanent place of residence, included two who became well known authors: Magnus Gross and Anton Eickhoff. Magnus Gross already had an interesting life in Germany. (16) He was born 28 September 1817 in Fulda in Electoral Hessia. After attending the gymnasium there, he worked for six years as an apprentice, then as an assistant in an apothecary, and then went to the University of Giessen in 1838, where he studied the natural sciences, especially chemistry with Liebig. He completed his studies at the University of Marburg with the chemist Bunsen in 1842. A discovery of his in the art of dying, which was patented by the Bavarian government, causing him to design factories, and led to his being called as a professor of chemistry to the agricultural school at Schleisheim near Munich.

The illness of his brother in the U.S. caused him to remove there before he had taken on this position, however, and he landed in New Orleans in spring 1846, from when he went to St. Louis.   There he designed a candle and soap factory, but soon got involved in politics, quickly becoming familiar with American conditions. He became a correspondent for the *Deutsche Schnellpost* in New York and worked part time for the *Anzeiger des Westens* in St. Louis during the Mexican War, 1846-48. He was a decided Democrat, as most Germans were at the time, and worked in 1848 for the election of General Cass as president. From then on, he worked as a political journalist. Here and there, he tried his hand at publishing newspapers, first in Louisville, then in Cincinnati, until he found a permanent place of residence in New York in 1854, and a position with the *Abendzeitung*. Journalists in this country are a wandering breed, and so we next find him in Philadelphia after 1854, but only till 1856, in which year he settled in Washington.

There he took on the publication of campaigning publications during the Fremont campaign on behalf of the National Executive Committee of the Democratic Party.

At this time in particular, Gross aroused a great deal of hostility. Most of the prominent German journalists and politicians had joined the Republican Party. The recently arrived German immigrants, although previously (before 1856) joining the Democrats, got involved in the election, and exerted a great deal of influence if not by their number of votes at least by their speeches and publications. These Germans, who in spite of the changes suffered by the older political parties, of which the Democratic Party had taken a questionable path, still clung to their old love for the Democrats, but now danced around on the issues of the day and Gross understandably was not spared.

For a long time, he seems to have lost his interest in politics, because he opened an apothecary at Washington and practiced pharmacy and chemistry. However, as the election of 1860 approached, he could not resist getting involved. Like an old battle horse at the sound of the trumpet he plunged right into the campaign, sold his business, accompanied Douglas on his campaign trip through New York and worked for him by giving speeches and speaking on his behalf. He remained there and worked as an editor for the political section of the *New Yorker Staats-Zeitung*, 1860-69.

As much as he lacked of thoroughness and concentration in the first years of his political career, as he made his way through by trial and error, we cannot deny that in the course of time he finely developed into a fine author. That he was the political editor of such an outstanding paper as the *Staats-Zeitung* is the best proof for this. He also however actively got involved in politics. From 1863 to 1870, Gross participated in the state conventions of the Democratic Party. In 1867, he was elected by the people to the convention for the revision of the state constitution, an office that generally called for those known for their knowledge and standing. In 1869, he was appointed to the board of education of the City of New York, a position just as important, and here he accomplished a great deal on behalf of the introduction of German into the public schools.

A more adventurous life is that of Anton Eickhoff, whose life was rich with changing destinies. Born 11 September 1827 at Lippstadt in Westphalia, he received his first education in the school of his hometown, and then attended the school at Lippstadt and began at age sixteen to write prose and poetry, publishing them in the newspapers of the province, which gladly supported this youthful talent. His first written works were a bit to political for a Prussian subject and although he had passed his 1846 exam to become a teacher, court proceedings were instituted against him, causing him to immigrate. In October 1846, he boarded ship at Bremen. A journey lasting eighty-four days ensued, and he landed in New Orleans on 1 January 1847, a foretaste of the sad fate that awaited him early on in America.

It is told that several young educated Germans at the time of their arrival in St. Louis found themselves forced to work for low pay studying the geology of area stone quarries. With Eickhoff it is certain that he had to earn his daily bread working on steam boats on the rivers of the West. Only he who knows from his own experience how terribly hard this work is can understand how much a young man of education, and one additionally with a poetical vein, must have suffered in this situation. He traveled on the Mississippi, from its mouth all the way up to the falls in Minnesota, on the Arkansas to Little Rock, on the Ohio to its origin and finally on the Missouri to points beyond the borders of civilization. In summer 1847, he spent several weeks in the territory reserved for the Cherokees at the blossoming Indian colony in present day Kansas, located west of Missouri.

On return to St. Louis in 1848, he obtained a position as a teacher at the Jesuit school known as the University of St. Louis. From a steamboat worked to a teacher at such a well-off and popular educational institution is a quick jump to make and the best proof that either impatience or the lack of positions must have caused him to make the wrong first step in America, which is one that sometimes cannot later be made good.

Already in summer 1848, he founded in St. Louis a journal that appeared twice weekly, the *St. Louis Zeitung*. The year 1849 was an unfortunate one for St. Louis and for him. In May, a great fire destroyed many steamboats in the harbor and almost the entire business district of the city, and cholera came on with seemingly endless strength, driving a great number of people away in the course of the summer. His business came to a sudden end. He rushed to Dubuque to become editor of *Der Nordwestliche Demokrat*. His course from now on, for a number of years, was like that of a comet. In the following winter, an illness caused him to go to Louisiana, in the spring we find him then in Louisville, where he edited the *Beobachter am Ohio* for a time. Then he moved back to New York, where he edited the *Abendzeitung*. From 1854-56, he edited the *New Yorker Staats-Zeitung*, later the *New Yorker Journal*, and for a short time, the *Presse*.

During the Civil War after the battle of Gettysburg (1-4 July 1863) Eickhoff was appointed by Governor Seymour of New York to the position of commissar with the responsibility providing for the care and subsistence of the New York troops, a position he executed to the satisfaction of all. In the same year he was elected to the state legislature on the Democratic ticket, but declined to stand for election for the following term. Problems in the City of New York together with the corruption in the Democratic Party caused him to turn away from politics for several years, and he did not participate in public affairs again until the party had re-organized itself. In 1872, he became secretary of the Democratic General Committee, and in 1873 he was elected to the office of coroner, one of the most important and responsible offices of New York City.

Thereafter, his party nominated him for Congress to represent the seventh district of the state of New York, and he took office in March 1877, hold it then till March 1879. In the previous election, he had been defeated by a German, Edwin Einstein, who was born in Ohio. In the meantime, Congressional work did not suit his interests. He felt that he had lost fluency for public speaking by his long absence from public life. However, his speeches do not confirm this at all, as evidence by h is speech presented in Congress on the death of Schleicher.

Eickhoff won his main importance as a political author. He belonged to the time
in which Germans, who devoted themselves to politics, first had to become familiar with
the history of the land and the character of its statesmen. This was a time when one would
have to make great efforts to edit together the news for the readers of newspapers, as
there were no telegraphic reports, and Congressional and legislative reports, as extensive
as they were, would have to be studied, as one did not get a hold of these in abridged
format or verbally. Eickhoff had spoken in almost all states, where there were Germans,
and personally knew most politicians and had become quite familiar with the character of
the people, with its political past and present that he could and did exert great influence
as a journalist. He still is in the age that permits him to have a great deal of influence.

The *Katholische Kirchzeitung*, which had earlier appeared in Baltimore and them
moved to New York has been edited for many years by Maximilan Oertel, one of the
most brilliant journalists among the Germans in this country. (17) Educated in theology at
German universities, Oertel joined the Old Lutheran Church, of which so much was
heard in the 1830s and early 1840s. The well-known Bishop Stephan, who looked more
like a retired Prussian officer than a Bishop of the Lutheran Church, and was supported
and protected by the Saxon pietistic minister of Einsiedel, was the guiding light of this
religious community. Oertel came with him and many other pastors in early 1839 to St.
Louis., and belonged to the most pious of the pious. Whether it was the deception that he
suffered and the community suffered because of Stephan, who soon revealed himself
after their arrival as a domineering and selfish person obsesses with free love, to wander
from the teachings of the group, or if it was he sought further confirmation of his
salvation than the most strict, orthodox Lutheran dogma offered, Oertel was transformed
from the most devoted student of the burner of papal bulls to a staunch believing
Catholic. (18)

Regardless whether he was Old Lutheran or Ultramontane, there was always gay
and free view of life that had the upper hand with him. A healthy, oft sharp sense of
humor adorned his works, which reminds us frequently of the splendid old Abraham a
Santa Clara. There is always something mischievous about him, and many an honorably

Catholic has often had difficulty establishing whether he actually was a friend of foe of the Catholic Church, and if he was making fun of it. The Pope, who in the meantime must know the facts better than others, had no doubt in the faith of "Father Oertel" (as he is often called, although he was not ordained), because if we are not mistaken, he named him a knight in the Holy Gregorian Order. Oertel lives on Long Island near New York and does not seem to have lost his sense of humor. Aside from his religious views, which we do not have to pass judgment on, he usually hits the nail on the head in all other questions of the day and is without doubt one of the most interesting characters among German authors in America.

The German-American element counts to its ranks one of the most well educated and intellectual women in history, Mrs. Robinson, better known under her pen name of "Talvj." Therese Albertine Louise Robinson nee Jakob, the youngest daughter of the political and philosophical writer, Ludwig Heinrich von Jakob, was born 26 January 1797 in Halle, where her father was a professor of philosophy at the university there. (19) After the university was dissolved (1806), she accompanied her father to Kharkov in southern Russia and in 1809 to St. Petersburg, where Professor von Jakob held important governmental positions, mainly concerned with the revision of the criminal laws of Russia. The daughter, who was already a diligent student in her youth, became very well acquainted with the Russian language and literature. In 1816, he returned with her father to Halle, and studied classical languages, especially Latin, for which she had not had time in Russia.

Around this time, she began to develop as an author, but for a long time was against publishing her own works, and only later on published some of her stories under the title *Psyche* (Halle 1825) and others in almanacs under the pen name of Talvj, which was made up of the beginning letters of her name T(herese) A(libertine) L(ouise) v(on) J(akob). The desire to learn Serbian arose in her at this time as a result of the reviews of Jakob Grimm of the Serbian folk songs. With the encouragement of Wuk Stephanowitsch and B. Kopitar she translated the *Volkslieder der Serben*, which appeared due to the support of Goethe in Halle (2 vols., 1825-26; 3rd edition, 1853). This was a new field and secured not only the lasting friendship of the old master Goethe, but also contacts with Jakob Grimm, Wilhelm and Alexander von Humboldt, Fr. K. von Savigny and others.

After she married Professor Edward Robinson in 1828, they both came to America in 1830, where she diligently studied the languages of the Native Americans, the fruits of which appeared by means of her German translation of Pickering's work *Essay on a Uniform Orthography of the Indian Languages of North America* (Leipzig, 1834). She also wrote a numberof articles for the *Biblical Respository*, which had been founded by her husband, and a number of essays on the topic *Historical View of the Slavic Languages*, which appeared as a German edition by K. von Oelberg (Berlin, 1837), and which she later expanded, and then brought out in the U.S. (New York, 1850). Jakob Grimm on her first edition: "It is a work that reflects a thorough knowledge of the topic." A new German translation of the expanded edition of 1850 appeared later (Leipzig: Brühl, 1852).

From 1837 to 1840, she visited Europe with her children, while her husband undertook a research trip to Palestine. She then published her *Versuch einer geschichtlichen Charakteristik der Volkslieder germanischer Nationen, mit einer Uebersicht der Lieder aussereuropäischer Völkerschaften.* (Leipzig, 1840) and the the small but very influential work: *Die Unächtheit der Lieder Ossians.* (Leipzig, 1840), which appeared in English as: *Ossian Not Genuine.* (Dublin, 1841). Parts of the first mentioned work had appeared earlier in the *North American Review.* By means of her critical study on Ossian Mrs. Robinson had brought an end to the debate surround the originality of MacPherson's edition of Ossian from the previous century. She based her work on the research of O'Reilly and Drummond, and then showed that the work was a falsification, as it was all too artistically produced, was full of mistakes in the Gaelic dialect, there was no direct story line and the descriptions of nature were all too veiled and all encompassing, as they had been inserted into the story here and there by MacPherson, as had been a number of mangled versions of old Irish folk songs. There certainly was a flood of criticism against her work, but they failed to shake the weight and thorough research of Mrs. Robinson.

After returning to New York, where her husband was a professor of Biblical Literature from 1837 until his death in 1863 at Union Theological Seminary, she devoted herself to the study of American history, and published as a result of her research *Eine Geschichte des Kapitän John Smith* (Leipzig, 1847) and in the same year *Die Kolonisation von New England* (Leipzig, 1847). A poor translation of the latter appeared in London in 1851.

Her acquaintance with Washington Irving, which dated back to Irvining's return from Spain (1846), led her to the field of literature, and from which the following novellas emerged: *Heloise, or the Unrevealed Secret* (New York, 1850; German editdion, Leipzig, 1850); *Life's Discipline, A Tale of the Annals of Hungary* (New York, 1851); and *Die Auswanderer* (Leipzig, 1852), which she translated and published as *The Exiles* (New York, 1853), and which also appeared later as: *Woodhill* (1856). Aside from this, Mrs. Robinson also published numerous essays on scholarly and literary-historical topics in American and German journals. After the death of her husband (1863), she returned to Europe with her family.

Mrs. Robinson was without questions one of the most important women writers. "Her style is simple," according to Duyckinck, "and not overdone, making good use of her knowledge and scholarship in the presentation of literary-historical topics, as with her discussions of Slavic works of literature. She also possesses the talent of a fine poetic education so as to enable her to cite the original ballads in German or English as she so desires." There are few German authors who have enjoyed such a great success in transmitting works in both languages (English and German) as has Mrs. Robinson. Her association with scholars and literary authors in America and Europe was extensive. Aside from those already mentioned, we can also make note of the following: K.W.L. Heyse, Franz Bopp and Wilhelm Grimm in Germany; Bancroft, Motley, George Ticknor, Longfellow, Bayard Taylor and Duyckinck in America; Kashin and Makarow in Russia; Dawidowitsch and Mikosch in Serbia; and many others.

Her husband, an outstanding American scholar devoted to Biblical Studies, certainly could thank her for a great deal of his knowledge of the German language and literature, and made great contributions in the field of Biblical criticism and exegesis, and especially contributed to transmitting a knowledge of German research on these topics to American scholars.

Albert Bierstadt and Thomas Nast, both of whom now reside in New York, came to America as children, so that they hardly could be considered German-Americans if the first had not received his artistic training in Germany and the latter had not systematically studied drawing with Theodor Kaufmann in New York.

Bierstadt was born in Solingen, Westphalia in 1830, and arrived in America at the age of three with his parents, who settled in Bedford, Massachusetts. (20) In his early youth, he showed great artistic talent for drawing, and in spite of the fact that another career had been planned for him; he was determined to study art. It can be assumed that in Boston that there were ample opportunities to study art, where for generations the arts had been patronized more than elsewhere in America, and where there was a collection of paintings and statues at the Athenaeum. In 1853, he attended the Art Academy at Düsseldorf, and while he had earlier only painted scenes of New England landscapes, he now found new sources for his paintings in Germany, Switzerland, and Italy. The year 1857 brought him back to America. He traveled in the beautiful states of the American West, and the magnificent alp-like scenes of the mountains and the Sierra Nevada seized him with such force that they provided the sources for his paintings from now on. Many of his best paintings are quite large. Several have made the trip across the ocean, such as: *Landers Park* (6' by 10'), *Sturm in den Felsengebirgen* (7' by 12'), and *Ansicht in Sierra* (6' by 10').

Bierstadt mainly painted landscapes and acquired the best reputation in this area amongst the painters of America. His style was realistic. He places nothing into this landscapes that is not already there. But he is so daring in the way he depicts the extraordinary phenomena of nature. He has often therefore tried to attain the impossible.

With such a productive artist, whose works number more than a hundred, there were some not as great as the rest. His early works, done before his study in Europe, can certainly not be placed on the same plateau as his later works, and he actually attained his zenith in the decade after his return from Germany, and since one always measures one against one's own works and his later works were not considered as surpassing others, some of his envious detractors asserted that his later works were proof that his talents had declined.

His gigantic panoramic paintings are undoubtedly his best. He is, as a critic has said, a heroic landscape painter. In coloration, which till now has been the mark of a master, Bierstadt towers above most of the Düsseldorf painters. His use of light is the most daring in the area of landscape painting. Bierstadt spent the years 1867-69 in Europe for the purpose of study. He is a member of the Art Academy of New York and resides on his estate known as Irvington not far from the city.

Thomas Nast, born 27 September 1840 at Landau in the Rheinpfalz, came to America as a six your old with his mother, arriving in New York in 1846; his father came several years thereafter. (21) He was not able to attend school, as his parents lived in poor circumstances. Like Leutze and Bierstadt, he defied all odds, and built on his inborn talents, dismissing any other kind of career, and attended a drawing school for about six months and then tried to make his living by means of his craft. For three years, he drew for low wages at *Leslie's Illustrirte Zeitung*, while sketching classical topics and models evenings in the Academy of Design. He then joined the *New York Illustrated News*, and went to London in commission of this journal, to illustrate the story of two well known boxers in a prize match there. From there he went to Genoa, to join Garibaldi and his Red Shirts and sketch the conquest of Sicily and Naples. His sketches of this romantic and adventurous campaign appeared in the two related journals, the *Illustrated News* of New York and London and in the *Monde Illustree* of London.

After his return in 1860, the field opened up that was destined for him. At the outbreak of the Civil War he became the caricaturist for *Harper's Weekly*, which had transformed itself from a very conservative journal that handled the topic of slavery with glove to one of the most radical journals of the Union. Nast understood as no other to give expression to the feelings for the Union and the nation by means of allegories, as well as to make the aspirations of its opponents appear to be utterly ridiculous by means of caricatures. However, in this field he was an imitator of the somewhat course English style, as best expressed in the satirical woodcuts that appeared in *Punch*. He always beckons with an open gate, but leaves with beholder with nothing to guess. So that nothing is left in the dark, he leaves, when necessary, his figures with a note hung on the mouth.

He has no concept of the subtleties of the French caricaturists or a Keppler, the publisher and illustrator of the *New York Puck.* , and that is that was his good fortune, as he draws for the masses. He could do better, if was not dammed to serve on party. The true satirist, however, as to take sides. Nast is undoubtedly a genius and many of his caricatures surpass those in the *London Punch*, but nevertheless he has passed judgment on himself, which is much too hard, but indicates his artistic perspective. He apparently often said: "I often cast my glance too high and in so doing stumbled into a manure pile." His talent and his working abilities made him free from worry and he can still accomplish much greater things if he would rid himself of his political ties.

Chapter Eight

Germans in New York State

Buffalo – German Newspapers – Philipp Dorschheimer – Wilhelm Dorschheimer – German Societies – Dr. Franz Brunck – German Singing Society – the 1848 Revolution – Influence of the Germans in Western New York – Dr Friedrich Heinrich Quitmann – General Adolph von Steinwehr
■■

Only after completion of the Erie Canal in spring 1826 did the city of Buffalo really being to flourish. Ernst Grey (Grau), a quite intelligent man from Heilbronn arrived there in 1828, and found only a few German families. German Protestant and Catholic congregations were soon formed, so that by 1850, five Protestant and three large Catholic churches had been built, as well as that many in the surrounding Erie County. By 1831, Germans started coming in great numbers to Buffalo and by 1837 the population had grown enough to justify publication of a German newspaper. Georg Zahm from Zweibrücken, who had learned the book printing trade there and later became a school teacher, published the first issue of this paper on 2 December 1837, and is described as an honorable and sociable man. Stephan Molitor was the editor. (1) However, the editorship soon was taken over by Zahm. No less a name was chosen for this first German newspaper than that of *Der Weltbürger*, and it is most noteworthy that the paper still exists with the same name and appears as a weekly, while another paper there, the *Buffalo Demokrat* appears as a daily.

The first political demonstration of Germans took place on 23 December 1837 after two hundred of them issued a proclamation, calling on Germans not to participate in any illegal undertakings against Canada. In 1838, Philipp Dorschheimer who had settled down in Buffalo in 1836 was appointed by the federal government to the office of postmaster, a prize position already then, which was sought after by politicians. (2) At the time, he was owner of the Farmers Hotel. Only the already then significant political influence of the Germans and the belief, which Dorschheimer very cleverly manipulated, that the German vote was in his hands, won him the position. It later would be shown that he really was a man one had to reckon with.

Philipp Dorschheimer was born in 1797 in Wöllstein, now in Rheinhessen, the son of a well-to-do miller. He attended school there, which was poorly administered under the French administration of the time, to his fourteenth year. He then entered his father's business, but decided to immigrate to America in 1816 at age nineteen. He first found work in Pennsylvania in his trade, and after several years took charge of a mill in Lyons, Wayne County, New York, which later became (1834) the first guesthouse in that town. In Pennsylvania as well as in New York, he dealt mainly with Americans. He learned to speak English quite fluently as spoken in the normal course of business exchange. But with a care better applied elsewhere he preserved his unique Palatine dialect, which gave a folksy and amusing flavor to his speech. He had almost totally forgotten German, but learned it again after coming to Buffalo by coming into contact with other Germans.

If his English was fluent, but had a foreign ring to it, his German was almost more amusing. He read English with ease, and loved to read, especially newspapers. He also thoroughly studied political writings, becoming quite familiar with the history of his new homeland. He was quite knowledgeable, especially of the political history of the U.S. and his remarkable memory made him a walking encyclopedia on the topic. He wrote English as poorly as German, but when one met him, one recognized that he was quite unique. He was a Nibelung-like figure of average size, had a relatively large head and an intelligent looking face. He must have impressed everyone. "His abilities of understanding," wrote one of his closest friends, "left nothing to be desired." His knowledge of people was extensive and in official positions he knew how to surround himself with competent assistants, so that he was an excellent administrator.

While the gift of public speaking escaped him, he possessed an extraordinary ability of persuasion in private conversations that avoided all intentionality, becoming therefore all that more effective and were almost irresistible. He knew how to convince influential people, when the opportunity offered itself to speak with them, that he was not only the most important and influential German in the City of Buffalo, but also the entire United States. His success in political life was due to his gift of human relations and his association with many important people. The victory of the Whig Party in 1840 cost him his postmaster position, which had had not brought him any wealth. Soon thereafter, he acquired one of the first guesthouses (Mansion House), which he maintained till 1864.

In 1848, he joined the free soil wing of the Democratic Party, and campaigned and voted for Van Buren. He saw much earlier than most Democrats in the North that the pretensions of the South, especially after the Mexican War which benefitted the South, that this would be dangerous for them, and that sooner or later the majority of the population of the North would have to go on the defense and that this would seal the fate of the Democratic Party for a some time. And, as so many others of his fellow Democrats, especially Germans did, he also therefore joined the Republican Party in 1854, or to be more accurate, helped found it.

He had become acquainted with Fremont, who at that time lived in New York, and with the approaching presidential election of 1856, Dorschheimer became one of the first to endorse him, and then actively campaigned for him with all his energy and diplomacy. He calmly and confidently rejected all kinds of objections raised against Fremont in a manner that exuded confidence in victory, so that that he convinced all those in doubt. In the Republican convention held in Philadelphia in June 1856, one saw him in the packed auditorium of the Musical Academy filled with delegates from all the northern states, including governors, senators, judges, journalists, lawyers, and members of Congress, and which one could almost say was like a national summit meeting. And here he made his way to the podium with ease to nominate Fremont. Everyone asked: Who is this man, as they took note of this large man. The usual answer was: He is just an old German, not a politician. However, he could tell the convention that he knew his countrymen and they would rather vote for Fremont than anyone else. He was right, as it developed. No one actually understood each word he spoke in his splendid Palatine-English dialect. But this was what did the trick. Everyone heard that the German vote was for Fremont and that no one could win without it. He left the podium amidst the greatest applause. Fremont was nominated, but did lose the election, winning 1,342,000 against Buchanan's 1,866,000, and Fillmore's 874,000. In 1859, the Republican Party elected Dorschheimer as treasurer for New York and in 1863, President Lincoln appointed him as tax collector for the district in which Buffalo is located, one of the most sought after positions in the state. Both positions were ones of trust and required sureties of hundreds of thousands of dollars. We can only confirm what a friend wrote of him:

> Dorschheimer was a very gentle-minded, calm and benevolent person, always
> ready to assist by word and deed and therefore was of great service to his
> countrymen. If he had been blessed with greater wealth, he no doubt would have
> been one of the most philanthropic persons on earth. His kindness won him more
> and more friends in the course of time, so that at the time of his death he was
> more beloved and popular than when he first became postmaster.

If one considers the high offices he held, offices that if dishonestly administered can lead to great wealth, then one can only view this as the best proof of his integrity that he only obtained the kind of income that sufficed to make the last years of his life carefree and this was due particularly to the profitable sale of his hotel in 1864. He died in 1868 at the age of 71.

His son William Dorschheimer, who had the same stature as his father, enjoyed the best possible education. He is a lawyer, highly educated, loves literature, and earlier, wrote well received articles for the best journals. During the hundred days when Fremont had command of the entire West he served on his staff as major, and later became the U.S. district attorney for the northern part of the state of New York. He was elected twice as vice-governor of New York, and just like his father had helped make Fremont a presidential candidate, so too did he work harder than anyone for Tilden at the Democratic national convention in St. Louis in 1876. He was an excellent and knowledgeable pubic speaker, and best described as a revised and expanded edition of his father as a politician.

Philipp Dorschheimer is like many Germans active in politics, but of a special brilliant order. In many smaller areas, in cities, and in quarters of cities, there are of course hundreds of Dorschheimers among the Germans. These lower echelon politicians all have the unique quality that raises them above the masses. The main reason for their success is that they use all their strengths to cause others to place a higher value on themselves. Naturally, we refer here not to the mercenary and intriguing kinds of electioneers and officer-chasers, but rather people who are honest and well-meaning as Dorschheimer was to the highest degree.

The first militia company was formed in Buffalo in February 1838. By 1841, there were already three such companies in the city. In that year, they organized together as a battalion, which was commanded by Major Georg Zahm, publisher of the *Weltbürger*. The names of the companies were: Steuben, Lafayette and Jefferson Guard. Dr. Friedrich Dellenbach, Lieutenant in the Steuben Guard, became the first German elected to the city council in 1839. First active in politics, he later on returned to private affairs, becoming the first director of the Savings Bank of Buffalo, and is one of the most respected citizens of the city.

At about the same time, Pastor A.A. Grabau, earlier pastor in Erfurt, settled down in Buffalo as the head of the Old Lutheran congregation in Buffalo. After many sorrows and privations, Grabau succeeded in founding competent schools and in 1840 a school for the education of teachers, which later received its charter under the name "German Martin Luther College." (3)

In July 1840, a second German paper appeared, the *Volksfreund*, an organ of the Whig Party, edited by W.A. Meier. The paper did not last much long after the election of that year, and Meier then devoted himself to other business matters and was also elected to the city council.

In 1841, a society was formed to support German instruction and literature, and the establishment of a German library. It was founded by: F.A. Georg, Jakob Beyer, Dr. Joahnn Hauenstein, Karl Neidhart, Adam Schlagter, Georg Pfeifer, Georg Beyer, Stephan Beltinger and Wilhelm Rudolf. Among these nine founders, only one was a German, five were Alsatians, one a Lothringian, and two were Swiss. It is interesting to note here that Alsatians and German Lothringians joined together with Germans in this undertaking. In an area of Illinois across from St.Louis the Alsatians and Lothringians also joined together with Germans there. Although there was a nearby French settlement, they had little contact with it. Ancestry wins out. All the aforementioned men supported every undertaking for the common good and did honor to the German name with regard to educational and commercial success. (4)

Der Freimütige, a Whig paper saw the light of day in December 1842, and was published and edited by Alexander Krause, a well educated and honorable man. This journal changed hands in 1845, going over to Ernst Oesten, who tried to make it a daily publication. After a short time, it ceased publication, but from its ashes there arose in November of the same year another Whig paper, the *Telegraph*. The *Weltbürger*, which had been founded by Georg Zahm, was acquired by Brunk and Damidion after Zahm's death.

Dr. Franz Brunck is so important for the political life of the state that a sketch of his life is the best way to offer insight into the role played by the German element in the political history of Buffalo and the western part of the state. (5) Dr. Brunck, a true child of the blissful Palatinate, was born in 1810 in the canton of Obermoschel. At an early age he lost his father, a well off owner of an estate. In fall 1829, he attended the University of Würzburg, continuing his studies the following year in Munich, where as a member of the Germania Burschenschaft he was involved in the unrest during December and was therefore confined for a month in the Isar Tower. Due to the efforts of a relative, the liberal deputy Ritter and other deputies of the Rhine district, he succeeded in obtaining release on the bases of a surety, while other political prisoners were only set free after four months by means of a decree from the appellate court of Landshut.

He made the decision to immigrate to America on completion of his studies if there was no change for the better in German political conditions. Thereafter, he continued his studies till 1833 and immigrated in 1834. He first settled in Lyons, New York, married an upstanding and refined American lady, and got involved in politics in Lyon and the surrounding area. He became studied the best commentaries on the federal constitution, and read widely, including the entire works of Jefferson and other statesmen, as well as of course newspapers. By means of his wife and contacts with other Americans he soon became fluent in speaking English. His considerable inheritance seemed to weigh upon him, however. The desire for country life, which he acquired in his youth, awakened within him again. He reached to the wanderer's staff in 1836, purchased a section of land (640 acres) in the wildest part of northern Indiana, and began to clear and plow land. Two years later, he got tired of the so-called wilderness just like Lenau had earlier, and gave his land to another, and moved back to Buffalo in spring 1839 after having lost almost his last dollar, and began his law practice anew. The old saying was true for him: No one succeeds in America till he has lost his European money.

As a university student Brunck had been a fellow brimming with life. Tall and slender in appearance with fresh brown complexion, his sparkling eyes, which were constantly in motion, were covered by dark black eyebrows. His liveliness never left him. Perhaps due to Dorschheimer, whom had gotten to know in Lyons and now found again in Buffalo, Brunk in 1840 dived into politics during the presidential campaign between van Buren and Harrison. He appeared at several Democratic meetings as a speaker and defeated the German-Bohemian F.W. Lassack in a debate at Rochester, winning a victorious bouquet there; Lassack had been a Democrat, and was elected as such to the state legislature by the Germans of Buffalo, but in 1840 had switched to the party of his opponents. Brunck always spoke extemporaneously in English as well as German. Written notes confused him. He followed the inspiration of the moment and needed a participatory audience to speak joyfully. With him it was not so much a matter of rhetorical skills, as he was lifted off and carried away by an agreeable audience. He had the gift of being able to capture the interest of his listeners, with the result that he won great victories in the process.

After Van Buren was defeated in 1842, he made a round-trip to the west, and was greeted everywhere, especially by Germans, who do not change their views as a result of victories or defeats. The Germans of Buffalo gave him a torch-lit parade in which 3,000/4,000 Germans are said to have participated, according to the Democratic press. Dr. Brunk spoke on behalf of Van Buren. Germans were very actively involved in the campaign of 1844 between Polk and Clay. The Democrats did everything to avenge the defeat of 1840. We also find our Dr. Brunk again on the stump not only in Buffalo, but also in important places between Albany and Detroit, Michigan. In this year, he came to Erie, Pennsylvania for a debate with Otto Hoffmann, a talented adventurer from a respected family in Darmstadt, who edited the so-called gigantic paper in Harrisburg, *Der Deutsche in Amerika*. This measured sixty inches in length and forty-two inches in width. Naturally, both sides claimed victory.

In fall 1845, Brunk and his business partner, J. Domedion, a practical printer, acquired the *Welbürger* from Zahm's widow. His medical practice that he had thus far successfully and advantageously carried on was now given up completely and he devoted himself with the great diligence and enthusiasm unique to him to this new undertaking. As lively and enthusiastic as Brunck was on the stump, so too was he now calm and thoughtful as editor, without need to shine or arouse excitement, a definitely rare kind of individual. The growth of the German population of Buffalo and the surrounding area (estimated at 7,000 in 1842 and by von Löher at 12,000 in 1846; the latter certainly to high a figure), the attention that Brunck gave to the paper, and his wide circle of acquaintances acquired from political life, contributed greatly to the ever increasing circulation of his paper. It was the strongest German paper of the Democrats in the northwestern part of New York, in northern Ohio and northern Indiana, and blossomed into a very profitable and splendid business enterprise.

It goes without saying that Brunck was actively involved in the various political campaigns. When in 1856 his best Democratic friends, and especially the leaders of the German Democrats, left their old party almost without exception to found the Republican Party, this made him waver for a short time, but could not tear him away from the party that he loved.

He refused several nominations to office, such as to the state senate and to the state treasurer of New York, but was elected in 1863 as treasurer of Erie County and state and county tax collector for the City of Buffalo. This office left him evening hours free for his paper, which had been a daily for several years now. The office was not only a very responsible position, but also a very well paid one. It is the only office that he ever held. But he participated in many affairs for the public good, especially those that aimed to improve the status of Germans.

In 1868, he made a long trip to Europe and in 1875 he brought his family to Europe for two years after having profitably sold his share of his business to his partner, F. Held. During this time, he corresponded with the paper, and his travel sketches were known for their clarity, accuracy, and valuable and noteworthy information they contained. In summer 1878, he again returned to Europe, so as to especially study Italy more thoroughly. A cheerful light heartedness, an uncommon intellectual and physical agility accompanied him up into old age.

On 13 April 1844, the first German singing society was formed in Buffalo: *Der Deutsche Gesangverein*, which became the still existing *Liedertafel* in 1848. In 1847, the *Arbeiterverein* was formed and after it was dissolved, the *Sängerbund* arose out of its musical section. The director and first members belonged to those who had immigrated earlier.

There was no lack of political societies in Buffalo. On the whole, the Germans of Buffalo have always been interested in politics. In 1845, they participated very actively in collecting funds for Dr. Seidensticker, who was imprisoned at the time. Upon his release a public meeting was held at the instigation of the *Deutsche Jung-Männer-Gesellschaft* to for the purpose of expressing joy by means of resolutions to that effect and to heartily welcome his forthcoming arrival in the U.S. Collections were also undertaken for Professor Jordan at the same time.

The French February Revolution in 1848 was welcomed with a grand demonstration and a torch-lit parade, to which the French were also invited. On the great open square in front of the Mansion House there waved the French and American flags from the well known Liberty Pole. At the head of the procession waved the black-red-gold German flag. In 1845, Karl Eslinger, who later moved to Wisconsin, was elected to the city council. Salomon Scheu, who had immigrated from the Rheinpfalz in 1839, was elected four times to city council and later to the office of mayor. An older brother of his, Jakob, was elected six times to the city council. Philipp Becker was mayor in 1875. Dr. Dewinning, who had immigrated in the 1830s, was elected twice to the state legislature. Richard Flach, who arrived here in 1848, was elected several times to the city council and later to the state legislature. In like manner, Johann G. Langner, as well as Philipp Becker, long time publisher of the *Buffalo Telegraph*, was also members of the state legislature.

J.F. Schöllkopf certainly deserves to be mentioned as one of the great businessmen not only of Buffalo, but also of the northwest. Born in Kirchheim, Württemberg, he arrived in Buffalo in 1841. His large mills and tanning companies were spread throughout several states, but did not stop him from supporting affairs for the common good, especially on behalf of the German element. He was a member of the *Deutsche Jung-Männer-Gesellschaft* and contributed generously to all beneficial collections. He was one of the founders and first directors of the Buffalo German Insurance Company and the German Bank. Both institutions developed into mighty corporations with great capital holdings and deposits. The Buffalo Savings Bank, which was founded in 1846 and in whose board of directors Germans were well represented, had in 1878 not less than five million seven hundred and fifty thousand dollars of deposits. A perhaps too great admirer of past times (*laudatory temporis acti*) speaks as follows about Buffalo's past:

> Everything that has been done to the present time by Germans and what has been preserved in memory of the German immigration, was accomplished by Germans who came before 1850.

In the early German settlements along the Schoharie and the upper Hudson the intellectual life of the German element was not as lively as in the larger cities. (6) German cultural life consisted there of several descendants of the German immigration of an earlier time period. This includes Dr. Friedrich Heinrich Quitmann, the Lutheran minister, who was born 7 August 1760 in the Westphalian town of Cleve (d. 1832, Rhinebeck, New York), where his father was inspector of the Prussian military stationed there. Quitmann was also slated for a life as a soldier. As his father was not without means, he wanted to give his son a good education so as to improve his future career in the army, and therefore sent him to Halle, where he attended school and then the university.

Halle was especially known then as the center of Protestant Pietism, borne on by such men as Niemeyer, Semler, Knapp, Schulze and others. Quitmann also became a Pietist while he was there, and instead of taking a military path chose the field of theology, much to the displeasure of his father. It was in any event a highly unusual decision as Quitmann seemed predestined for the life of a soldier. Of large, almost colossal stature, - already at the time of his entrance at the university one of the professors said: "Quanta osse! Quantum robur!!" – He possessed moreover an energetic, decisive nature and that "Semper pararus" emerged as a particular personal trait that was with him always.

Peremptorily stopped in his theological studies by his father, Quitmann then became a teacher in the princely Waldeck family, which however did not suit his tastes, causing him to take leave to Holland, so as to continue his theological studies there.

Ordained a minister, he then reported to the Lutheran consistory of the Netherlands for missionary service and was sent as a pastor to a congregation in the Dutch colony Curacao, near the Venezuelan coast. During his twelve year stay there, he married the daughter of a merchant, Anna Elisabeth Huyck, and then returned to Europe (1793) retired by the Dutch government.

The political events that shook Europe at the time caused Dr. Quitmann and his family to immigrate to New York (1795), obviously with the intention of returning to Holland or Germany after peace had been established. Conditions however took such a course that he changed his mind and decided to make America his permanent home. He reported to the Lutheran Synod and obtained a call to the united churches at Schoharie and Kobleskill. He remained there till 1798, in which year he took over the churches at Rhinebeck, Württemberg, Germantown and Livingston. In 1815, in which year he was elected to the state legislature, he resigned from his ministerial position most of the latter churches, and in 1824 also from the one in Württemberg. In 1828, when his health left him, he then completely retired from all ministerial functions. He passed away at Rhinebeck on 25 June 1832.

Dr. Quitmann was highly regarded not only in church circles, but also in the political realm. He was an intimate friend of Governor Daniel Tomkins, Edward Livingston, Governor William C. Bouck, Martin Van Buren and other political greats of the Democratic Party. Asides from his one term in the state legislature (he refused re-election) he held no other political offices. On the other hand, he was chairman and president of the Hartwick Seminary and after Dr. Kunze's death, president of the Lutheran Ministerium of New York from 1807 to 1828, in which capacity he knew how to protect the German congregations from the influences of American pietism, i.e. the so-called revival movement. As these revivals went hand in hand with the downfall of the German language, the work of Dr. Quitmann could be said to have accomplished a great deal for the preservation of the German language.

"His position in society," says Dr. Wackernagel "was outstanding and highly respected. His exemplary knowledge, his manners, and his unforced, actually elegant behavior, made him sought after and admired by all. As an educator in the princely family of Waldeck he was accustomed to moving in the upper echelons of society and after settling down as pastor at Rhinebeck, he entertained the highest members of New York society at his home." "He had," so write Governor Bouch, "only the slightest contact with common folk, something that must be ascribed to his serious expression. He had a tall and stately figure that commanded respect and provided his appearance with an impressive and sublime character."

In learning he was second to none among the Lutheran theologians of the country. He fluently spoke German, English, Dutch, French, and Spanish, and preached often in the first three languages, and had spoken Dutch, Spanish, and French in Curacao.

He frequently advised on political and scholarly questions and his understanding of the characteristics of personalities, his outstanding memory and his striking arguments, spiced with wit that never failed him and bordered on biting sarcasm but which did not offend, made him a beloved oracle at all times.

He was also active as an author, and published the following: *A Treatise on Magic, or the Intercourse between Spirit and Men* (1810); *An Evangelical Catechism* (1814); *Three Sermons on the Reformation by Luther* (1817); and a *Psalmbuch* (1817).

His son, Johann Anton Quitmann, born at Rhinebeck on 1 September 1798, was an important figure in American history. (7) He began his career as a professor of German at Mount Airy College in Pennsylvania (1819); became a lawyer in Chillicothe, Ohio; moved to Natchez, Mississippi, became chancellor of the state supreme court and a member of the state legislature and senate of Mississippi, serving as president of the latter body (1832-35), and in this capacity also served as interim governor of the state (1835). He then took part in the Texas war of independence (1836), visited Germany and France in 1839 and on his return, was appointed a judge in the supreme court of Mississippi. At the outbreak of the Mexican War, he joined as a volunteer and was appointed by President Polk in 1846 to the rank of Brigade General and in 1847 to Major General. For his heroism at the Battle of Monterey he was presented with an honorary dagger by Congress.

General Quitmann, although born in the U.S., was a German through and through, enjoying friendly relations with the not very sizable German population of Natchez, and always assisting German immigrants by word and deed. As early as 1839, he was one of the founders of the German Reading Society in Natchez, to which he presented a great deal of books that he had brought from Germany, and he often visited its reading rooms. From 1840 to the outbreak of the Mexican War, he hired a German teacher, who provided instruction to the children of German parents. A German lady, who lived at the time in Natchez, assured us that General Quitmann was always interested in the settlement and advancement of Germans in Natchez.

Before we conclude our discussion of New York, we must note a man who was not a resident of the state early on, but acquired fame as the head of a New York regiment in the Civil War and after the end of the same took up permanent residence in the state. We, of course, refer to Adolph Wilhelm August Friedrich von Steinwehr. (8) He was born 25 September 1822 at Blankenburg in the duchy of Braunschweig. His father and grandfather were both higher officers in the army, and so it was natural that Steinwehr, after he had finished his schooling, entered the military academy in 1841 in Braunschweig and later joined the army at the rank of lieutenant. The outbreak of the Mexican War in 1846 led him to the U.S., where he joined a regiment of volunteers in Alabama, and was elected an officer and served under General Scott.

After the war ended, Steinwehr found a position as a geometer in the U.S. Border and Coastal Survey Department and came to Mobile with his corps in 1849, where he married an American lady. In 1851, he again tried in vain to gain acceptance into the regular army as an officer. Displeased at the results, he traveled with this family to

Germany, but returned in 1854, settling on a farm in the vicinity of Wallingford, Connecticut.

With the outbreak of the Civil War, he could no longer remain home. He organized the 29th (German) New York Vol. Regiment that was ordered to the brigade of Blenker and took part in the unfortunate first Battle of Bull Run (July 1861), in which Blenker's brigade formed the reserve and did not see action and avoided the general panic that ensued, taking up a firm position covering the wild flight of the troops and so saved Washington from an attack by the Confederates.

With the re-organization of the army under McClellan in the fall, Steinwehr, whose military skill had been recognized, was appointed Brigade General. His brigade was sent through the mountains of Virginia at the roughest time of year on a march during which the entire division had to travel on almost impassable roads and suffered greatly due to the lack of food for the purpose of assisting Fremont, and participated then in the Battle at Cross Keys. Later transferred to the corps of General Sigel, Steinwehr took part as commander of a division in a series of battles that ended with the defeat of the commanding general Pope at Bull Run (August 1862). He also took part in the bloody battles of Fredericksburg (1862), Chancellorsville and Gettysburg, excelling especially at the latter (2 May 1863), when he offered decisive resistance to the victorious enemy and held them at bay till the right flank, which had come under attack, could re-organize.

In the murderous Battle of Gettysburg (1-3 July 1863), in which Confederate General Lee was forced to retreat form Pennsylvania across the Potomac, Steinwehr also excelled by seizing several favorable positions, holding them firmly.

After the Battle of Chickamauga, Tennessee (20-21 September 1863), which was so unfortunate for the Union troops, re-enforcements from the Army of the Potomac were hurried to the army now under the command of General Grant, and Steinwehr's division was chosen to do the job. It did so enthusiastically, participating in the skirmishes and battles there, especially at Lookout Valley and Lookout Mountain.

Steinwehr resigned from the army on 5 July 1865 after not seeing active duty for the last months of the war due to ill health. Among the German generals, Steinwehr was recognized as one of the most competent, as he combined courage and decisiveness with his outstanding military knowledge.

On returning to private life, he chose Albany, New York as his place of residence, and occupied himself writing in the field of geography and statistics. He published an excellent geography for use in schools that appeared in Cincinnati in 1866 with maps like those done by Stieler, for whose atlas Steinwehr had done the maps of America. In 1876, his *Centennial Gazeteer of the United States* appeared in Philadelphia. H.A. Rattermann says in his superb biography of Steinwehr that "undoubtedly the main work of his life remains unfinished," namely, an atlas of the U.S. with thirty-two maps in folio format. The copper plates had already been done by the famous Royal Geographer, Keef Johnston, in Edinburgh, Scotland. The two that were completed remain true masterpieces. The lithographed plates were in Geneva ready for printing.

From Cincinnati, where he was occupied with the second edition of his school geography, he traveled on his way back home to Albany, when in the night of 24 November 1877 he stopped for a short time in Buffalo, where he met an unexpected death. He was busy writing a letter to his daughter in Koblenz with pen in hand, when he suddenly sank back into his chair, departing life apparently without battle. He was buried with full military honors at Albany. At the time of his death, his family was in Germany, with the exception of a son who was a student at Yale. Rattermann closed his aforementioned biography of Steinwehr as follows:

He was a soldier in the truest sense of the word, and a nobleman not merely by birth and name, but also through his deeds. One cannot really imagine a more pleasant and sociable gentleman than Steinwehr. He was a man of towering education, of cavalier-like behavior, and thoroughly intelligent at all times. (9)

Chapter Nine
Germans in New Jersey

The Germans in New Jersey – Johann A. Roebling
■■

There now is a relatively large percentage of Germans in the towns and cities of New Jersey, but forty years ago there was really not much to speak of in terms of the German element. We may assume that especially in Newark, Hoboken, and Jersey City, which actually are suburbs of New York City that Germans there, like their neighbors in New York, actively participated in public affairs and furthered the German heritage. Indeed, in 1839, we find a German public school in Newark.

In 1848, a man settled down in New Jersey, of whom Germany and German-Americans can be very proud of. We refer to Johann August Roebling, one of the foremost engineers of recent times, who is not only the equal of Robert Stephenson, but actually surpasses him. (1) Roebling comes from a large and respectable family in Thüringen and in particular from Schwarzenburg-Sonderhausen. He was born 12 June 1806 in Mühlhausen, attended elementary school there, and was then educated in Erfurt and Berlin, where he studied engineering. As much as he was interested in this field, his inquiring mind also took in active interest in philosophy as well, and he attended the lectures of Hegel.

From 1827 to 1831, he served as an assistant for the construction of roads in the province of Westphalia. It was at this time that an immigration society was formed in Mühlhausen, which counted a number of educated people among its membership. If we are not mistaken, Emil Angelrodt, who later on played an important role in St. Louis, was also a member, as was perhaps also von Dachröden, who also came from the same region and settled in the vicinity of St. Louis at Lewis Ferry on the Missouri River. (2)

Roebling joined this immigration society, whose membership included an unusual genius by the name of Etzler. He had lived in America for a period of time and had aroused considerable attention in the press and in the U.S. congress by means of his daring and dynamic proposals as to how to monitor weather mechanically. He undoubtedly possessed an extraordinary amount of theoretical knowledge and succeeded in winning the confidence of Roebling. It appears that many other diligent and educated Germans had gotten the idea at this time of founding a German colony in the U.S. with a constitution based on humanity and brotherhood.

Nothing came of a colony in the original sense as conceived of by its founders, but some of the members of the Mühlhausen Immigration Society did settle down in an attractive area of Beaver County, Pennsylvania, not far from Rapp's colony. (3) Roebling became a farmer, and served as a delegate at the German-American conventions held in Philipsburg in 1838, which aimed at establishing a German teachers' seminary. However, he fortunately became recalled his training as an engineer and again took up his profession.

He surveyed for the central railway in Pennsylvania, as well as for the construction of several canals. In 1841, he began producing wire cable, which was first used on the Alleghany Portage road. In 1844, the Pennsylvania canal aqueduct across the Alleghany River to Pittsburgh was hung with cable, and aroused a great deal of attention at the time, and laid the foundation for his reputation as an engineer.

He then built the beautiful Monongahela Suspension Bridge at Pittsburgh (1,500 feet in length with eight spans). In 1848, he moved to Trenton, New Jersey, where he set up his great cable-making factory. A wonderful construction of an 800 foot span over the Niagara, a mile below the falls, was built over the water raging through the gorge there. Above the bridge for vehicles and pedestrians there is another for trains. The structure is of the greatest elegance, and has demonstrated its solidity for more than thirty years; it was completed in 1852. Soon thereafter, he built a bridge that was just as beautiful and elegant on the Ohio River, connecting Cincinnati, Ohio with Covington, Kentucky. It has a span of 1,200 feet.

His last great work was his plan for the colossal bridge on the East River, connecting New York with Brooklyn. He had been considering the project for a decade and had thought and figured through everything. He then drew up plans after having overcome numerous problems, including some strong opposition to his plans, by the sheer force of his strong will power, when suddenly the great engineer was snatched away from us. A beam crushed his left foot, and four toes had to be amputated. The wound began to heal and the danger overcome, when lockjaw appeared, causing this powerful man to pass away on 20 June 1869 after a long period of suffering.

The great work was then completed by his sons, who had worked and thought through everything together with their father. The resulting bridge is 5,000 feet long with a central span that is 1,600 feet long over the surface of the East River.

Roebling was not only one of the most outstanding members of his profession, but one of the best and finest persons. The minister who presided at his funeral, which attracted more than 5,000 people, said: "With him Trenton has lost one of its best citizens, the poor one of their greatest benefactors, and the world an illuminated mind." He was the sole supporter of an orphanage, and also gave generously to various charities. He left a great fortune, and provides for many charitable bequests in his will.

Roebling was an extraordinary man. He had a strong, high forehead, with energetic eyebrows covering his somewhat deeply set eyes, from whence genius flashed like lightning. His nose and mouth showed strength and boldness. He was an impressive figure, and at first glance, one might not have expected that here was man of great kind-heartedness, modesty, and friendliness. In an obituary, which the shareholders of the Covington & Cincinnati Bridge Company dedicated to him, it was stated: "In the field to which he devoted the greatest part of his life there was no one like him. While he respected the experts of his profession, he nevertheless did not feel bound to their opinions. Honor is due to him for having built reliable bridges across the Niagara and the Ohio, while leaving canals open and untouched. His last completed work will stand in our city for centuries as an official blessing and monument of his talent."

Chapter Ten
Germans in New England

**New England – German Immigration since 1820 – Dr. Karl Beck – Karl Follen –
Franz Lieber – Germans in Boston – Wilhelm and Robert Wesselhöft –
Leopold Morse (Maass)**
■■

German immigration commenced anew in the second decade of the nineteenth century, but hardly touched the states of New England. The population there had become more firmly entrenched than anywhere else, and remained essentially closed to other ethnic elements. Commerce, shipping, and fishing flourished along the coasts, while industry developed inland after the disruptions due to the war with England. The land was not suitable for agriculture, but there were more than enough of the necessary natural resources available to provide for business and industry. In these colonies, which were much like the English motherland, there was a lack of the cosmopolitan spirit that could more or less be found in New York, Pennsylvania, and the western states.

The region therefore lacked the power of attraction with regard to immigration. On the other hand, New England was well endowed with educational points of attraction, with Yale University in New Haven, Connecticut and Harvard in Cambridge, near Boston, towering above all other educational institutions. A quite important intellectual life thrived in Boston in particular. Many of the professors and authors there had visited Europe, especially Germany, and German scholars were quite well received there.

In the 1820s, we therefore find Franz J. Grund as professor of mathematics at Cambridge, Gräter as professor of drawing and modern languages, and a bit later Dr. Karl Beck as professor of Latin language and literature. (1) The latter was born 19 August 1798 at Heidelberg, studied theology and philology at Berlin and Tübingen, and graduated with a Ph.D. in philosophy. As a result of his involvement in the student movement, he was forced to flee due to fear of being arrested. He first found refuge in Switzerland with his stepfather, the famous theologian DeWette, in Basel, and then sailed to America in 1824. At first, he served as a school teacher in Northampton on the Hudson till 1832, when he received the aforementioned professorship, a position he held for almost twenty years.

He published several philological works, was a man of great common sense, and served honorably in the Civil War with the sanitation commission, and thereafter wrote and worked on behalf of the freedmen. His entire fortune was devoted almost exclusively to public projects for the common good. He served for two years as a member of the state legislature of Massachusetts, and died in March 1866 at Cambridge as one of the most widely respected citizens of the state and was grieved by many beyond the borders of Massachusetts.

Among all Germans, however, who settled in New England, Karl Follen was undoubtedly the most interesting and intriguing person. (2) His father (Follenius) was a judge and court councilor in Giessen at the time of his birth. He was a strict, law-abiding and honorable man, but with a ferocious temper, although he was more indulgent and trusting towards Karl than his other children. Karl's place of birth was not in Giessen, but rather in Romrod, where his grandfather had been the forester. His mother had been sent there before his birth, as Giessen at the time was in a state of unrest due to the troop movements there. He was born 4 September 1796. (3)

A brother two years older, Adolph, co-author with Karl Follen of the *Freie Stimmen frischer Jugend*, was literarily inclined. Caught up in the investigations of revolutionary activity, he was imprisoned for two years in Berlin for interrogation, then went to Switzerland, where he studied medieval German literature, held professorships, tried farming, and even became a member of the council in Bern, finally passing away in 1855. A sister Louise married the later the later professor Vogt in Giessen and was the mother of the natural history researcher, Karl Vogt. His youngest brother, Paul, a competent jurist, immigrated to America in 1834.

Karl Follen received a splendid education at the gymnasium in Giessen. He did extraordinarily well, and aside from classical languages also studied Hebrew, French, and even Italian. In 1813, hardly seventeen years old, he entered the University of Giessen to study law, but left in the fall with his brother Adolph to join a Hessian volunteer battalion in the French campaign under the command of Prince Emil. His corps moved through Strassburg into the Franche Comte as far as Lyon to serve as the reserve force for the large army under Schwarzenberg. The conquest of Paris brought an end to the campaign that had its share of hard marches and deprivations, but did not actually come head to head in battle with the enemy. Paul, who was hardly fifteen years old and who had not received the permission of his father to join the army, had joined a Hessian front line regiment, and distinguished himself in several battles by means of his bravery.

In spring 1814, Karl continued his studies, and it was in Giessen that conceived of the idea of reforming student life and of merging the existing student organizations into a general German organization (*Burschenschaft*). He was ahead of all others in terms of his daring enthusiasm and his unshakable persistence in striving to realize this goal. His scholarly and moral approach, his uncommon speaking ability, a certain kind of personal magnetism, which one usually ascribes to prophets and apostles, assured him an almost irresistible influence on all of his idealistic fellow students. This influence however also brought him some bitter enemies in student circles, and under suspicion with university and governmental authorities, the latter of which still lived in the traditions of the Confederation of the Rhine, which feared and therefore hated all ideologues more than their protector.

Karl Follen was also at the time a Turner in good physical condition, an excellent fencer and swimmer, attributes that only added to his influence. No one could say he lacked courage in his reforming endeavors, especially those aimed at limiting duels to those judged admissible by an honorific court. After diligently completing his studies with the outstanding legal scholars Löhr and Grollmann, he then received the doctoral degree not surprisingly at the top of his class in 1817, and then began lecturing as a private docent on the topic of Roman law.

However, at the university he had already developed an interest in philosophical and religious studies. He eagerly studied the philosophical works of Spinoza, Hume, Kant and Fries. After completing his studies, he turned all that more seriously to the study of philosophy and theology. As a practicing lawyer, he represented several communities in Oberhessen, which were in danger of losing their communal rights by means of new legislation. He composed their petitions to the state ministry, but attracted the hatred of the government as a result of winning the cases, and suffered continual harassment and persecution. He therefore left Giessen in 1818 and established himself as a private docent in Jena, and began lecturing there. As in Giessen, he soon attracted an enthusiastic following. Oken, Fries and other outstanding professors held him in high regard, although in many political questions he did not agree with Fries.

Among those who gathered around Follen mention must be made of Karl Sand for whom Follen had become a hero. (4) The unconditional manner with which Follen expressed his political theories, the decisiveness that he insisted upon in carrying out an idea without regard to the consequences may have exerted an influence on Sand that Follen could not have foreseen. That he, however, motivated Sand to assassinate Kotzebue in 1819 is a charge that remains unproven despite the countless investigations and the interviews with Follen and his colleagues. Follen, however, was not cleared by the government of the unfortunate deed of Sand, and the later persecutions against him were based on the suspicion that he had founded an organization with definite treasonous tendencies.

In the meantime it became quite clear that it was no longer safe for Follen due to the ever increasing political reaction and the expanding activity of the investigatory commission of the Bundestag. After a short stay in Jena, he left his beloved homeland, which he was never to see again. Traveling from Strassburg, he went to Paris and visited with Lafayette, Benjamin Constant und other important men of the time; with the former he always enjoyed the warmest friendship. From Paris, he went to Switzerland, where he received a call to the school of Chur in Graubünden as professor of history. During his stay there, demands were made by the Prussian government to the cantonal council, unsuccessfully calling for the extradition of Follen. In 1821, he moved from his position in Chur to a professorship at the recently re-organized University of Basel and held lectures on natural, Roman and church law, as well as logic and other branches of philosophy. His stay there was just as honorable and pleasant only interrupted by a second visit to Paris, and lasted till 1824. However, the council of Basel was bombarded with requests from Prussia, Austria and Hessia, Follen's own homeland, as well as from other Swiss cantons, such as Bern, Zürich, and Luzern, responding to the pressure of the other powers, demanding his extradition, so that the government in Basel finally decided to arrest him. However, they informed him of this decision so that he would have enough time to make to possible for him to take flight and avoid imprisonment.

With a fake passport he succeeded in escaping to Paris and on 1 November 1824, he disembarked at La Havre for New York. Traveling with him was Dr. Karl Beck, who had already made a name for himself after several years in America by means of his outstanding philological scholarship, and held a professorship of Latin language and literature at the University of Cambridge in Massachusetts. He had also contributed to the fame of the German name in scholarly circles by means of his exemplary character as well as his wealth of knowledge.

After the quite stormy journey, which brought his ship first to the coast of Bermuda, Karl Follen finally landed on our shores on 20 December 1824. During stays in New York and Philadelphia he made the acquaintance of many important and influential people. This was especially due to Lafayette, who at that time was triumphantly traveling through the country. Those he met included Du Ponceau and George Ticknor, the latter of whom, as well as Alexander Everett he brought the warmest recommendations from his earlier teacher, Professor Welker in Bonn. (5) He then went to Cambridge, and there obtained a position at Harvard as a teacher of German through the influence of the aforementioned persons. With iron-like determination he threw himself into the study of the English language, so that he successfully administered his position, although he had only begun to study English on his journey to America. At the same time, he gave private lectures on Roman law.

It was his intention to only read the best English. William Ellery Channing, perhaps the best stylist in the English language, was his model, not only through his writings, but also by means of conversations with him, for which there was ample opportunity, resulting eventually in a close friendship with this knowledgeable and noble gentleman. (6) It is almost unbelievable how quickly he was able to penetrate into the spirit and fine points of the English language, but it was his thorough knowledge of classical and modern languages, his endless energy, and his rhythmically finely tuned ear, which enabled him to so successfully master a new language so well that even in his works written soon after his arrival we rarely find a non-idiomatic expression. Eventually, he wrote and spoke masterfully and with such enthusiasm and natural eloquence. However, there was no lack of deliberation and moderation on his part, and he had no fear of not being the equal of the native-born.

He was an improviser. Even his best speeches and sermons were based on brief notes, and in the main he was given to the inspiration of the moment. Of course, he had a rich treasure of thoughts to draw from and was a thinker, a deep one. If an in-born inclination to philosophy and theology had not held him from studying jurisprudence, and if he had turned to the practice of law and politics he no doubt would have become famous either in the courtroom or the halls of Congress and would have held a very high position.

He stood out not only because of the nobility of his character and his natural eloquence, but also because of his thoroughly sensible ideas on the state of the economy, and especially with regard to legislation and politics in general. He was a student of Adam Smith, Bentham, and Macintosh. The few places in his only partly preserved correspondence, which was collected in his biography so affectionately written by his widow, and which relate to politics, is where we find his very fine understanding of all the issues facing the U.S. at the time, as well as his shrewd assessment of the leading statesmen as well.

He had hardly taken office when he took on the task of compiling a German-English grammar, which went through many editions and for many years was considered the best in the country. He also completed several German textbooks that especially stood forth because of the methodical and intelligent selection of examples. Already in spring 1826, he opened a gymnastic school for students and the general public, the first on this side of the ocean, and one which received great support.

Meanwhile he had not yet given up the idea of studying law. In the winter, he lectured in Boston on the history of Roman law and became acquainted with Judge Story, Judge Davis and other outstanding legal scholars, as well as with John Quincy Adams, then President of the United States. (7) The latter himself understood and appreciated the German language. He sought council and advice from Follen, especially with regard to German literature. When Adams left Germany at the end of the previous century, the most popular authors were Goethe, Klopstock, Wieland, Voss, Musäus, Schiller, and as he wrote Follen, especially Bürger. Adams completely translated Wieland's *Oberon*, but did not publish it, because an Englishman had beaten him to the punch. Wieland himself felt that Adams' translation was truer to his, but that Sotheby's was more poetical. Adams now asked Follen to provide him with information on two new authors, Jean Paul and Tieck, a request that Follen fulfilled by providing a very positive and balanced critique of the two. From the correspondence of the President with Follen it becomes clear that Adams quickly perceived the importance of this man and paid him the appropriate respect.

After his appointment to a position as an instructor of German at Harvard, Follen began a serious of lectures on moral philosophy and ethics at the theological seminary at Cambridge. The close contact with Channing and other important people, who all belonged to the Unitarian Church, did not fail in turning his religiously inclined nature to the study of theology. His first attempts at poetry, as well as those of his brother Adolph

(*Freie Stimmen frischer Jugend*) bear witness of his deep poetic feelings. Was not the student movement, which Follen had so diligently helped to build not only one that cultivated patriotism and the desire for freedom, but also Christianity as well? To be sure it remained quite undecided as to what kind of Christianity should fill the heart of Germany's youth, and as a result the German student movement emancipated itself from religious questions after several years.

With someone like Follen it was natural that neither orthodoxy nor pietism could quell his religious quest. The Unitarians, who did not maintain a binding dogma, not even recognizing some articles of the Christian faith, and were completely independent in terms of church organization, knowing no synods or religious authorities, but were completely dependent on the individuality of independent congregations, must have been something particularly attractive to Follen, whose most decisive character trait was that of self-determination. And, they must have been even more attractive with members, such as Channing, Theodore Parker and Alexander Everett. They were the most eloquent clergy of the church, and almost all the literary and scholarly notables of New England more or less adhered to the principles of the Unitarians.

It was self-evident that such a knowledgeable expert of German philosophy, which Follen was, would belong to the liberal wing of this most liberal religious denomination. In summer 1828, he was accepted as a candidate for preacher and as he had just married Elise Cabot, a lady equal to him in spirit and temperament, it was his desire to be called to a congregation so that he could obtain a more independent position. In order to keep him at Harvard, he was appointed to a position as instructor of church history and ethics at the theological school, where he had previously lectured, so that he could now look forward to a somewhat sizable income.

Finally in 1830, he was called to the first professorship for German language and literature by means of voluntary contributions to fund the position for the period of five years. However, it was not till fall 1831 that he took on the position. His work here was richly blessed, and from this time on, the efforts can be dated to attract the best teachers of German scholarship and literature to America. To be sure, men like Ticknor, Bancroft, Longfellow and John Quincy Adams had already completed their education in Germany, and Channing, Ware, and Parker had studied German philosophy, but it was Follen who awakened a love of German literature and scholarship on a much grander scale. The Prescotts, Motleys and the Emersons were directly or indirectly inspired by him to study German intellectual life. Follen did not confine himself to his lectures at the university, but also held lectures on German authors, first in Boston, later in New York and in many others states. As an apostle of German scholarship he successfully planted the German seed in America, gifted as he was by his noble sense of enthusiasm and his natural and animated eloquence.

Almost at the same time, his friend and travel companion across the ocean, Dr. Beck, had obtained a permanent position at Harvard as a professor of Latin. He had also acquired a great circle of scholarly friends and like Follen cultivated and promoted German scholarship.

Against the wish of many of his friends, Follen joined the Anti-Slavery Society in 1833. This led to a great material loss on his part. Even if the population in rural areas and small towns supported its principles, this was by no means the case in the centers of business and industry, and the business aristocracy viewed this movement with horror, which eventually developed into hatred. Even the educational institutions looked with mistrust at the every increasingly vocal party, and sought to distance itself in every way from the widely despised abolitionists, so as to do not stem the flow of students from the South.

One had hoped that after the successful attempt at establishing a professorship in German from private sources that after a period of five years that the academic authorities would establish this as a permanent position. This did not happen and it may certainly be assumed that Follen's participation in the anti-slavery movement was the main reason for this. Follen was well aware of this, but he was not the kind of man to neglect his duty as a result of the possible consequences. He had sufficient political experience to see that the agitation against slavery could not always be carried on within the appropriate channels. He well knew that many hotheads were given to overstepping their bounds and that instead of attacking slavery as an institution and opposing it as far as the Constitution allowed, they had vented the bitterest verbal abuse against the slaveholders. He knew that they would definitely make their principles known without the slightest regard to material interests, which so strongly influences the decision making process, as well as without regard to historical traditions or the impact on their own education. On the other hand, however, the opposition to the abolitionists was so hateful that in its efforts at destroying the party it ruthlessly attacked some of the most sacred rights granted by the Constitution and laws of the land, including the freedom of speech, freedom of the press, freedom of assembly, that there is no doubt that Follen was attracted to the movement more by the attacks on it than by its principles.

If one reads his correspondence, the addresses he wrote, and the speeches he held at meetings of the party, one find that he did not support an agitation against slavery outside the law. The only demands that he considered supportable were the elimination of slavery in the District of Columbia and the territories, over which the Congress had the lawmaking authority, and also the ban on the slavery trade between the states, which he felt vindicated by Congress under the clause that this body had the right to regulate trade. Above all, he also wanted to maintain the rights of free speech and free assembly as rights granted by the Constitution. We especially find this last point advanced by him in the thoughtful debates, which a committee of the Anti-Slavery Party had with a committee of the state legislature of Massachusetts.

The legislatures of various southern states had issued proclamations in which they denounced the abolitionists as hostile to the Union and called on state legislatures in New England to take the appropriate steps against them. These decrees were transmitted via a message of the governor of Massachusetts to the legislature and a special committee was appointed to review them.

The abolitionists did not actually fear any active involvement of the legislature, but rather a report of its committee and a statement of the legislature that would condemn the work of the Anti-Slavery Party and arouse the public anew to violence. It therefore requested a hearing before the committee and Follen was appointed its representative. His testimony before the committee was exemplary in terms of content and style. The well known author, Harriet Martinau, was in the audience (March 1835), and wrote the following in his travel work about America (*Retrospect of Western Travel*. New York, 1838, p. 128):

> The hall of the senate was crowded full and filled with shouts of approval when the speaker (Follen) crushed one accusation after the other, or successfully denounced the impertinence of the chairman. They interrupted Follen, when he showed that the critical position statements of public meetings against the abolitionists had resulted in mob actions against them. The chairman demanded his silence, and that he treat the committee with respect, whereupon he responded with his gentle but resounding voice: "Am I given to understand that if I condemn storming groups of mobs that I do not show the proper respect to the committee?" The chairman then played a pitiful role despite the shouts of approval thereafter. However, Dr. Follen conquered the field inch by inch, and succeeded in saying everything that he had in mind.

However, it is particularly of note that his name was brought before the public when in 1836 he wrote an address to the American people on behalf the Anti-Slavery Party in which he explained its basic principles in the loftiest and most moderate manner. This was sent to all members of Congress, to all members of state government in the various states, but in the end did not exert a great deal of influence, however. Naturally, there was no lack of opposition to this statement and part of the press arose against it and its author. From several sides it was mentioned that it was least of all inappropriate for a refugee who enjoyed the hospitality of the country to act as a firebrand in the social and political life of his new homeland.

This therefore became the opportunity for him to defend the rights of immigrants and he did this on the speaker's platform as well as in his writings in the most courageous, penetrating and convincing manner. He struck the strongest blows of the time against the rising tide of nativism and while he always expressed himself moderately, the noblest sense of pride came through his words. " He said: "Should he deny the principles in this country, whose people so loudly proclaim its freedom and which proclaims the principles of its Declaration of Independence as natural rights, which he had defended in the old country and which he offered himself up for, leaving his mother earth and his beloved parents, sisters and friends?"

After Follen had been ordained a minister in the Unitarian Church in Boston, he accepted a call to a congregation in New York, remaining there till spring 1838. However, he did not devote all his time to this position, but also held lectures on political topics, such as, for example, "True Republicanism" and "The Duties of an American Citizen;" he also successfully wrote articles for the best journals of the time on religion, church, and other topics. A series of lectures in winter 1837/38 on Schiller enjoyed a select, but sizable audience.

After returning to Boston, he continued to write, and focused especially on a work on psychology, which he viewed as his *Magnus opus*, but did not complete in spite of the years of preparation and work on individual parts of it. He also held a number of highly successful lectures in Boston, first on pantheism, and later on the history of Switzerland.

Soon after his return to Boston, he obtained a permanent position as minister at a church in East Lexington. This was a congregation that was just as independently minded as its minister, and shared the confession of faith expressed by him at various times in various ways, but summarized best as follows: "The Christian faith has value only if it is the result of a completely open minded and rational study." In winter 1839/40, he received an invitation to New York from the mercantile library society to lecture on German literature. He traveled there on the steamboat *Lexington* and his lectures were enthusiastically received, but had to be interrupted, because he had promised to return to help dedicate the newly constructed church of his congregation on 15 January 1840.

His wife in the meantime had become seriously ill in New York and so he wrote to the board of his church, requesting that the dedication be postponed for a week. He placed it at the disposal of the church as to making a final decision and offered to be there if it was in the interest of the congregation to be there on the planned for date. The board, which due to the gentility of Follen's letter, decided that it was not so serious, and urged him to come, and although Follen was very unpleasantly surprised by this news and his wife urged him not to go, he considered it unworthy not to hold to his promise. On 13 February 1840, he boarded the same steamboat, which in the same night went up in flames. Only one or two sailors saved themselves on floating bales of cotton. As great as the number was of those who lost their lives, it was Follen who was so greatly mourned across the U.S. Even those who had bitterly opposed him because of his resoluteness in the slavery matter respected and honored him as a man and a thinker with a transparent character filled with the purest of feelings.

His works were published in two large volumes and join those of his noble teacher and friend, William Ellerly Channing. There was no doubt that the life and work of this German man did not disappear in the river, but exerted a great deal of influence on the spirit of the American people.

Only several years later (1827), another exile, Franz Lieber, followed in the footsteps of Follen. If Follen was lost to his new homeland in the best years of his life, then it was fate that granted the more fortunate Lieber the opportunity of developing himself here intellectually and working for the benefit of his fellow citizens in the most productive manner. (8) The intellectual atmosphere of Boston exerted the same attractive influence that it had on other Germans who had settled there.

Born in March 1800, Lieber's youthful years fell into the time of the iron rule of France when Prussia fortified itself by means of the spirit and work of Stein, Scharnhorst,

Fichte, Jahn, Gneisenau and Schőn. His father, Friedrich Wilhelm, lived in meager circumstances; frugality and renunciation were the rules of life, as were doing one's duty and honoring the parental teachings. Franz showed himself to be a diligent and industrious student, was a favorite of his teachers and also a sprightly gymnast and swimmer, a second Friesen, "without reproach in body and soul."

Both of his older brothers, who had joined in the War of Liberation in 1813, returned home as wounded officers. "Boys, take your rifles from the wall!" called out his father in March 1815, as he entered the room, where Franz was occupied with studies, "he is on the loose again – Napoleon. He is back from Elba."

The one brother, who had recovered from his wounds, returned to his regiment, and Franz and his two years older brother, both too young for military service, joined as volunteers. On the day that they were to be mustered in (they had chosen the proud and well known Colberg Regiment), both boys came to their father. "Greetings, we go now, if it is alright with you?" "Go to your mother," answered their father, "go to your mother."

"Our hearts," said Lieber, "sank; she had suffered so much during the first campaign." With a half-choked up voice I said to her: "Mother, we are going to leave and join the service, if this is alright?" She embraced us both, crying loudly. "Go." That was all she could say.

George Sand, speaking of Schiller's Karl and Franz Moor, said: "I would have liked to have known the lion, which bore such youths." At this point in Lieber's *Letters to a Gentleman in Germany* I was seized by the same desire of wanting to have known this German mother. (9)

With the kind of joyous and lofty feelings that north Germans greet the Rhine, the young Lieber crossed this famous German river. The volunteer *Jäger* company was put into service in Belgium. Lieber received his first baptism in fire in the Battle at Ligny (16 June 1815), in which a bloody battle was fought around the village of Ligny in the evening. His comrades in arms fell to the right and left of him. His brother was wounded. When the retreat was called late in the evening, only thirty remained from a company of 150.

After the most difficult marches on roads washed away by rainstorms, his regiment joined the battle of Waterloo on the evening of 18 June. Lieber made it out of this intensely fought battle unscathed, which was fought on the right flank of the French by Planchenois, and which actually decided the fate of the battle, only then to be severely wounded twice the following day a few minutes after a carelessly planned attack on Namur, where Grouchy's troops had retreated to.

It was a miracle that he survived. Many months were spent in the hospitals of Lüttich, Aachen, and Köln, and only long after peace was concluded did he recover so that he could return home to his family in Berlin. He continued his studies, first at the gymnasium and then at the university in his hometown. As he did not shed his love of homeland and his enthusiasm for freedom he soon came under governmental suspicion like other freedom fighters, such as his Turner teacher Jahn, and was imprisoned several months for interrogation. After he was released, his attendance at Prussian universities was forbidden, so he went to Jena, which at that time was not the place for one to cool off his ideas on German unity and freedom. All prospects of a career in Prussia were finished, however. After he had changed his place of residence several times, we then find him in Dresden. Here he got the idea of joining the freedom fighters, which were then assembling in France and Germany to assist in the battle for the independence of Greece.

The struggle in Greece exerted a tremendous influence, which can hardly be imagined today, on the younger generation due to its classical education, even in the U.S. In spite of all hindrances, which the European governments placed in the way of the collection of funds and forces headed to Greece, there were hundreds of Germans streaming through Switzerland and France, all of them more or less in military order on their way to the glorious "Hellas." Most of their bones now lay on the battlefields of

Artas and Peta, where they met a heroic death, disgustingly deserted by the "brave" Greeks, or before the walls of Athens and Napoli de Romania, where they were shot down, or succumbed to the fever.

Enthusiasm was followed by the bitterest disappointment. Like so many others so too did Lieber leave Greece with a much better opinion of the Turks than the Greeks. But one has to be fair. The idea of supporting the Greeks with armed forces was a mistake in and of itself. What the Greeks needed was money, weapons, munitions, medicine, and of course some competent staff and engineering officers. The European volunteers, which Lieber himself admits, consisted only in the minority of those who went there for the love of the cause. For the most part, they were soldiers, who had been unlucky at home, and hoped that they could win back or improve their previous rank. Then there were adventurers of all nations who soon came to quarrel among themselves. There were enough soldiers there already, and volunteers that came from civilized countries were already disciplined to some extent and wanted to fight in a way they were accustomed to, and could not accommodate themselves to the guerilla-style warfare begin waged there by the self-elected "Capitanos." They hardly paid the latter any allegiance and were not concerned with the government, whose manner of waging war consisted of attacking at night, and when successful culminated in the decapitation of prisoners.

Lieber remained only three months in Greece. At the end of March, he landed in Ancona almost with any means and with great difficulty reached Rome. In difficult straits due to his lack of personal identification papers, without which no government would grant him residence, he turned to the Prussian ambassador, who at that time was none other than Niebuhr. (10) This great historian immediately recognized Lieber's significance. He promised him shelter, and invited him to lunch. When Lieber tried to apologize because of his ragged clothing, Niebuhr replied: "You are wrong young man to say so. Do you think that a diplomat is heartless? I am none other than the one who lectured in Berlin?" Moreover, it soon turned out that Niebuhr appointed him to teach his oldest son, Markus. And so Lieber lived in Rome in the rich intellectual environment of

Niehbuhr's home (Palazzo Orsini) for a year, and also devoted himself to the serious study of the antiquities and art treasures in Rome.

The King of Prussia, Friedrich Wilhelm III, then visited Rome, and dwelt at the residence of the ambassador, who urgently pressed him to not cause Lieber any further difficulties in Prussia. After the latter had accompanied Niebuhr to Naples and had traveled with him through Italy all the way to Vienna, he then returned to Berlin, basing his decision on the word of the King. However, he was again arrested and brought to the fortress at Köpnick, where he wrote his *Wein- und Wonnelieder*. (11) Finally, he was released thanks to the efforts of Niebuhr. So as to escape further persecution, he fled to London. There he made out a meager existence as a correspondent for German newspapers and also giving German instruction, and then finally decided to immigrate to the U.S. in 1827.

We then find him in Boston, where he organized a swimming school, just as Follen before him had organized a gymnastic school. Letters of recommendation from Nieburhr provided him with a welcome reception in Boston. He made friends and acquaintances that lasted the rest of his life. Among his friends, and we must also add, his admirers, we find Josiah Quincy, the president of Harvard; the noble and highly gifted William Ellery Channing; and the equally scholarly and intellectual Professor Felton, the first legal scholar of America who enjoyed a great reputation in Europe; Judge Story; two historians Prescott and Bancroft; George Ticknor; the poet Longfellow; and above all Charles Sumner, with whom he formed a lasting friendship.

Soon thereafter, he undertook the difficult task of translating the Brockhaus encyclopedia, basing this task on his inexhaustible energy. Written for Americans, he tactfully deleted many articles that were of interest to German readers, and enriched the work with others, drawing on many contributors, who wrote articles focusing on English and especially American history, geography, and literature. This appeared under the title: *Encyclopedia Americana, based on the Conversation Lexicon*, and proved to be epoch-

making and attained the widest possible circulation. (12) It now forms the basis for the
latest editions of the encyclopedia, which naturally have to be updated with time.

For five years, till 1832, he was occupied with the preparation of this work, which
lent him an honorable literary name at the very beginning of his American career. This
work was an accomplishment. If we consider that the German work was the product of
German authors, that a handbook could deal with all possible topics so objectively, and
that it reflected the spirit and perception of its authors, then we can realize that this spirit
and perception could not but have had other than a great influence on its readers. And, it
is exactly this encyclopedia, which the educated have used for instructional purposes,
thus providing them with the greatest possible influence. It is not an irrelevant question as
to whether a people, which had no encyclopedia, now used a German, French, or English
one. That a strong breath of German spirit flowed through this work (13 volumes) into
American intellectual life is a fact that cannot be denied.

An engagement belonged to the romantic life of young German scholars, and
dates usually to their student days. Already two years after his immigration, Lieber had
such a firm position that his fiancé could follow him, accompanied by her brother. The
marriage took place in New York (21 September 1829) in the St. Thomas Church. Only
in the rarest of cases do we find a noble and competent man without a noble and
competent wife. His friends admired not only her intellectual gifts, but also her genuine
sensibility and her kindliness. "They have a happy home of the rarest kind," wrote
Sumner, who frequently makes reference to their beautiful family life. While he was still
occupied with the encyclopedia (1831), Lieber also translated a work on the July
Revolution and a work by Anselm Feuerbach about Kaspar Hauser, a work which his
wife aided him with. (13)

Lieber then received a commission from Philadelphia to work on the curriculum
of the Girard College that was being established there. He soon found himself at home
there and became acquainted with many of its most important people, also becoming
friends with many. We name here only Nicholas Biddle, the president of the board of

trustees of the Girard Foundation, as well as the U.S. National Bank; Horace Binney, one of the foremost legal scholars of the country; Charles J. Ingersoll, statesman and jurist; Judge Thayer, likewise well known in the law and literary realm; and also as particularly ex-king Joseph Bonaparte. (14) In 1835, he accepted a call to a professorship of history and national economy at South Carolina College, one of the best colleges in the South, and moved to the state's capital with his family. A full twenty years were devoted there to the teaching profession with loyalty, diligence, and great success.

It was here that he created the works that gave him a name and a lasting reputation not only in this country, but in Europe as well. In 1838, his *Manual of Political Ethics* appeared in two large volumes, which was later on re-issued (1876) having been edited by Theodore D. Woolsey, professor of political science. In 1839, he published *Prinzipien der auslegung der bürgerlichen und politischen Gesetze* (1 volume) and *Bürgerliche Freiheit und Selbstregierung* (2 volumes). We lack the space here to cite all the positive comments made by the many well known reviewers of these works. If we mention the following names, then it reflects in a small way the reputation that Lieber's name enjoyed: in the U.S.: Story, Kanzeler, Kent, Sumner, William H. Prescott, Professor Greenleaf and George Bancroft; in England: Henry Hallam and Professor Creasy; in Germany: Mittermaier, von Mohl and Bluntschi; in France: Laboulaye and de Tocqueville; in Belgium: in Belgium: Rolin and Jacquemeyns, who wrote him a deeply felt obituary in the *Revue Internationale*; and in Italy: Pierantoni and Gavelli. His major works were used as textbooks in all the universities of the U.S., were also published in England, and many of his smaller works also were translated into German.

Those who were closest to him regarded it as his greatest misfortune that he took a position in the South. If you take into consideration the fact that his son Oskar, who had studied in Germany and who was described as a highly talented and kindly person, had his fate thereby interwoven with the South, and that he opposed his father while his younger brother fought bravely in the Union Army and he on the other hand supported the Rebellion, perishing in one of the first battles (near Williamsburg), then one can readily understand this regret. However, for Lieber's entire educational experience his stay in the South and his acquaintances with statesmen like Calhoun, William K. Preston, Legaree, De Sausure, and Pettigrŭ were not inconsequential. His circle of acquaintances in the field of American politics was thereby expanded greatly and it gave him the best opportunity to become acquainted with the other side on a variety of issues, and his search for truth could only benefit from this.

In 1857, Lieber accepted a call to Columbia College in New York as professor of history, national economics, and political science, and he held this position till his death. During the Civil War he spent a great deal of time in Washington, D.C. as an advisor on difficult international and war-related issues. In commission of the highest commanding officer, General Halleck, he worked on instructions for the behavior of soldiers in the field, which was published by the General Staff as Order No. 100 and was sent to all staff officers of the U.S. Army. Laboulaye referred to this as a masterpiece. Bluntschli gave it the greatest praise in the preface to his *Droit International codifie* and included it as an appendix to his work. After the war, he was asked by the government to organize and catalog the archives of the Confederacy. In 1870, he was appointed as an arbitrator of an international commission to decide outstanding claims between the U.S. and Mexico, a position he held till his death.

His publication activity was one of the most fruitful and all encompassing, lasting to the time of his death. He worked on a great work dealing with the development of the U.S. Constitution, when he unexpectedly passed away in 1872. Aside from the works already he mentioned, he was also always writing for journals here and abroad, and during the war wrote as President of the Society for Loyal Publications many pamphlets, such as: *No Part Now, All for Our Country*; *Lincoln or McClellan*; *Slavery, Plantations and the Yeomanry*, etc. At the same time, he maintained an extraordinarily extensive correspondence, writing in the most thorough and comprehensive manner. He was a member of the Institute de France and many other scholarly societies and remained in written contact with many of his colleagues. Aside from his many correspondents in the U.S., he also corresponded with such individuals as Humboldt, Niebuhr, Bunsen, Julius, Mittermaier, Holzendorf, Laboulaye, de Tocqueville, Jacquemeyns, and others.

Additionally, the task often fell to him to deliver an address at the opening of public institutions, the dedication of monuments, receptions, etc.

One would have to think that a man of such thorough and universal scholarship, whose works reflect knowledge of world literature, and who spent the greater part of his life teaching, researching in libraries, and writing at his desk, would have been of necessity a not very sociable person, and inclined to pedantry. However, this would be an error. He was a child with children, a fencer, Turner, swimmer with young people, an intelligent, witty, good spirited, friendly and sociable person. Everyone was attracted and charmed by his vivaciousness and love of life. He was hardly of medium size, but strong and well built. A highly arched thinker's forehead above his thick strong eyebrows and the somewhat deeply set eyes gave him an appearance that, in the opinion of many, was like that of Daniel Webster.

Let us hear the thoughts of Americans about him. One who knew him the best was Judge Thayer, who said of him: "Only few people have combined greatness and strength with such kindliness." Sumner wrote in one of his letters: "I owe him a great deal of gratitude;" in another he writes: "My heart beats for you and my thoughts are always on your works." Judge Story: "His conversation is always fresh, original and sparkling with reminiscences." At another place, he said of him: "He always makes me think." William H. Prescott said: "Your book (*Political Ethics*) is full of so many suggestions that when the reader is only half done he is led to follow its thesis till he has finished the work." Chancellor Kent said: "Lieber's eminence as a scholar in history, national economics, moral philosophy, and geology and the humanities would be enough to establish the reputation of any university in our country. His talents, his scholarship, his great moral value are widely recognized by the foremost scholars and jurists of our country."

Professor Greenleaf expresses himself as follows with regard to Lieber's works: "He first dives into the deepest water and then comes up as a good swimmer." Sumner wrote of him in 1841: "I wish that your place of residence (South Carolina) was more in accordance with your heart, but you have the sources of the greatest satisfaction where you are. A happy home of the rarest kind, a permanent and honorable sphere of activity, a well known name, a good conscience for doing good and furthering the cause of truth, education and a good government! I know few people, who have so much cause to be thankful to God as you do."

Judge Thayer said in his masterful memorial address about Lieber: "He hated a demagogue worse than a tyrant." As proof he referred to a passage in Lieber's *Civil Liberty* that closes with the words: "Woe to the country where political hypocrisy first calls the people almighty, then posits the teaching that the voice of the people is the voice of God, then calls the cry of the street the true voice of the people, and in the end creates the voice that is desired." Thayer continued: "The influence of this important work by Lieber was great for intellectuals in Europe as well as especially in America."

America is deeply indebted to Lieber. Hardly any other man instructed our countrymen in the truth of history, in the rules of moral philosophy and the principles of political science as Lieber, who taught in the most appealing way. He loved his listeners and they loved him. He used every chance to awaken the noblest feelings in the hearts of his students, so that he could in truth say to them (from the preface to his *Civil Liberty and Self-Government*):

> I always sought to show you how you will bear witness that a human being bears an indestructible individuality and that democratic society is a living organism that grants no rights without duties, no freedom without the majesty of law, that nothing great can be attained without patience, that there can be no true greatness without selflessness."

Native-born Americans praise him that he became a thorough-going American. It is true that when he visited the old country in 1849 that he refused many offers personally made to him by Friedrich Wilhelm IV to entice him back to Berlin. It is also likewise true that he lovingly embraced his new homeland and he devoted everything he could to it, except his intellectual independence. However, no German immigrant remained more German than Lieber. His untiring energy for work, his thoroughness, his love for literature and the fine arts, his naturalness and his humor, his love for intellectual freedom and independence, his thirst for truth, his hatred for all affectedness, his scorn for all that was low, his striving to lead youth to the ideal and above all his ever present sense of duty mark him as a man of German descent. These characteristics are rarely united together, and only found in Germany with the noblest and best minds.

His correspondence always reflected a warm interest for the old country. Its unity and strength were always of great interest to him. He had already said that the ideas that had inspired him as a youth now appeared to be fulfilled and that kings and ministers now spoke words that had once landed him in jail. At the outbreak of the Franco-Prussian War the enthusiasm of an 1815 volunteer arose within him again. In a letter dated 20 June 1870, he wrote: "I write throughout the day, but my soul is full of one word, one feeling, and one thought – Germany. Streams of blood will flow, not for long, but they will be wide like the sea and just as deep." And on 18 August: "My correspondence from Germany bears witness that all Germans are motivated by the noblest feelings and are ready to offer everything, money and life, for the defense of the fatherland. Even family fathers cannot be turned back; high officials join as volunteers and serve as privates. And I sit here and write like a philistine. It is too hard."

A saying in large letters in the entrance hall to his home in New York expresses in a few words the best characterization of this man: *Patria cara, carior libertas, veritas charisma* (Precious is my country, more precious is freedom, most precious is truth).

By this year, the German population of Boston had significantly increased. Löher, obviously estimating to high, writes that there were 3,000 at the time. (15) Robert Wesselhöft had already settled in Cambridge near Boston in 1841, and his brother Wilhelm in Boston, both as doctors. They practiced homeopathy, which was then very being very well received in New England. Robert in later years constructed the large water cure institute in Brattelboro, Vermont that became so well known. In 1846, the first

German newspaper, the *New England Zeitung*, was founded, followed later by the *Boston Merkur*, both of which no longer exist.

The German population in the other four states of New England during the time period under discussion was so small that we can not talk about the influence of immigration on the character of the population there. A detailed study would probably show that there were Germans here and there in the various excellent educational and beneficial institutions of New England, as is the case elsewhere. In later years, especially in Connecticut, the German element made a great deal of progress in New England, contributing greatly to its development. (16)

Only in recent years has attention been drawn to one German in Massachusetts, whose name was hidden behind an English-sounding name. We refer here to Leopold Maas, who was known in Boston as Morse. He was born in 1831 in Wachenheim in the Rheinpfalz, and came to the U.S. in his youth, devoting himself to salesmanship. He also appears to have actively participated in politics, serving twice as a delegate at the Democratic national conventions, twice as an unsuccessful candidate for Congress, but then finally winning in 1876, and then getting re-elected in 1878. He is the only elected Democrat among the eleven congressional representatives of Massachusetts in Congress. (17)

The German Element in the Northeast

III. Editor's Conclusion

Editor's Conclusion

Gustav Koerner provides us with a portrait of the German element in Pennsylvania, New York, New Jersey, and New England by means of his biographical focus. His history certainly is the appropriate point of departure for anyone interested in exploring influences and contributions to this area. Certainly many of the persons and topics he covers are worthy of further exploration and examination, and hopefully this work will contribute to further research and study.

Although Koerner does make occasional use of statistics, it might be helpful here by to provide some statistical information regarding the size of the German **element** in Pennsylvania, New York, New Jersey, and New England to get an idea of the size of the populations we are dealing with. A good source of such data is Alexander Schem's *Deutsch-Amerikanisches Konversations-Lexikon*, a German-American encyclopedia that was published after the Civil War and provides data with regard to the German element in various states, including information on German-American churches, societies, newspapers, etc. Unless otherwise noted, the information that follows is drawn from this source. (1)

Pennsylvania

By the time of the publication of Koerner's German-American history (1880) the German element had grown substantially since the beginning of the nineteenth century. As to areas of settlement, the German element by this time was concentrated in the following cities: Philadelphia, Pittsburgh, Alleghany, Scranton, and Reading; and the following counties: Philadelphia, Alleghany, Luzerne, Schuylkill, Erie, Lancaster and Berks.

Although Koerner does make mention of the Civil War service of various individuals, he does not focus on the topic, and so it might be well to provide the following basic information about the role played by the German element. The German-born troops from Pennsylvania in the Union Army numbered 17,208 and the units with German-born troops consisted of the following: the 21st (later the 98th), 27th, 73rd, 74th, and the 75th infantry regiments. In addition to the German-born troops, there were 100,000 American-born troops of German descent, and their units consisted of the following: the 4th, 8th, 9th, 10th, 11th, 14th, 15th, 16th, 48th, 50th, 51st, 56th, 65th, 79th, 88th, 96th, 97th, 98th infantry regiments, as well as the 112th, 113th, and 115th artillery regiments. Together this makes for a total of 117,208 soldiers and 26 regiments, thereby demonstrating that the German element of Pennsylvania indeed played significant role on behalf of the Union cause in the War Between the States. (2)

By 1870 the foreign-born population from the German-speaking countries numbered: 160,146 from Germany; 1,536 from Switzerland; and 5,765 from Switzerland, for a total population of 167,447. The German-speaking population, however, was much greater than the foreign-born population, and was estimated at 1.5 million out of a total state population of 3,521,791, or almost half the population of the state. Such a large percentage was no doubt due to the inclusion in this estimate not only the descendants of the foreign-born population, but also the American-born born population descended from the German immigrations of the colonial era.

A little more than a century after the publication of Koerner's history (1990), the population of German descent registered at 36.3% of the state's population, or 4,314,762 out of a total population of 11,981,643. (3) The population of German descent today, therefore, is more than one-third of the state's population, and the German-speaking population may well have numbered much more than that before World War One. The substantial growth and development of the German element was no doubt due to the waves of immigration reaching back to the colonial era, which then rose greatly throughout the course of the nineteenth century, continuing on into the twentieth century.

New York

In 1870, the total population of New York State was 4,382,759. The population of foreign-born from the German-speaking countries was 328,721, with 316,882 German-born; 3,928 Austrian-born; and 7,911 Swiss-born. The German-speaking population was estimated at between 600,000 and 700,000, or roughly twice the population of the foreign-born element.

Not surprisingly, about one-half of the German-born population, or 151,216, was in New York County (includes New York City). The German-born population was then mainly located in the following other counties of the state: 40,112 in King's County; 31,150 in Erie County; 11,663 in Monroe County; 8,319 in Westchester County; 7,909 in Albany County; 6,553 in Queens County; 6,348 in Onondaga County; and 5,664 in Oneida County.

In 1869, German instruction was introduced into the public schools of New York City, and was also available in many other cities, such as Buffalo, Albany, etc. The secular and religious organizations were numerous by this time: Altogether there were at least 350 German-American societies and approximately 250 congregations. The German-language press was equally as impressive, with a total of 56 publications for New York State (27 in New York City alone).

Given these statistics, it is not surprising that the New York Germans played an important role in the Civil War. They provided a quite substantial contribution to the Union Army with a total of 16 infantry regiments that were either entirely or partly German; 6 artillery units, and 2 cavalry units. A full 21% of the Union forces from New York, or 256,252 consisted of the German-born. (4)

New Jersey

In 1870, the total population of New Jersey was 906,096. The population of the foreign-born from German-speaking countries was 56,062, with the German-born numbering 54,001 and the Swiss-born 2,061. The German-born population was concentrated in Essex County (including Newark) with 17,810 and Hudson County (including Jersey City and Hoboken) with 17,091. The population here amounted to approximately two-thirds of the German-born population. The German-speaking population at this time was estimated at 120,000, or roughly twice that of the foreign-born population.

There were well over a hundred secular societies and organizations, and approximately thirty religious congregations at the time. The German-language press was fairly large given the size of the population, and stood at 18 publications (7 in Newark alone). When it came to the Civil War, the New Jersey Germans also responded to Lincoln's call for troops, forming a total of three military units (1 cavalry unit and 2 artillery units). (5)

New England

Since Koerner focuses his discussion on Massachusetts when it comes to New England, the focus here likewise will be on the German element there. In 1870, the total population of Massachusetts was 1,104,319, with the German-born population numbering 13,072 and the Swiss-born 491. This amounts to a total population of 13,563 from the German-speaking countries of Europe. Almost half of this number, or 5,000, lived in Boston.

German-American secular and religious organizations and institutions were not surprisingly concentrated in Boston, where there were some half dozen religious congregations, and several German-American societies. The Boston Turnerverein was formed in 1849, and in 1869 the Germania Society was formed to unite the existing

German societies into one central organization. In the following year a German Theater Society was formed, thereby reflecting the cultural interests of the German element of Boston. At the time, there were a total of two German-language newspapers. Reference might also be made here to the number of scholars who were either German-born or of German descent, who taught at the institutions of higher learning in the state of Masachusetts.

During the Civil War, there were two infantry regiments that consisted partly of German-born troops. It might also be mentioned that the only other German units from New England that served in the Civil War were from Connecticut. The population of Connecticut in 1870 was 650,000, and the German-born population stood at that time at 8,525. (6)

A Basic Source

Since the publication of Koerner's history in 1880, German immigration continued on up to the present time, thereby contributing to the growth of the population of German ancestry. The German element experienced some tumultuous times in the first half of the 20th century with the advent of two world wars against the ancestral homeland, which brought with them a tragic display of anti-German hysteria and sentiment. However, the second half of the 20th century brought with it many positive events that have contributed to renewed interest in German heritage and culture throughout the U.S. This included the celebration of the German-American Tricentennial in 1983, the establishment of German-American Day in 1987, and the unification of Germany in 1990. The story of these intervening years since the late nineteenth century is properly the topic for another work dealing with the German element in the states covered by this volume, but one which of necessity would have to take a look at Koerner's work as one of the basic sources for that history.

IV. Appendices

Appendix A

Germans in Colonial Pennsylvania

Oswald Seidensticker notes in his history of the German Society of Pennsylvania that: "There is also a wide range of extraordinarily different estimates as to the total number of Germans in Pennsylvania. Ebeling (*Erdbeschreibung und Geschichte von Amerika*, vol. 4, p. 203) estimates that in 1754 there were 90,000 Germans in a total population of 190,000. A larger estimate as to their proportion of the population, namely three-fifths of the total, comes from Governor George Thomas. Franklin's estimate is more conservative. In a hearing before the British House of Commons (1764) he was asked about the population of Pennsylvania, which he estimated at 160,000, of which one-third was estimated as German. Additionally, he did note: "I cannot state this with certainty." (*Testimony of Dr. Benjamin Franklin*. Philadelphia, 1776, p. 6) The *Encyclopedia Brittanica*, printed in Philadelphia, notes that 40,000 Germans had arrived up to the year 1776. We will therefore not be off the mark if we estimate the total number of Germans in Pennsylvania in the middle of the eighteenth century at some where between 70,000 and 80,000." (1)

Appendix B

German Immigration, 1820-78

Theodore Poesche, Washington, D.C. compiled the following statistics relating to German immigration based on published government sources.

1820	999	1835	10,250	1849	63,148	1864	60,462
1821	476	1836	23,352	1850*)	83,921	1865	88,213
1822	458	1837	26,632	1851	82,909	1866	123,163
1823	430	1838	13,681	1852	152,106	1867	140,861
1824	633	1839	25,235	1853	150,004	1868	128,718
1825	916	1840	33,004	1854	229,562	1869	133,299
1826	1,056	1841	18,542	1855	79,351	1870	101,337
1827	1,529	1842	23,153	1856	76,408	1871	117,714
1828	4,843	1843†)	16,004	1857	95,061	1872	172,758
1829	1,211	1844	23,170	1858	47,966	1873	149,590
1830	2,058	1845	38,626	1859	43,917	1874	71,506
1831	3,476	1846	63,550	1860	57,404	1875	49,292
1832*)	14,323	1847	84,473	1861	33,867	1876	42,817
1833	10,622	1848	62,684	1862	29,866	1877	36,547
1834	20,675	......		1863	34,809	1878	41,822

Total........................ 528,187

Total von 1849—1878... 2,718,497

"   "   1820—1848... 528,187

Total von 1820—1878.. 3,246,084

N.B.: This table includes the German-speaking immigration as listed for Germany, Prussia, Austria, and Switzerland in the indicated time periods. For France half of the immigration was included, as more than half of the immigration undoubtedly consisted of German-speaking immigrants from Alsace-Lorraine. The Russian Germans, which includes the many German Mennonites who have come to the U.S., are excluded, as this table includes Slavs who were part of the German and Austrian immigration. We, therefore, exclude the one to account for the other. (2)

Appendix C

The Pittsburgh Convention

The original version of Speyrer's motion was as follows:

That in all states, counties and townships, where the German citizens constitute a majority, sessions of court be held in the German language, that officials be appointed who are fluent in both English and German, and that laws be printed in German as well, and that all means at the disposal of the convention be applied to attain this goal.

Von Löher's history speaks with great indignation that this motion was passed in a much milder version. He does not seem to have understood the confusion that would have arisen, if, for example, in one county if all court business, including reports and documents, were kept in one language, and then in the neighboring county were in another language, while the higher courts and lawmaking bodies were maintained in the language of the majority of the population.

Since the officials in all states at that time were elected by the people, this would have required a change in the language qualifications for public office. Both motions were unfeasible. In practice things are worked out on site. In lower courts it often happens, especially in the western states that the judge, parties and witnesses are all Germans, and so the trials are held in German, while due to appeals all protocol reports and summons and other court orders are maintained in English. Von Löher therefore seems to have based his judgment of the Pittsburgh convention entirely on oral tradition. There really was no discussion of "enormous plans for German states," as he calls them, and there was also no "spirit of obstinacy, dissatisfaction and hostility," but rather the exact opposite. (3)

Sources

The sources Koerner used for his German-American history were predominantly in the German language. A copy of them follows for those interested in further research with these source materials. References to more recent sources are provided in the notes for this edition. For further references to primary and secondary sources, see the following bibliographies by the editor of this volume: *German-Americana: A Bibliography*. (Metuchen, New Jersey: Scarecrow Press, 1975), and also by the same author: *Catalog of the German-Americana Collection, University of Cincinnati*. (München: K.G. Saur, 1990). And, for a general history of the German element in America, see the author's: *The German-American Experience*. A Revised and Expanded Edition of Theodore Huebener's The Germans in America. (Amherst, New York: Humanity Books, 2000).

Quellen.

Eine sehr ausgedehnte Korrespondenz, sowohl mit vielen der Männer, die in diesem Buche erwähnt werden, als auch mit Literaten und Redakteuren deutscher Zeitungen in den Vereinigten Staaten, hat uns die werthvollsten Mittheilungen gebracht und uns, nebst eigenen Ergänzungen, das größte Material geliefert. Die nachstehenden Schriften sind außerdem die vorzüglichsten, welche wir benutzt haben:

1. CHARLES FOLLEN's WORKS, edited by his widow E. C. FOLLEN, 3 vol., Boston, 1846.
2. Life of CHARLES FOLLEN. By same.
3. Franz Löher. „Geschichte und Zustände der Deutschen in Amerika". Cincinnati, Eggers und Wulkop, 1847; Leipzig, bei K. F. Köhler.
4. Friedrich Kapp. „Geschichte der deutschen Einwanderung im Staate New York, bis zum Anfang des 19. Jahrhunderts". 8. Auflage. New York, E. Steiger.
5. Friedrich Münch. „Erinnerungen aus Deutschland's trübster Zeit". St. Louis und Neustadt a. d. Hardt, Konrad Witter.
6. Reise Sr. Hoheit des Herzogs Bernhard zu Sachsen-Weimar-Eisenach durch Nord Amerika in den Jahren 1825 und 1826. Herausgegeben von Heinrich Luden. 2 Theile. Weimar, Wilhelm Hoffmann, 1828.
7. W. D. von Horn. „Johann Jakob Astor". New York, E. Steiger, 1868.
8. Ferdinand Ernst. „Bemerkungen auf einer Reise durch das Innere der vereinigten Staaten von Nordamerika im Jahre 1819". Hildesheim bei Gerstenberg, 1820.
9. Reisebericht der Familien Köpfli und Suppiger aus Neu-Schweizerland, Illinois. Sursee, 1833.
10. Theodor C. Hilgard. „Erinnerungen". Als Manuskript gedruckt. Heidelberg.
11. „Anzeiger des Westens". St. Louis. Jahrgänge 1835—1850.
12. „Belleville Beobachter". Belleville, 1844.
13. „Bellevillier Zeitung". Belleville, Jahrgang 1849.
14. „Alte und Neue Welt". Philadelphia, Jahrgänge 1834—1844.
15. „Cincinnati Volksblatt". Jahrgänge 1836—1850.
16. „Der Hochwächter". (Georg Walker.) Cincinnati, Jahrgänge 1845—49.
17. „Der Deutsche Pionier". Monatsschrift des deutschen Pionierlebens in Amerika. Cincinnati, Jahrgänge 1—11 (1869—1879).
18. Life and Letters of Washington Irving. 4 volumes. New York, Putnam and Co.

434   Das deutsche Element in den Ver. Staaten 1818—1848.

19. WASHINGTON IRVING. "Astoria". Philadelphia, Carey, Lee and Blanchard, 1826.
20. Gert Göbel. „Länger als ein Menschenleben in Missouri". St. Louis, Konrad Witter, 1877.
21. PIERCE. "Charles Sumner's Memoirs and Letters". Boston, 1877.
22. FRANCIS LIEBER. "Political Ethics".
23. FRANCIS LIEBER. "Letters to a Gentleman in Germany". Philadelphia, 1834.
24. Franz Lieber. „Tagebuch meines Aufenthalt's in Griechenland". Leipzig, bei Brockhaus, 1823.
25. Life, Character and Writings of Francis Lieber. A discourse delivered before the Historical Society of Pennsylvania, by M. Russel Thayer. Philadelphia, 1873.
26. Lieber's Writings and Pamphlets.
27. Dr. Oswald Seidensticker. „Geschichte der „Deutschen Gesellschaft" von Pennsylvanien von 1764—1876". Philadelphia, Ignaß Kohler und Schäfer und Korabi, 1876.
28. J. G. Besselhöft. „Selbstbiographie". Manuskript.
29. FRANCIS S. DRAKE. "Dictionary of American Biography". Boston, Osgood and Co., 1872.
30. E. A. and GEO. L. DUYCKINCK. "Cyclopædia of American Literature". New York, Chas. Scribner, 1856.
31. Dr. J. G. Büttner. „Die Vereinigten Staaten von Nord Amerika". 2 Bände. Hamburg, 1844.
32. Dr. J. G. Büttner. „Briefe aus und über die Vereinigten Staaten". 2 Bände. Dresden, 1846.
33. Emil Klauprecht. „Deutsche Chronik in der Geschichte des Ohiothales". Cincinnati, Hof und Jakobi, 1864.
34. „Das Westland". Nordamerikanische Zeitschrift für Deutschland von Dr. G. Engelmann und Karl Neyfeld. Heidelberg, bei Engelmann, 1837—1838.
35. Alexander Schem. „Deutsch-amerikanisches Konversations-Lexicon". 11 Bände, New York, 1869—1874.
36. CHARLES NORDHOFF. "The Cotton States." New York, Scribner, 1876.
37. CHARLES NORDHOFF's Works, generally.
38. Rudolph A. Koß. „Milwaukee." Milwaukee, Verlag des „Herold", 1872.
39. Armin Tenner. „Cincinnati Sonst und Jeßt". Cincinnati, Mecklenborg und Rosenthal, 1878.
40. M. JOBLIN AND JAMES LANDY. "Cincinnati Past and Present". Cincinnati, 1872.
41. The Biographical Encyclopædia of Ohio of the 19. Century. Cincinnati and Philadelphia, Galaxy Publishing Company. 1876.
42. American Biographical Dictionary for Illinois. New York, 1873.
43. WM. H. EGLE. "History of the Commonwealth of Pennsylvania". Harrisburg, 1877.
44. WHITELAW REID, "Ohio in the War". 2. Vol., Cincinnati, 1868.
45. „Der deutsche Kirchenfreund". Redigirt von Dr. Ph. Schaff. Mercersburg, Pennsylvanien, 1848—1850.

Quellen.   435

46. Wm. B. Sprague. "Annals of the American Lutheran Pulpit". New-York, 1869.
47. L. Stierlin. „Der Staat Kentucky und die Stadt Louisville". 1873.
48. Ferdinand Römer. „Texas". Bonn, 1849.
49. Hermann Ehrenberg. „Texas und die Revolution." Leipzig, 1843.
50. Reports of the Santa Rita Silver Mining Company. Cincinnati, 1859 —1860.
51. Reports of the Sonora Exploring and Mining Company. Cincinnati, 1856, 1858—1860.
52. Dr. Th. Logan. "Memoir of the Life and Services of Dr. C. A. Luetzenburg". New Orleans, 1848.
53. H. A. Rattermann. „General Johann Andreas Wagener. Eine biographische Skizze". Cincinnati, 1877.
54. Schriftliche Notizen über Ferd. Rud. Haßler, von seinen Töchtern.
55. Emil Sichoffe. „Ingenieur F. R. Haßler." Aarau, Sauerländer 1877.

Notes

Editor's Preface

1. See; Gustav Koerner, *Das deutsche Element in den Vereinigten Staaten von Nordamerika, 1818-1848.* (Cincinnati: A.E. Wilde & Co., 1880).

2. See: Don Heinrich Tolzmann, ed., *Illinois' German Heritage.* (Milford, Ohio: Little Miami Pub. Co., 2005), and by the same editor: *Missouri's German Heritage.* 2nd edition. (Milford, Ohio: Little Miami Pub. Co., 2006).

3. In the future, the editor plans on translating and editing chapters from Koerner's history that deal with Ohio, Kentucky and Indiana for a volume focusing on the German element in the Ohio Valley.

Editor's Introduction

1. For further information on Koerner, see: Evarts B. Greene, "Gustave Koerner," in: Tolzmann, ed., *Illinois' German Heritage*, pp. 93-103.

2. Regarding the *Burschenschaft*, see: Tolzmann, ed., *Missouri's German Heriatge*, pp. 1. For further information about the uprising of 1832-33 in Germany, see: Joachim Kermann, Gehard Nestler and Dieter Schiffmann, eds., *Freiheit, Einheit und Europa: Das Hambacher Fest von 1832 – Ursachen, Ziele und Wirkungen.* (Ludwighafen: Verlag Pro Message, 2006).

3. Regarding Koerner's involvement in the Frankfurt Uprising, see: Greene, "Gustave Koerner," p. 96.

4. For a discussion of Duden and the importance of his book about America, see: Dorris Keeven-Franke, "Gottfried Duden: The Man behind the Book," in: Tolzmann, ed., *Missouri's German Heritage*, pp. 85-95.

5. For Koerner's history of Belleville and southern Illinois, see: Gustav Koerner, "Southern Illinois," in: Tolzmann, ed., *Illinois' German Heritage*, pp. 5-42.

6. See: Koerner, *Das deutsche Element*, p. 6.

7. For references to Koerner's correspondence with Lincoln, see: Tolzmann, ed., *Illinois' German Heritage*, p. 105.

8. For Koerner's autobiography, see Gustav Koerner, *Memoirs of Gustave Koerner, 1809-1896: Life Sketches Written at the Suggestion of His Children*. 2 vols. Edited by Thomas J. McCormack. (Cedar Rapids, Iowa: The Torch Press, 1909).

9. See: Julius Goebel, "Gustav Koerner," *Dictionary of American Biography*.

10. See: Friedrich Kapp, *Geschichte der Deutschen im Staate New York bis zum Anfange des neuenzehnten Jahrhudnerts: Geschichte der deutschen Einwanderung in Amerika*. Dreitte, vermehrte Auflage. (New York: Ernst Steiger, 1869). Friedrich Kapp (1824-84) was a Forty-Eighter, who lived in America from 1850-70, editing German-American newspapers and writing several German-American historical works, then returned to Germany, where he served in the Reichstag. For biographical information, see: Horst Dippel, "Kapp, Friedrich," in: *Neue Deutsche Biographie*, Vol. 11, pp. 134ff. Also, see: H.A. Rattermann, "Friedrich Kapp," *Deusch-Amerikanisches Magazin*. 1(1887): 16-36, 226-238, and 360-373. Rattermann also provides a bibliography of Kapp's writings, pp. 371-73, including essays, articles, as well as book publications.

11. See: Koerner, *Das deutsche Element*, p. 5

12. Ibid, 6.

13. Ibid.

14. Ibid.

15. Ibid, p. 7.

16. Ibid, p. 9.

17. Ibid, pp. 11-12.

18. Ibid, p. 11.

19. Ibid, pp. 20-21.

20. Ibid, p. 8.

21. Ibid, pp. 16-17.

I.   Pennsylvania
Chapter One

1. For a survey of German immigration to Pennsylvania, see the following two "classic" works: Oswald Seidensticker and Max Heinrici, *Geschichte der Deutschen Gesellschaft von Pennsylvanien, 1764-1917.* (Philadelphia: Graf & Breuninger, 1917), pp. 7-36, and also his: *Bilder aus der Deutsch-Pennsylvanischen Geschichte.* (New York: Ernst Steiger, 1883). For reference to more recent works on the topic, see the editor's two bibliographies: *German-Americana: A Bibliography.* (Metuchen, New Jersey: Scarecrow Press, 1975), pp. 53-61, and: *Catalog of the German-Americana Collection, University of Cincinnati.* (München: K.G. Saur, 1990), Vol. 1, pp. 204-26.

2. Regarding the impact and influence of the Pennsylvania Germans on the way in Pennsylvania, see: Benjamin Rush, "An Account of the Manners of the German Inhabitants of Pennsylvania. Introduction and Annotations by Theodore E. Schmauk. Notes By I. Daniel Rupp, revised," in: *Pennsylvania German Society Proceedings and Addresses.* 19(1910): 3-128; reprinted in: Don Heinrich Tolzmann, ed., *German Pioneer Life: A Social History.* (Bowie, Maryland: Heritage Books, Inc., 1992). Also, see: W.J. Mann, *Die gute alte Zeit in Pennsylvanien.* (Philadelphia: J.G. Kohler, 1882), pp. 23-46, and James Owensd Knauss, Jr. *The Pennsylvania Germans: James Owens Knauss, Jr.'s Social History.* Edited by Don Heinrich Tolzmann. (Bowie, Maryland: Heritage Books, Inc., 2001), pp. 119-40.

3. For a discussion of the interrelationships between the Pennsylvania Germans and the more recently arrived German immigrants of the nineteenth century, see: Don Yoder, "The Dutchman and the 'Deutschlenner': The New World Confronts the Old," *Yearbook of German-American Studies*, 23(1988): 1-17. Koerner argues that both groups more or less blended together, with the more recent immigrants assuming leadership of the German-American press, churches and secular organizations. A good case in point would be the German Society of Pennsylvania, whose leadership passed into the hands of the more recent immigrants in the course of the nineteenth century. Don Yoder takes a closer look

at the interrelationships of the older Pennsylvania German element and the more recently arrived immigrants and identifies the ways the latter influenced the former. He discusses three areas of influence: "First of all, the immigrant Germans who settled in Pennsylvania served their apprenticeship in America, in a sense, by serving the already existing Pennsylvania Dutch culture in industry, business, church and press." Secondly, he notes that "the 'Deutschlenner' enriched Pennsylvania Dutch folklore. In dealing with the lore repertoire of the Pennsylvania Dutch, one sees not all of it crossed the Atlantic with the colonial migration…The third influence is the most important of all. The presence of the 'Deutschlenner' among them in Pennsylvania, and visible from the Midwest through the German-American press, stimulated the Pennsylvania Dutch to decide who they were, ethnically speaking. By comparing themselves to the newcomers, they saw that after all they were not 'Germans in America' nor even 'German-Americans' but Pennsylvania Dutch, different from the new immigrants in almost every aspect of their culture," See: Yoder: "The Dutchman…," p. 15.

4. Regarding ethnic humor in the early nineteenth century as it relates to German-Americans, see: Dale T. Knobel, "'Hans' and the Historian: Ethnic Stereotypes and American Popular Culture," *Journal of German-American Stuides*. 15:3-4(1980): 65-74.

5. For further information about the Mühlenberg family, see: Paul A.W. Wallace, *The Muhlenbergs of Pennsylvania*. (Philadelphia: University of Pennsylvania Press, 1950).

6. For this time period of Pennsylvania German history, see: William T. Parsons, *The Pennsylvania Dutch*. (Boston: Twayne Publishers, 1976).

7. For a survey of Pennsylvania German newspapers, see: Daniel Miller, *Early German-American Newspapers: Daniel Miller's History*. Edited by Don Heinrich Tolzmann. (Bowie, Maryland: Heritage Books, Inc., 2001).

8. With regard to the religious life of the Pennsylvania Germans, see: Knauss, *The Pennsylvania Germans*, pp. 35-57; and: Jesse Leonard Rosenberger, *The Pennsylvania Germans: Jesse Leonard Rosenberger's Sketch of their History and*

Life. Edited by Don Heinrich Tolzmann. (Bowie, Maryland: Heritage Books, Inc., 1998), pp. 69-85. Also, see: Rush, "An Account...," pp. 93-103.

9. The system of indentured servitude is well summarized in: Bittinger, *The Germans in Colonial Times*, pp. 215-29.

10. The formation of the German Society of Pennsylvania is described in Seidensticker and Heinrici, *Geschichte...*, pp. 37-50.

11. Ibid, pp. 40.

12. For a directory of the officers of the German Society of Pennsylvania, see; Ibid, pp. 439-591.

13. Rahel Levin (1771-1833) was a German author, whose home "became the meeting-place of men like Schlegel, Schelling, Steffens, Schack, Schleiermacher, Alexander and Wilhelm von Humboldt, Lamotte-Fouque, Baron Brückmann, Ludwig Tieck, Jean Paul Richter, and F. von Gentz. During a visit to Carlsbad in 1795 she was introduced to Goethe, whom she saw again in 1815, at Frankfort-on-the-Main." See; *The Jewish Encyclopedia*.

14. Bohlen's biography can be found in the history of the German Society of Pennsylvania: See: Seidensticker and Heinrici, *Geschichte...*, p. 464-66.

15. For a popular folk-song about Koseritz, see: Koerner, *Das deutsche Element*, p. 424.

16. Blenker (1812-63) was one of the well-known German Forty-Eighters, who served in the Union Army in the Civil War. See: Don Heinrich Tolzmann, ed., *The German-American Forty-Eighters, 1848-1998*. (Indinanapolis: Max Kade German-American Center, Indiana University-Purdue University & Indiana German Heritage Society, 1998), p. 92. For information regarding the role played by the Pennsylvania Germans in the Civil War: See David L. Valuska and Christian B. Keller, *Damn Dutch: Pennsylvania Germans at Gettysburg*. (Mechanicsburg, Pennsylvania: Stackpole Books, 2004).

17. Sigel (1824-1902) was one of the most well-known and popular of the German Forty-Eighters, who also served in the Union Army in the Civil War. See: Tolzmann, ed., *The German-American Forty-Eighters*, pp. 87-88.

18. For information about the Moravians, see: Lucy F. Bittinger, *The Germans in Colonial Times*. (Rpt., 1901; Bowie, Maryland: Heritage Books, Inc., 1986), pp. 168-83, and in: Phene Earle Gibbons, *Pennsylvania Dutch & other Essays, with an Introduction by Don Yoder*. (Mechanicsburg, Pa.: Stackpole Books, 2001), pp. 173-205. For further references, see Tolzmann, *German-Americana: A Bibliography*, pp. 207-12, and also by the same author: *Catalog*, Vol. 2, pp. 317-18.

19. See: Karl J.R. Arndt, *George Rapp's Harmony Society, 1785-1847*. (Rutherford: Fairleigh Dickinson University Press, 1871).

20. For the Duke's report, see: Bernhard, Duke of Saxe-Weimar-Eisenach, *Travels of His Highness duke Bernhard of Saxe-Weimar-Eisenach through North America in the Years 1825 and 1826*. Translated by William Jeronimus and edited by C.J. Jeronimus. (Lanham, Maryland: University Press of America, 2001).

21. For a history of the settlement along the Ohio River, see: Karl J.R. Arndt, ed., *George Rapp's Years of Glory: Economy on the Ohio*. (New York: Peter Lang Pub. Co., 1987).

22. See: Karl J.R. Arndt, *A Documentary History of the Indiana Decade of the Harmony Society, 1814-1824*. 2 vols. (Indianapolis: Indiana Historical Society, 1975).

23. For further information regarding the travel reports that Koerner mentions here, see: Reuben Gold Thwaites, ed., *Early Western Travels, 1748-1846: A Series of Annotated Reprints of Some of the Best and Rarest Contemporary Volumes of Travel, Description of the Aborigines and Social and Economic Conditions in the Middle and Far West, During the Period of the Early American Settlement*. 32 vols. (Cleveland, Ohio: A.H. Clark, 1904-07).

24. Regarding Astor (1763-1848), and his family, see: Lucy Kavaler, *The Astors: AN American Legend*. (New York: Dodd, Mead, 1968), and also by the same author: *The Astors: A Family Chronicle of Pomp and Circumstance*. (New York: Dodd, Mead, 1966).

Chapter Two

1. As Koerner refers to many German newspapers in this chapter that are too numerous to reference here, the reader is referred for further information to: Karl J.R. Arndt and May E. Olson, *The German-Language Press of the Americas: Vol. I: U.S.A.* (München: Verlag Dokumentation, 1976), pp. 501-605. For a general survey of the newspapers of this period, see: Carl Wittke, *The German Language Press of America*. (Lexington: University of Kentucky Press, 1957), pp. 36-58.

2. For further biographical information on Johann Georg Ritter (1771-1839), see: H.A. Rattermann, *Gesammelte ausgewählte Werke*. (Cincinnati: Selbstverlag des Verfassers, 1911), Vol. 10, pp. 171-80. According to Rattermann, Ritter's German book store was located at 263 North Second Street in Philadelphia.

3. According to Robert E. Cazden, "During the 1830s no one more single-mindedly championed the cause of German culture than Johann Georg Wesselhöft (1804-1859), publisher of the *Alt und Neue Welt* and for a short time the premier German bookseller in the land." See: Cazden, *A Social History of the German Book Trade in America to the Civil War*. (Camden, South Caroina: Camden House, 1984), p. 82. For further information, see also: Cazden, "Johann Georg Wesselhöft and the German Book Trade in America," in: Gerhard Friesen, ed., *The German Contribution to the Building of the Americas: Studies in Honor of Karl J.R. Arndt*. (Hanover, New Hampshire: Clark University Press, 1977), pp. 217-34, and: Rattermann, *Werke*, Vol. 11, pp. 387-400.

4. Johanna Schopenhauer (1766-1838), the mother of German philosopher Arthur Schopenhauer, was a well published author in her own right. See; J.G. Robertson, *A History of German Literature*. Fifth edition revised and enlarged by Edna Purdie. (Edinburgh: British Book Centre, 1968), p. 401.

5. Heinrich Zschokke (1771-1848), a prolific German author, was especially well known for his many popular novels. See: Robertson, *A History...*, p. 412. Some of Wesselhöft's correspondence with him can be found in: Robert E. Cazden, "Johann Georg Wesslhöft and the German Book Trade in America," pp. 217-34.

6. Gottfried Duden (1785-1855) came to the U.S. I n1824, and lived for several years on a farm in Missouri, and after his return published a book in 1829 on his

experiences that one on to become one of the most influential books in the history of the German immigration to America. For further information, see: Tolzmann, ed., *Missouri's German Heritage*, pp. 28-29.

7. The reference here is to the 1832-33 uprising in Germany. For further information about them, see: Tolzmann, *The German-American Experience*, pp. 166-67.

8. Karl Follen (1796-1840), Karl Beck (1798-1866), and Francis Lieber (1798-1872) immigrated to the U.S. after the Napoleonic wars as a result of the restoration of the old order in Europe in search of the political freedoms offered in America. They greatly contributed to an appreciation of German culture in America, while also actively becoming involved in the political life of their new homeland. Follen became the first professor of German in the U.S. at Harvard, and was active in the abolitionist movement. For further information about him, see: Franz Mehring, *Deutsch-Amerikanischer Freiheitskämpfer*. (Giessen, 2004). Also, see: Rattermann, *Werke*, Vol. 10, pp. 81-120. Beck taught gymnastic (*Turnunterricht*) and Latin at the Round Hill School in Northhampton, Massachusetts, and later became a professor of Latin at Harvard. For further information about him, see: Rattermann, *Werke*, Vol. 10, pp. 121-30. Lieber became a professor of history and economics at South Carolina College, and published numerous works on related topics. For further information about him, see: Charles R. Mack, ed., *Francis Lieber and the Culture of the Mind*. (Columbia, University of South Carlina Press, 2005), and also: Rattermann, *Werke*, Vol. 10, pp. 29-66. George Ticknor (1791-1871) was a literary historian, who served as professor of literature and Romance languages and literatures at Harvard. For information about him, see: George Stillman Hillard, ed., *The Life, Letters and Journals of George Ticknor*. (Boston, 1876).

9. Francis Joseph Grund (1805-63) was active in public and political affairs before the Civil War, but lost much of his influence due to his tendency of switching political parties. For further information about him, see: Rattermann, *Werke*, Vol. 10, pp. 67-80.

10. Koerner refers here to Wesselhöft's unpublished manuscript autobiography, which had had access to in writing his history, but which now apparently is lost.

11. Samuel Ludvigh (1801-69) was a German born from Hungary, who came to America in 1837 after being forced to leave Europe as a result of his writings against Metternich. His free thought views earned him the title as the "Fackelträger," or "Torchbearer." He is buried at Spring Grove Cemetery in Cincinnnati, Ohio. For further information about him, see: Rattermann, *Werke*, Vol. 12, pp. 203-24.

12. Cazden notes that Wesselhöft sent Radde to New York in 1834 to open a branch of his store there, and that: "Radde, an experienced printer and friend of Wesselhöft's from Europe, built up a remunerative book business and even attempted some publishing of his own during the 1830s. Eventually, Radde became a fixture of the New York book trade and a wealthy purveyor of German-language literature." See: Cazden, "Johann Georg Wesselhöft and the German Book Trade in America," p. 220.

13. Wesselhöft traveled widely, visiting places where he sought to sell German books. For example, Cazden notes that his travels in 1842-43 brought him to the following places: Baltimore, Washington, D.C., New York, Canada, Cleveland, Cincinnati, Louisville, St. Louis, New Orleans, Vicksburg, and Pittsburgh. See: Ibid, p. 224.

14. For further information about Hermann, Missouri, see: Tolzmann, ed., *Missouri's German Heritage*, pp. 23ff.

15. The idea of establishing a German state in the West arose in the early nineteenth century. For further information, see: Ibid, pp. 8ff.

16. Cazden notes that Wesselhöft's physical ailments, and the decision of his son to forsake bookselling for farming, finally compelled him to retire in 1854; but by then St. Louis was on the way to becoming a major Midwestern center of the German-American book trade." See: Cazden, "The German Book Trade in St. Louis," in: Don Heinrich Tolzmann, ed., *German-American Literature*. (Metuchen, New Jersey: Scarecrow Press, 1977), p. 55.

17. With regard to his burial site, Lois Puchta, Gasconade County Historical Society, informed me that: "Yes, Wesselhoeft is buried in the Hermann City Cemetery; date of death is 26 January 1859. There is no marker but the location of the grae

can, of course, be determined." E-Mail to the editor from Lois Puchta (3 February 2008).

18. The *Alte und Neue Welt* "was ably edited and full of information on a great variety of topics, and was widely copied by other German papers throughout the United States...its style was superior to that of most German papers, and its editorials and news comments were generally dignified." See: Wittke, *The German Language Press*, p. 43.

19. Wilhelm Weber (1808-52) came to America in 1834, settling in St. Clair County, Illinois, but eventually moving to St. Louis, where he became involved in the German-American press. For further information about him, see: Tolzmann, ed., *Missouri's German Heritage*, pp. 34, 40-45.

20. Kapp's comments on German-American reading interests obviously must have been negative, causing Koerner to go out of his way to show that they were unfounded. Also, see footnote no. 10, Chapter One.

21. Wilhelm Ludwig Jakob Kiderlen (1813-77) came to the U.S. in 1836, and founded the book store of Kiderlen & Stollmeyer in Philadelphia. In 1843, it was sold to Wesselhöft, and Kiderlen turned to editing various German-American newspapers. For further information, see: Rattermann, *Werke*, Vol. 12, pp. 318-19.

22. One of the papers that Kiderlen edited was *Der Deutsche Republikaner* in Cincinnati, which was later on edited by Emil Klauprecht. For further information, see: Arndt and Olson, *The German Language Press*, pp. 441-42.

23. Wilhelm Schmöle (1811-90) came to America in 1833, and participated actively in German-American affairs in Pennsylvania. For further information about him, see: Rattermann, *Werke*, Vol. 11, pp. 485-87.

24. Ludwig August Wollenweber (1807-88) came to the U.S. in 1832. He worked on the staff of several German-American papers, and published a number of literary and historical works. For further information, see: Rattermann, *Werke*, Vol. 11. 474-88.

25. Friedrich Wilhelm Thomas (1808-77) came to the U.S. in 1837, and settled down in Philadelphia, where he established his well-known publishing company. For

further information about him and his press, see: Rattermann, *Werke*, Vol. 12, pp. 315-17.

26. Victor Scriba (dates unknown) came to America in the 1820s, and edited German-American newspapers in Chambersburg, Pennsylvania before moving to Pittsburgh in 1836, where he became a German newspaper published and editor. For information about him, see: Rattermann, *Werke*, Vol. 10, pp. 433-35.

27. Emil Klauprecht (1815-96) came to the U.S. in 1832, eventually settling in Cincinnati, where he edited several German newspapers and published several literary and historical works. For further information about him, see: Emil Klauprecht, *Cincinnati, or the Mysteries of the West: Emil Klauprecht's German-American Novel.* Translated by Steven Rowan and edited by Don Heinrich Tolzmann. (New York: Peter Lang Pub. Co., 1996, pp. xi-xxv.

28. Nikolaus Lenau (1802-50) was an Austrian from Hungary, who came to America in 1832, and lived for a time in Ohio, but spent most of his time at the Harmony Society at Economy. Arndt writes of him: "No letter of introduction to the Society has been found but it is known that Lenau had letters of introduction to two well-known Pittsburghers at this time, Volz and von Bonnhorst. Both were attorneys of the Harmony Society, and both were particularly busy with Society business at this time. Lenau presented his letter of introduction to Volz within two weeks after his arrival in Baltimore and only eighteen days after his arrival in the United States he had, with the help of the Harmonists, who had previously received such men as Duke Bernhard zu Sachsen-Weimar-Eisenach, purchased land in Ohio. The Harmonists themselves had for a quarter of a century been interested in Ohio real estate and would have settled there themselves if they had been able to get a section large enough for their extensive needs." See Karl J.R. Arndt, "The Effect of America on Lenau's Life and Work," in: Alexander Ritter, ed., *Deutschlands literarisches Amerikabild: Neuere Forschungen zur Amerikarezeption der deutschen Literatur.* (Hildesheim: Olms Verlag, 1977), p. 259. Lenau's visit at Economy took place from October 1832 through March 1833. Arndt also notes about the Harmonists that: "Economy at this time was the home of some of the most cultured and clever men in America. They had little respect for worldly

matters, but were financial geniuses in dealing with them. They were ascetics, who firmly believed with Jacob Boehme that man in his present state was the ugly descendant of that Adam who in falling away from God had acquired bestial organs and had lost the divine image. Because of this they believed that it was the duty of every serious Christian to live a simple, ascetic life and not to propagate man's bestial image with which he had become burdened when he fell." He also noted that many considered Rapp's followers "slaves of Father Rapp and thought he was using them for his own material benefit. This point of view was strengthened by the fact they lived an ascetic life. Yet they played a decisive part in establishing the industrial might of the entire Pittsburgh area...During his stay at Economy Lenau lived for the most part of the time in the home of the Baker family, which overlooked the Ohio River. It is still standing and has become part of the Harmony Society Museum which now belongs to the Commonwealth of Pennsylvania," pp. 260-61. For further information on Lenau's stay in Ohio, see: Rattermann, *Werke*, Vol. 11, pp. 401-22.

29. Although the idea of a national German-American convention was widely discussed in the German-American press, the general concensus was that such a meeting should be held in Pittsburgh due to its central location between the eastern and western states.

Chapter Three

1. Rattermann planned a multi-part article on the conventions held in Pittsburgh and Philippsburg, but only the first two of the series appeared. See: H.A. Rattermann, "Geschichte der deutschen Konventionen zu Pittsburgh und Philipsburg, (1837-1842)," *Deutsch-Amerikanisches Magazin.* 1(1886): 87-104, 447-58. This indicates that the *Alte und Neue Welt* endorsed the plans for the conventions (17 June 1837, and that a committee was formed in Philadelphia to get in touch with the organizers in Pittsburgh. The Philadelphia committee consisted of: Dr. Wilhelm Schmöle, J.N. Kuhlenkampff, W.L.J. Kiderlen, J. Schmauck, E.L. Walz, and a Mr. Walz.

2. The Pittsburgh committee consisted of: David Kämmerer, Eduard Fendrich, Friedrich Braun, Nikolaus Võgtly, jun., J.G. Backofen, sen., Martin Schwer, and Joseph Beyerly.

3. Rattermann reports that Schmöle published the agenda of topics to be discussed at the convention, which appeared in the *Alte und Neue Welt* (12 August 1837). Wilhelm Weber responded to these agenda items, endorsing them in an article published in a St. Louis paper, the *Anzeiger des Westens* (13 September 1837), placing particular emphasis on the preservation of the German language by means of educational institutions, as well as the preservation of German customs and traditions as natural rights that Germans in America were entitled to as American citizens. See: Rattermann, "Geschichte...," p. 457.

4. Peter Kaufmann (1800-69) came to America in 1820, and was responsible for establishing the settlement of Teutonia in Columbiana County, Ohio. He also published and edited German-American newspapers, and published several fascinating works in German and English. For further information about him, see: Karl J.R. Arndt, *Teutonic Visions of Social Perfection for Emerson: Verheissung und Erfüllung: A Documentary History of Peter Kaufmann's Quest for Social Perfection from George Rapp to Ralph Waldo Emerson.* (Worcester, Massachusetts: The Harmony Society Press, 1988). This consists of Kaufmann's autobiography, which he sent to Emerson, wherein he proposed greater cultural cooperation between Anglo- and German-Americans.

5. Johann August Roebling (1806-69) came to America in 1831 with his brother as representatives of the Mühlhausen Immigration Society, which established the settlement of Saxonburg, Pennsylvania. For further information about him, see: Don Heinrich Tolzmann, *John A. Roebling and His Suspension Bridge on the Ohio River.* (Milford, Ohio: Little Miami Publishing Co., 2007).

6. Reference here is made to the anti-immigrant Know-Nothing Movement that rose in response to the rising tide of immigration to the U.S.

7. For the fascinating and bizarre biography of Count Leon and the story of his settlement in Louisiana, see: Karl J.R. Arndt, "The Life of Count Leon," *American-German Review.* 6(1940): 5-8-15-19, and also by the same author: "The

Genesis of Germantown, Louisiana," *Louisiana Historical Quarterly*. 24(1941): 378-433. Also, see: Louis Voss, *Louisiana's German Heritage: Louis Voss' Introductory History*. Edited by Don Heinrich Tolzmann. (Bowie, Maryland: Heritage Books, Inc., 1994).

8. Eduard Muehl (1800-54) came to the U.S. in 1836, and published and edited German-American newspapers in Cincinnati, Ohio and Hermann, Missouri. For further information about him, see: Tolzmann, ed., *Missouri's German Heritage*, pp. 25-36.

9. Bűttner served as pastor of a German Evangelical church in St. Louis, and later as a professor of theology at a German Reformed theological seminary in Ohio. For further information about him, see: Ibid, pp. 49, 61.

10. Koerner notes here that the reason the teachers' seminary failed was that German-Americans generally sent their children to schools maintained by their particular religious denomination, and were more than reluctant to send them to secular schools, especially one that freethinkers were so closely associated with.

11. The majority of the convention opposed the idea of forming German states in the West. However, one minority group strongly supported the idea, while another advocated assimilation. The convention seemed to come down on the side of the realities of the German-American experience, supporting German districts and settlements, and emphasizing the importance of preserving German language, culture, customs, and traditions.

12. This quote is from a letter by Sumner, written in June 1837. See: Francis Joseph Grund, *Aristocracy in America: From the Sketch-Book of a German Nobleman, With an Introduction by George E. Probst*. (New York: Harper Torchbooks, 1959), p. viii.

13. See: Francis Joseph Grund, *Martin Van Buren als Staatsmann und künftiger Präsident der Vereinigten Staaten von Nord-Amerika*. (New York: n.p., 1835). This work is worthy of further analysis to ascertain how Grund appealed for the German vote.

14. See: Francis Joseph Grund, *Aufruf an die deutschen Wähler: General Harrison's Leben und Wirken*. ({Philadelphia: Gedr. bei C.F. Stollmeyer, 1840). A

comparison of this campaign biography with that of Van Buren would make for an interesting study of German-American campaign literature.

15. See; Francis Joseph Grund, *Speech of Francis J. Grund, at the Union League Rooms*. (Philadelphia: n.p., 1863). The fact that Grund's speech was published at this late date in his career indicates that he still exerted some political influence.

16. Koerner here refers to a Capuchin, a member of the Franciscan order of the Catholic Church, in the service of Albrecht von Wallenstein (1583-1634), who commanded the Catholic forces during the Thirty Years War. For further information, see: Hellmut Diwald, *Wallenstein. Eine Biographie*. (Berlin:Ullstein TB-Verlag, 1987). The other reference is to Abraham a Santa Clara (1644-1709), a Catholic priest and author, was an especially popular preacher in the German-speaking countries. For further information about him, see: Franz M. Eybi, *Abraham a Santa Clara. Vom Prediger zum Schriftsteller*. (Tübingen: Niemeyer, 1992).

Chapter Four

1. For a history of the printing of federal and state publications in German, see: Heinz Kloss, *The American Bilingual Tradition*. (Rowley, Massachusetts: Newbury House, 1977), especially pp. 107-62.

2. Regarding school laws in Pennsylvania, see: Ibid, pp. 147-51.

3. For information regarding the militia companies in New York, see: Koerner, *Das deutsche Element*, pp. 108ff.

4. The reference here is to the poem "Der Deutschen Vaterland" by Ernst Moritz Arndt (1769-1860), which was a well known poem during the War of Liberation against Napoleon.

5. Regarding Koseritz, see footnote 15, Chapter One.

6. The July Revolution refers to the French Revolution of July 1830, which resulted in King Charles X being overthrown, and being replaced by his cousin Louis-Philippe, who himself was then overthrown during the 1848 revolution that swept across Europe. The Polish Revolution of 1830-31, also known as the November Uprising, began in November 1830, and aimed at the liberation of Poland from

Russia. Both of these uprising exerted a great deal of influence on those seeking change in the German states, and no doubt inspired the German revolutions of 1832-33.

7. For the full report of the Bundestag, see: *Darlegung der Hauptresultate aus den wegen der revolutionären Komplotte der neueren Zeit in Deutschland geführten Untersuchungen, durch eine Kommission des deutschen Bundestags, veröffentlicht im Jahre 1838.* (Frankfurt am Main: In der Bundes-Präsidial-Druckerei, 1838).

8. Regarding the Frankfurt uprising and Koerner's involvement, see: Tolzmann, ed., *Illinois' German Heritage*, p. 96.

9. Koerner here is no doubt referring to the Second Seminole War in Florida that was fought from 1835 to 1842. For further information on this war, see: John K. Mahon, *History of the Second Seminole War, 1835-1842.* (Gainesville, Florida: University of Florida Press, 1967).

10. The German student union known as the *Burschenschaft* had branches across Germany. It had visions of a united Germany under a republican form of government, and for that reason was considered as a threat to the status quo by governmental authorities.

11. For further information on the German singing societies of Philadelphia, see: Martha Crary Halpern, *Greman Singing Societies of 19th Century Philadelphia.* (Philadelphia: German Society of Pennsylvania, 1988).

12. Bertel Thorvaldsen (1770-1844) was a Danish sculptor, who was well known for his historical works, such as of Maximilian I in München. For further information about him, see: Harald Tesan, *Thorvaldsen und seine Bildhauerei in Rom.* (Köln: Böhlau, 1998).

13. Haratio Greenough (1805-52) was an American sculptor, who was well known for his historical works, such as of George Washington. For further information on him, see: Nathalia Wright, *Horatio Greenough, the First American Sculptor.* (Philadelphia: University of Pennsylvania Press, 1963).

14. Paul Heyse (1830-1914) was a well known German author of the nineteenth century, especially of novellas. For further information, see: Rainer Hillenbrand, *Heyses Novellen: ein literarischer Führer*. (Frankfurt am Main: Lang, 1998).

15. Hering (1800-80), considered the father of American homeopathy, came to America in 1833. For further information about him, see: Julian Winston, *The Faces of Homoepathy*. (Tawa, New Zealand: Great Auk Publishing, 1999).

16. Christian Friedrich Samuel Hahnemann (1755-1843) was a German physician, who is considered the founder of homeopathy. For further information about him, see: Robert Jütte, *Samuel Hahnemann, Begründer der Homöopathie*. (München: dtv premium, 2005). Among his many publications, see his: *Heilkunde der Erfahrung*. (Berlin: Wittich, 1805).

17. Friedrich von Raumer (178101873) was a well known German historian of the nineteenth century, who undertook many speaking trips throughout Europe and the U.S. After his trip the U.S. in 1843, he published a report a work on his impressions of America that appeared in German as: *Die Vereinigten Staaten von Nord America*. (Leipzig: F.A. Brockhaus, 1845) and in English as: *America and the American People*. (New York: J. & H.G. Langley, 1846).

18. Teutonia was located south of Clermont, Pennsylvania, and appears to have lasted till 1844, and came to an end after Ginal left the settlement and moved to Milwaukee, where he became an active member of the Freethinkers' Congregation. For further information about the settlement, see: Susan Tassin, *Pennsylvania Ghost Towns: Uncovering the Hidden Past*. (Mechanicsburg, Pennsylvania: Stackpole Books, 2007), pp. 1-3.

19. One can readily see by Koerner's account that there were a wide variety of German settlements established in Pennsylvania, ranging from those established by Rapp and Ginal to others, and that they each met with varying degrees of success.

Chapter Five

1. For further information on Schmöle, see footnote no. 23, Chapter Two.

2. For the background history of the *Dreissiger*, see: Wittke, *The German Forty-Eighters*, pp. 6-17.

3. Several German-American newspapers were banned in Germany due to their outspoken opposition to the prevalent political conditions in the German states. For further information, see: Cazden: *The German Book Trade*, pp. 581-669.

4. Karl von Rotteck (1775-1840) was a German historian at the University of Freiburg, who was well known for his liberal views. In 1833, he was overwhelmingly elected mayor of Freiburg, but due to pressure from the government of Baden, was forced into retirement, with his nephew taking his place in office. He was exceptionally popular with the *Dreissiger*, and his treatment was greatly resented as the suppression of the results of a democratic election, and as symbolic of the lack of true democracy in Germany. For further information about him, see: Hermann Kopf, *Karl von Rotteck zwischen Revolution and Restauration*. (Freiburg: Rombach, 1980).

5. Particpants and supports of the 1832/33 uprising received harsh treatment from the authorities. For example, Friedrich Ludwig Weidig, who Koerner mentions, was an Evangelical minister, who supported the teachings of Friedrich Ludwig Jahn during the War of Liberation against Napoleon, and thereafter was closely watched as a result by the police. He was then arrested in 1833 for having supported the 1832 uprising, and then removed from his position as a minister. Thereafter, he worked with Georg Büchner in publishing an underground journal, *Der Hessische Landbote*. This led to his being placed under house arrest in Darmstadt, where he was subject to physical abuse during his interrogation, ultimately leading him to commit suicide in 1837. For further information, see: Friedrich Wilhelm Schulz, *Der Tod des Pfarrers Dr. Friedrich Ludwig Weidig: Ein aktenmässiger und urkundlich belegter Beitrag zur Beurteilung des geheimen Strafprozesses und der politischen Zustände Deutschlands*. (Zürich: Liter. Comptoir, 1843).

6. Seidensticker received a term of life imprisonment, but was pardoned on the condition that he would seek immigration. See: Wittke, *The German Forty-Eighters*, p. 11.

7. Reference here is made to other participants in the 1832 Revolution.

8. Mention here is made to the German philosopher Karl Christian Friedrich Krause (1781-1832), whose views were not considered as popular in Germany, as they were elsewhere in Europe, especially in Spain. For a selection of his works, see his: *Ausgewählte Schriften*. Hrsg. von Enrique M. Urena und Erich Fuchs. 2 Vols. (Stuttgart: Frommann-Holzboog, 2007).

9. News of the 1848 Revolition was jubilantly received by German-Americans across the U.S. For further information, see: Wittke, *The German Forty-Eighters*, pp. 29-42.

10. Regarding the reception of these Forty-Eighters in America, see: Ibid, pp36-40.

11. Hecker's visit in Cincinnati resulted in the founding of the first Turner Society in America in 1848. See: Don Heinrich Tolzmann, *German Heritage Guide to the Greater Cincinnati Area*. Second edition. (Milford, Ohio: Little Miami Pub. Co., 2007), p. 80.

12. The German-American painter Emanuel Leutze (1816-68) is most well known for his famous painting of "Washington Crossing the Delaware" that was completed in 1851. See: Anne Hawkes Hutton, *Portrait of Patriotism: Washington Crossing the Delaware*. (Radnor, Pa.: Chilton, 1975).

13. See: Alexander Schem, *Deutsch-Amerikanischens Conversations-Lexikon*. (New York: Ernst Steiger, 1872), Vol. 6, p. 513.

14. Friedrich List (1789-1846) was one of the most innovative and creative German economic and political thinkers of his time, and focused on the idea of creating a German customs union as the vehicle for achieving not only German, but European unity as well. Such ideas, of course, were considered as a threat to the status quo, thereby forcing List to immigrate to America, only to return later on. For further information about him, see: William Henderson, *Friedrich List: Eine historische Biographie des Gründers des Deutschen Zollvereins und des ersten Visionärs eines vereinten Europas*. (Düsseldorf, 1984). Also, see: Rattermann, *Werke*, Vol. 11, pp. 443-53.

15. A more up-to-date edition of List's works can be found in: *Friedrich List, Schriften, Reden, Briefe*. Hrsg. von Erwin von Beckenrath & Karl Goeser. 10 Vols. (Berlin, 1927-36).

16. For further information about Ginal, see: Wittke, *The German Forty-Eighters*, pp. 10, 127.

17. Philipp Schaff (1819-93) was a well known German-American theologian and the author of numerous influential works. Wittke notes of him that: "He detested rabid atheists and agnostics who undermined religious faith with science and education, and excoriated freethinking Forty-Eighters as misguided and vicious individuals who were 'not only estranged...from all Christianity and the Church, but even from all higher morality and deserve rather to be called the pioneers of heathenism and a new barbarism than of civilization.'" Moreover, he felt that they could only bring "reproach and shame" on the German element. See: Wittke, *The German Forty-Eighters*, p. 137.

18. Schaff's views about America are best revealed in his fascinating portrait of the U.S.: *Amerika: Die politischen, socialen und kirchlich-religiösen Zustände der Vereinigten Staaten von Nordamerika, mit besonderer Rücksicht auf die Deutschen aus eigener Anschauung dargestellt*. (Berlin: Wiegandt & Grieben, 1854). This work was well received not only in the U.S, but in Germany as well. See the favorable review, for example in: *Literarisches Centralblatt für Deutschland*. No. 52(30 December 1854), p. 838. This review itself reflects the international reputation that Schaff enjoyed on both sides of the Atlantic. Koerner obviously felt that Schaff's view were too harsh.

19. Friedrich August Rauch (1806-40) came to America in 1831, therefore before the 1832/33 Revolution, but did so as a result of comments he made against the political order in Germany, in particular his favorable comments in support of Weidig (see footnote no. 5). For further information about him, see: Howard J.B. Ziegler, *Frederick August Rauch, American Hegelian*. (Lancaster, Pa.: Published by Order of the College, 1953).

20. For further information about Leeser (1806-68), who is considered the founding father of the American Jewish press, see: Lance J. Sussman, *Isaac Leeser and the Making of American Judaism.* (Detroit: Wayne State University Press, 1995).

21. Demetrius Augustins Gallitzin (1771-1840) is one of the several fascinating figures discussed by Koerner in this chapter. The son of a Russian prince and the daughter of a German field marshal, he was raised by his mother after his parents had separated, and spoke not only German, but also French, as was then customary among the nobility. For further information about him, see: Rattermann, *Werke*, Vol. 10, pp. 265-90.

22. The "princely fortune" mentioned here, was, according to his biographers, approximately $150,000. See the next footnote for references to these works.

23. The works referred to here are: Peter Heinrich Lemcke, *Leben und Wirken des Prinzen Demerius Gallitzin.* (Münster, 1861), which appeared in translation as: *Life and Work of Prince Demetrius Augustine Gallitzin.* (New York, 1941).

24. Joahnnes Nepomuk Neumann (1811-60) is now known as Saint John Nepomucene Neumann, having been canonized by Pope Paul VI in 1977). See: Donald Attwater and Catherine Rachel John, *The Penguine Dictionary of Saints.* 3rd edition. (New York: Penguin Books, 1993).

25. Drexel (1792-1863) represents another fascinating person discussed by Koerner in this chapter, who really deserves an up-to-date biography. For information see the exhibit catalog: *Francis Martin Drexel (1792-1863): An Artist turned Banker, the Drexel Museum Collection, Drexel University, Philadelphia, Pennsylvania, January 1976-December 1976.* (Philadelphia: Drexel University, 1975).

26. Oswald Seidensticker (1825-94) was one of the major German-American historians of this time, and published extensively in the historical journal, *Der Deutsche Pionier*, and was the author of several valuable works, including a history of the German Society of Pennsylvania (see footnote no. 1, Chapter One for the citation to this work). For a selection of his articles, see his: *Bilder aus der Geschichte der Deutsch-Pennsylvanischen Geschichte.* (New York: Ernst Steiger, 1885). Also, see his bibliography of the first century of German printing in America became the foundation for the following work: Karl John Richard Arndt

and Reimer C. Eck, eds. *The First Century of German Printing in the United States of America: A Bibliography based on the Studies of Oswald Seidensticker and Wilbur H. Oda.* Compiled by Gerd-J. Bötte and Werner Tanhof using a Preliminary Compilation by Annelies Müller. Publications of the Pennsylvania German Society, No. 21. 2 Vols. (Göttingen: Niedersächsische Staats- und Universitätsbibliothek, 1989). At the time of his death, the Pennsylvania German Society paid tribute to him as an "eminent scholar and author," and passed a resolution that was published in the *Pennsylvania German Society Proceedings and Addresses.* 4(1894): 153. This stated that:

> Whereas, in the course of Divine Providence, Dr. Oswald Seidensticker has been removed from the scene of his earthly labors and usefulness; and whereas, though he was not nominally a member of the Pennsylvania German Society, yet was always recognized by it as one of the most sympathetic, distinguished and valuable co-laborers in the work which the Society has set for itself; therefore resolved, that the Pennsylvania German Society herewith expresses its profound sense of the great loss to the community, to the literature of the Germans in America, and to the cause of the Pennsylvania Germans in particular, that has been sustained by the decease of Dr. Oswald Seidensticker, the eminent scholar, historian, and litterateur and distinguished representative of the best elements of our German-American citizenship. Resolved further, that the deep and sincere sympathy and condolence of the Society be conveyed to the bereaved family of the deceased, the pain of whose bereavement in the loss of so tender and true a husband and father must be unutterably great; and finally, resolved, that the above preamble and resolution be engrossed on the Minutes of the Pennsylvania German Society, and a copy of the same be sent to the family of the deceased.

II.   New York, New Jersey, and New England
Chapter Six

1. For a history of German immigration to New York in the period before that discussed by Koerner, see: Friedrich Kapp, *Geschichte der Deutschen im Staate New York bis zum Anfange des neunzehnten Jahrhunderts. Geschichte der deutschen Einwanderung in Amerika.* Dritte, vermehrte Auflage. (New York: E. Steiger, 1869, and also his: *Die Deutschen im Staate New York während des achtzehnten Jahrhunderts.* (New York: E. Steiger, 1884). Although there are more recent works on the topic, these are fairly comprehensive, and have, unfortunately, never been translated, but would make excellent candidates for translated editions. For more recent works, see: Don Heinrich Tolzmann, *German-Americana: A Bibliography.* (Metuchen, New Jersey: Scarecrow Press, 1975), pp. 47-49, and also by the same author: *Catalog of the German-Americana Collection, University of Cincinnati.* (München: K.G. Saur, 1990), Vol. 1, pp. 193-204.

2. For a history of the German Society of New York, see: Klaus Wust, *Guardian on the Hudson: The German Society of the City of New York, 1784-1984.* (New York: The German Society of New York, 1984).

3. Lutterloh and von Weissenfels were two of the many German officers who served in the American Revolution in the Continental Army. Baron von Weissenfels "an officer in the British Army, offered his services to Washington when the Revolution began. He had fought under Wolfe at Quebec and had seen that brave commander die on the Heights of Abraham. After the cessation of hostilities, he settled down as an English officer in New York. There he got married, with General von Steuben as his best man. During the Revolution, he defeated the British at White Plains, accompanied Washington over the Hudson, and took aprt in the battles of Trenton, Princeton, Saratoga, Monmouth Courthouse, and Newton. He died in 1806 in New Orleans." Heinrich Emanual Lutterloh was "major of the guard of the Duke of Brunswick, who met Franklin in London. He became colonel on Washington's staff in 1777, and three years later he was made Quarter-master General of the Army." See: Don Heinrich Tolzmann, *The*

German-American Experience: A Revised and Expanded Edition of Theodore Huebener's The Germans in America. (Amherst, New York: Humanity Books, 2000), pp. 106-07.

4. Friedrich Wilhelm von Steuben (1730-94) served as Inspector General of the Continental Army during the American Revolution. For a recent biography, see: Paul Douglas Lockhart, *The Drillmaster of Valley Forge: The Baron de Steuben and the Making of the American Army.* (New York: Collins, 2008). Also, see: Armin Brandt, *Friedrich Wilhelm von Steuben: Preussischer Offizer und amerikanischer Freiheitsheld.* (Halle: Mitteldeutscher Verlag, 2006), and: Jürgen Brüstle, *Friedrich Wilhelm von Steuben: Eine Biographie.* (Marburg: Tectum Verlag, 2006). For an older work, see: Rudolf Cronau, *The Army of the American Revoluition and its Organizer: Rudolf Cronau's Biography of Baron von Steuben.* Edited by Don Heinrich Tolzmann. (Bowie, MD: Heritage Books, 1998).

5. For a list of the presidents of the German Society of New York, see: Wust, *Guardian,* p. 64.

6. Johann Jakob Astor (1763-1848) came to America in 1784, and became one of the first multi-millionaires in the country by means of the fur trade, real estate, and other business enterprises. For a biography, see: Arthur Douglas Howden Smith, *John Jacob Astor: Landlord of New York.* (Philadelphia: J.B. Lippincott, 1929). Also, see: H.J. Ruetenik, *Berühmte deutsche Vorkämpfer für Fortschritt, Freieheit und Friede, von 1626 bis 1898: Einhunder und fünfzig Biographien mit Portraits.* (Cleveland: Forest City Bookbinding Co., 1899), pp. 134-44.

7. Friedrich Kapp (1824-84) was a Forty-Eighter, who lived in America from 1850-70, editing German-American newspapers and writing several German-American historical works, then returned to Germany, where he served in the Reichstag. For biographical information, see: Horst Dippel, "Kapp, Friedrich," in: *Neue Deutsche Biographie,* Vol. 11, pp. 134ff. Also, see: H.A. Rattermann, "Friedrich Kapp," *Deusch-Amerikanisches Magazin.* 1(1887): 16-36, 226-238, and 360-373. Rattermann also provides a bibliography of Kapp's writings, pp. 371-73, including essays, articles, as well as book publications. Also, see: Ruetenik, *Berühmte deutsche Vorkämpfer,* pp. 317-18.

8. The Heidelberg Catechism was the German Reformed catechism drawn up in the sixteen century in the Palatinate, and often referred to as the Palatine Catechism. It explains the German Reformed Church as did Luther's Catechism explain the Lutheran faith.

9. Kapp's quote was drawn from one his two works cited in footnote no. 1.

10. For a recent edition of this work, which originally appeared in 1839, see: Washington Irving, *Astoria: Adventure in the Pacific Northwest*. Introduction by Kaori O'Connor. (London: KPI Limited, 1987). Kaori O'Connor notes that Irving's work was "a literary *tour de force* that captured the restless, adventurous spirit of that pioneering and commercial age, captivated audiences for whom the West and the frontier were subjects of the deepest fascination, and celebrated the individualism that was then such a dominant note in the American character," p. xi. The work became a bestseller of its time, and was translated in several languages, including German, French, and Russian.

11. For further information about the library, see: Don Heinrich Tolzmann, Alfred Hessel, and Reuben Peiss, *The Memory of Mankind: The Story of Libraries since the Dawn of History*. (New Castle, Delaware: Oak Knoll Press, 2001). Here it is noted: "In 1848, the German-American merchant prince, John Jacob Astor, left $400,000 for the purpose of founding a library, which was incorporated in 1849," p. 120.

12. Astor also served as president of the German Society of New York from 1837 to 1840.

13. Albert Gallatin (1761-1849) came to America from Switzerland in the 1780s, and served as U.S. Secretary of the Treasury. For further information regarding his correspondence with Astor, see: Henry Adams, ed., *The Writings of Albert Gallatin*. 3 vols. (Philadelphia: Lippincott, 1879).

14. Prince Karl Bernhard von Sachsen-Weimar-Eisenach (1792-1862) was well known for his travel reports about his visit to America in the 1820s. See: Heinrich Luden, ed., *Reise Sr. Hoheit des Herzogs Bernhard von Sachsen-Weimar-Eisenach durch Nord-Amerika in den Jahren 1825 und 1826*. (Weimar: W. Hoffmann, 1828).

15. Charles Sealsfield was the pen name for Karl Postl (1793-1864) came to America in 1823, and traveled back and forth between Europe and the U.S., becoming a bestselling author through works published on both sides of the Atlantic. For an introduction to his work, see: Charlotte Branceforte, ed., *The Life and Works of Charles Sealsfield (Karl Postl) (1793-1864)*. (Madison: Max Kade Institute for German-American Studies, 1993). Also, see: H.A. Rattermann, "Charles Sealsfield: Sein Leben und seine Werke," in: H.A. Rattermann, *Gesammelte ausgewählte Werke*. (Cincinnati: Selbstverlag des Verfassers, 1912), Vol. 10, pp. 1-27.

16. See: Charles Sealsfield, *Sämtliche Werke, Bd. 3: Austria as It is: or Sketches of Continental Courts*. Bearbeitet von Karl J.R. Arndt. (Hildesheim: Olms, 1972).

17. August von Platen-Hallermünde (1796-1835) was a German poet. For further biographical information, see: Hartmut Bobzin, , ed., *August Graf von Platen: Leben, Werk, Wirkung*. (Paderborn: Schöningh, 1998).

18. See: Sealsfield, , *Sämtliche Werke, Bd. 8-9: Der Virey und die Aristokraten, oder Mexiko im Jajre 1812.*

19. For other titles by Sealsfield, see his collected works: Sealsfield, *Sämtliche Werke*. Bearbeitet von Karl J.R. Arndt. 24 vols. (Hildesheim: Olms, 1972-91).

20. For further information about Ottendorfer, see: Gerard Wilk, *Americans from Germany*. Edited by Don Heinrich Tolzmann. (Indianapolis: Max Kade German-American Center & Indiana German Heritage Society, 1995), pp. 37-38.

21. For further information on these and other papers mentioned by Koerner in this volume, see: Karl J.R. Arndt and May E. Olson, *The German Language Press of the Americas: Vol. 1: History and Bibliography, 1732-1968: United States of America*. (München: Verlag Dokumentation, 1976).

22. For further information about Schlüter, see: "Ein Veteran der deutsch-amerikanischen Presse aus dem Leben geschieden," *Der Deutsche Pionier*. 13(1881): 404.

23. For the history of the German-American book trade, see: Robert E. Cazden, *A Social History of the German Book Trade in America to the Civil War*. (Columbia, S.C.: Camden House, 1984).

24. For a fascinating account of the underside of life in New York by a German-American authors, see: Gustav Lenning, *Die Nachtseiten von New York und dessen Verbrecherwelt von der Fünften Avenue bis zu den Five Points: Eine vollständige Schilderung der Geheimnisse des New Yorker Lebens. Nach den Mitteilungen eines alten Mitgliedes der New Yorker Geheim-Polizei und nach anderen authentischen Quellen.* (New York: F. Gerhard, 1873).

25. For further information on Grund, see: Ruetenik, *Berühmte deutsche Vorkämpfer*, pp. 224-25.

26. Justus Falckner (1672-1723) was ordained as the first German Lutheran minister in America, and served congregations in New York, New Jersey, and Pennsylvania. For further information, see: Julius Sachse, *Justus Falckner, Mystic and Scholar, Devoit Pietist in Germany, Hermit on the Wissachickon, Missionary on the Hudson: A Bi-Centennial Memorial of the First Regular Ordination of an Orhtodox Pastor in America, Done November 23, 1703, at Gloria Dei, the Swedish Lutheran Church at Wisaco.* (Philadelphia: The Author, 1903).

27. Johann Christoph Kunze (1744-1807) served Lutheran congregations in Pennsylvania and New York, and was also a professor of classical languages at the University of Pennsylvania and Columbia College in New York. For further information about him, see: A.L. Gräbner, *Geschichte der lutherischen Kirche in Amerika.* (St. Louis: Concordia Publishing House, 1892), pp. 460-70.

28. The Old Lutherans were those Lutherans who opposed the merging of the Lutheran and the Reformed Church by the King of Prussia in 1817.Many of these Old Lutherans immigrated to America, including to New York, where they founded the Buffalo Synod. Others went to Missouri, where they established the Missouri Synod. For further information on German-American Lutheran history, see the work cited in footnote no. 28. Regarding the German immigration to Missouri, see; Don Heinrich Tolzmann, ed., *Missouri's German Heritage.* 2nd ed. (Milford, Ohio: Little Miami Pub. Co., 2006), pp. 39-40.

29. Regarding nativism in the nineteenth century, see: Tolzmann, *German-American Experience*, pp. 197-202.

30. August Belmont (1813-90) immigrated to America in 1837, and enjoyed a successful business and political career; he married the daughter of Commodore Matthew C. Perry (1794-1858) was responsible for opening Japan up to the West (Convention of Kanagawa, 1854). For further biographical information about him, see: Irving Katz, *August Belmont: A Political Biography*. (New York: Columbia University Press, 1968). Also, see: Ruetenik, *Berühmte deutsche Vorkämpfer*, pp. 417-20.

31. For further information about Blenker and his regiment, see: Wilhelm Kaufmann, *Germans in the American Civil War*. Translated by Steven Rowan and edited by Don Heinrich Tolzmann, Werner Mueller, and Robert E. Ward. (Carlisle, Pennsylvania: John Kallmann, Publishers, 1999), p. 279.

32. Karl Heinzen (1809-80) was a well known Forty-Eighter, who edited the journal, *Der Pionier*. For further information about his life and work, see: Carl Wittke, *Against the Current: The Life of Karl Heinzen (1809-80)*. (Chicago: University of Chicago Press, 1945).

33. Friedrich Hecker (1811-81) was undoubtedly the best known of the German Forty-Eighters, who came to America, settling near Belleville, Illinois. For his biography, see: Don Heinrich Tolzmann, ed., *The German-American Forty-Eighters, 1848-1998*. (Indianapolis: German-American Center at Indiana University-Purdue University & Indiana German Heritage Society, 1997). Also, see: Sabine Freitag, *Friedrich Hecker: Biographie eines Republikaners*. (Stuttgart: Franz Steiner Verlag, 1998). Also, see: Ruetenik, *Berühmte deutsche Vorkämpfer*, pp. 338-42.

Chapter Seven

1. Isaac Nordheimer (1809-42) was born in Memelsdorf, Germany, and came to New York in 1835. For further information, see: *Concise Dictionary of American Biography*. 2nd ed. (New York: Charles Scribner's Sons, 1977), p. 728.

2. For further information on George J. Adler (1821-68), see: *Who Was Who in America: Historical Volume, 1607-1896*. (Chicago: Marquis Who's Who, 1963), p. 2.

3. Johann Ludwig Tellkampf (1808-76) came to the U.S. in 1838, but returned to Germany shortly before the 1848 Revolution. For further information about him and his brother Theodor August, see: H.A. Rattermann, *Werke*, Vol. 12, pp. 55-66.

4. For further information on Theodor August Tellkampf (1812-83), see the footnote no. 3.

5. For further information on Göpp, see: Tolzmann, *German-American Experience*, p. 172. Also, see: Ruetenik, *Berühmte deutsche Vorkämpfer*, pp. 446-47.

6. Regarding the fascinating work entitled *E Pluribus Unum*, see: *Ibid.*

7. Regarding Theodor Poesche, see: *Ibid.*

8. Adolf Heinrich Strodtmann (1829-79) was a well known German-American author, who came to the U.S. in 1852. See: Robert E. Ward, *A Bio-Bibliography of German-American Writers, 1670-1970.* (White Plains, New York: Kraus, 1985), p. 295.

9. Caspar Butz (1825-85) came to America in 1849 after participating in the 1848 Revolution. For further information, see: Tolzmann, ed., *German-American Literature.* (Metuchen, New Jersey: Scarecrow Press, 1977), pp. 203-15.

10. Karl Nordhoff (1830-??) was born in Erwitte, Westphalia, Prussia, and came to America with his parents in 1835. For further information, see: *Concise Dictionary*, p. 728.

11. Dr. Joseph Hyppolyt Pulte (1811-84) was born in Meschede, Westphalia, and came to the U.S. 1834. He was a specialist in the field of homeopathy, and published many works on the topic. For further information, see: *Concise Dictionary*, p. 814. Wilhelm Nast (1807-99) was well known as the founding father of German Methodism. See: Carl Wittke, *William Nast: Patriarch of German Methodism.* (Detroit: Wayne State University Press, 1959).

12. Hermann Ernst Ludewig (1809-56) was especially well known for his valuable bibliographical work: *Literature of American Local History.* (New York: Privately Printed, 1846).

13. Karl Knortz (1841-1918) was born in Gasrbenheim, Rhenish Prussia, and came to America in 1864. He published many works dealing with American literature,

culture and ethnology, and also translated a great deal of American literature. See: Tolzmann, *German-American Literature*, pp. 222-27.

14. Hermann Kriege (1820-1850) was born in Westphalia, and came to the U.S. in 1845. For further information, see: Ward, *Dictionary*, p. 164.

15. Regarding the 1848 Revolution, see: A.E. Zucker, ed., *The Forty-Eighters: Political Refugees of the German Revolution of 1848*. (New York: Columbia University Press, 1950).

16. Anton Eickhoff (1827-1901) was born in Lippstadt, Westphalia, and came to America after participating in the 1848 Revolution. See: Zucker, *The Forty-Eighters*, pp. 290-91. Also, see: Ruetenik, *Berühmte deutsche Vorkämpfer*, pp. 447-50.

17. Maximilian Oertel (1811-82) was born in Ansbach, and came to the U.S. in 1837. For references to his various works, see: Ward, *Dictionary*, p. 218.

18. Martin Stephan (1777-1846) was born in Stramberg, Moravia and came to the U.S. in 1838 as the leader of the Saxon Lutheran immigration, but was soon expelled due to charges of misconduct. For further information, see: Don Heinrich Tolzmann, *Missouri's German Heritage*, pp. 39-40.

19. Therese Albertine Louise von Jakob (1797-1870) was born in Halle, and came to the U.S. with her husband Eduard Edward Robinson in 1828, and returned to Germany in 1864 after the death of her husband. For further information about her life and work, see: Ward, *Dictionary*, p. 241.

20. Albert Bierstadt (1830-1902) was the German-American artist, who was especially known for his paintings of the American West. For a biographical sketch of him, see: Wilk, *Americans from Germany*, p. 5-7.

21. Thomas Nast (1840-1902) became especially well known as a political cartoonist, and created the donkey symbol for the Democratic Party and the elephant symbol for the Republicans. In the 1860s, he also created the popular image of Santa Claus. For further information about him, see: Wilk, *Americans from Germany*, pp. 34-37. Also, see: Ruetenik, *Berühmte deutsche Vorkämpfer*, pp. 485-88.

Chapter Eight

1. Stephan Molitor (1806-73) was born in Choslitz in Oberfranken, came to America in 1830, and edited German-American newspapers in New York, Buffalo, and finally in Cincinnati. For further information, see: "Stephan Molitor," *Der Deutsche Pionier*. 5(1873): 191-92.

2. For further information about Philipp Dorschheimer (1797-1868), see: Gustav Koerner, "Phillipp Dorschheimer," *Der Deutsche Pionier*. 11(1879): 251-53. For further information about him and his son William Doschheimer (1832-88), see: *Geschichte der Deutschen in Buffalo und Erie County, N.H., mit Biographien und Illustrationen hervorragender Deutsch-Amerikaner, welche zur Entwicklung der Stadt Buffalo beigetragen haben.* (Buffalo, N.Y.: Verlag und Druck von Reinecke & Zesch, 1898), p. 24. This work together with an English translation is available at: http://archivaria.com/GdDbios/GdD1.html. Also, see: Ruetenik, *Berühmte deutsche Vorkämpfer*, pp. 188-92.

3. For information on Rev. A.A. Grabau, see: *Geschichte der Deutschen in Buffalo*, pp. 275-76.

4. Regarding the German element in Illinois, see: Don Heinrich Tolzmann, ed., *Illinois' German Heritage*. (Milford, Ohio: Little Miami Pub. Co.,

5. For further information about Dr. Franz C. Brunck (1810-87), see: *Geschichte der Deutschen in Buffalo*, p. 2.

6. Koerner does not provide any biographies of German-Americans from Rochester, most likely not having the information available to him at the time of the writing of his history. For further information on the German element there, see: Hermann Pfaefflin, *A 100-Year History of the German Community in Rochester, New York (1815-1915)*. Translated from the German by Rudolf Wallenberg and H.J. Swinney and edited by Hugo Huedepohl and Max Schaible. (Rochester, N.Y.: The Federation of German-American Societies, Rochester, N.Y., 2007).

7. Johann Anton Quitmann (1799-58) was born Rhinebeck, New York, and served as a brigadier general in the Mexican War, as governor of Mississippi, and also as a member of Congress. For further information about him, see: Tolzmann, *The

German-American Experience, pp. 197-99. Also, for information about him and his father, see: Ruetenik, *Berühmte deutsche Vorkämpfer*, pp. 144-50.

8. For further information about Adolf Steinwehr (1822-77), see: Kaufmann, *Germans in the American Civil War*, pp. 270-71. Also, see: Ruetenik, *Berühmte deutsche Vorkämpfer*, pp. 389-93.

9. Reference is here made to the following article: H.A. Rattermann, "General von Steinwehr," *Der Deutsche Pionier*. 9(1877): 17-29, 94-103, 160-66.

Chapter Nine

1. For further biographical information about Roebling, see: Don Heinrich Tolzmann, *John A. Roebling and His Suspension Bridge on the Ohio River*. (Milford, Ohio: Little Miami Pub. Co., 2005).

2. For information about Emil Angelrodt, see: Tolzmann, *Missouri's German Heritage*, p. 51.

3. For information on Rapp's colony, see: See: Karl J.R. Arndt, *George Rapp's Harmony Society, 1785-1847*. (Rutherford: Fairleigh Dickinson University Press, 1972), and also his: *George Rapp's Successors and Material Heirs, 1847-1916*. (Rutherford: Fairleigh Dickinson University Press, 1971). Also, see: Ruetenik, *Berühmte deutsche Vorkämpfer*, pp. 151-52.

Chapter Ten

1. For information about Franz Joseph Grund, see Chapter One, footnote no. 25.

2. For further information on Karl Follen (1796-1840), see: Frank Mehring, *Deutsch-Amerikanischer Freiheitskämpfer*. (Giessen, 2004). Also, see: H.A. Rattermann, *Werke*, Vol. 10: 81-120; Ruetenik, *Berühmte deutsche Vorkämpfer*, pp. 202-07; and: George Washington Spindler, *Karl Follen: A Biographical Study*. (Chicago: German-American Historical Society of Illinois, 1917). Spindler notes of Follen: "In the lecture room of the college, from the pulpit and political platform, and through the press, he contributed to the introduction of German ideals which, by fusing with the best spirit of American civilization, were to

become an important factor in the growth of our composite national culture," p. 225.

3. Paul Follen, or as he was generally known, Paul Follenius (1799-1844) was one of the pioneer organizers of German immigration to Missouri. For further information about him, see: Don Heinrich Tolzmann, ed. *Missouri's German Heritage*, pp. 12 and 33.

4. Karl Sand (1795-1820) was executed for the assassination of August von Kotzebue, who was considered a reactionary author.

5. Peter Stephen Du Ponceau (1760-1844) came to America with Baron von Steuben, and served as his secretary, and later served as president of the American Philosophical Society. See: *The Catholic* Encyclopedia, Vol. 5. George Ticknor (1791-1871) was a professor or Romance languages and literatures at Harvard, who studied in Germany and when "called back to a professorship, fought a long battle to reorganize Harvard, trying to raise the undergraduate college to the quality of a good German gymnasium, setting upon this a system of higher instruction like the "philosophische Fakultät," emphasizing lectures versus recitations, and allowing students t proceed at their own pace instead of the familiar lockstep." See: *Germans in Boston*. (Boston: Goethe Society of New England, 1981), p. 16. Edward Everett (1794-1865) served as president of Harvard as well as U.S. Secretary of State. See: Paul Revere Frothingham, *Edward Everett, Orator and Statesman*. (Boston: Houghton Mifflin Co., 1925).

6. William Ellery Channing (1780-1842) was a Unitarian minister at the Arlington Street Church in Boston. For further information about him, see: Charles Timothy Brooks, *William Ellery Channing, A Centennial Memory* (Boston: 1880).

7. John Quincy Adams (1767-1848) served as the sixth President of the United States, and took a great interest in German culture. For further information, see: Annaliese Harding, ed., *John Quincy Adams, Pioneer of German-American Literary Studies: Essays on the Occasion of an Exhibition of Documents, Manuscripts, Books and Prints in the Rare Book Exhibit Room.* (Boston: Boston Public Library, 1979). Erhard Staedler notes here that: "One of the earliest promoters of German-American cultural relations was John Quincy Adams, who acted as America's first ambassador to Prussia," p. 5.

8. For further information on Lieber (1798-1872), see: Charles R. Mack, ed., *Francis Lieber and the Culture of the Mind*. (Columbia: University of South Carolina Press, 2005), and H.A. Rattermann, *Werke*, Vol. 10, pp. 29-66. Also, see: Ruetenik, *Berühmte deutsche Vorkämpfer*, pp. 210-17.

9. See Lieber's *Letters to a Gentleman in Germany*. (Philadelphia: Care, Lea & Blanchard, 1834).

10. Barthold Georg Niebuhr (1776-1831) was a well known German historian, who served as the Prussian ambassador to Rome, 1816-23. For further information about his life and work, see: Gerrit Walther, *Niebuhrs Forschung*. (Stuttgart: Steiner, 1993).

11. For further information on this and other works by Lieber, see: Frank Freidel, *Francis Lieber, Nineteenth Century Liberal*. (Baton Rouge: Louisiana State University Press, 1947). Also, see: Tolzmann, *German-American Literature*, pp. 150-63.

12. See: Francis Lieber, ed., *Encyclopedia Americana*. (Philadelphia: Lea & Carey, 1832-35). This became a standard work before the Civil War, and apparently sold more than one hundred thousand sets.

13. The case of Kaspar Hauser (1812-33) is the incredible story of a child found in 1828 in Nürnberg, whose identity was unknown, but was thought by some to be the prince of Baden. For a recent article about this, see: Kim Carpenter, "I'm not human. I'm Kaspar. The Enigma of Kaspar Hauser," *German Life*. (August/September 2008): 34-37.

14. Joseph-Napoleon Bonaparte (1768-1844) was the elder brother of Napoleon, who went into French exile in America for seventeen years along with other French expatriates after the downfall of Napoleon. See: Patricia Tyson Stroud, *The Man Who had been King: The American Exile of Napoleon's Brother Joseph*. (Philadelphia: University of Pennsylvania Press, 2005).

15. The reference here is to the German-American history by Franz von Löher, *Geschichte und Zustände der Deutschen in Amerika*. (Cincinnati: Eggers & Wulkop, 1847).

16. For a recent study of Germans in New England, see: Robert Paul McCaffery, *Islands of Deutschtum: German-Americans in Manchester, New Hampshire and Lawrence, Massachusetts, 1870-1942.* New German-American Studies, Vol. 11. (New York: Peter Lang Pub. Co., 1996).

17. Leopold Morse (1831-92) was born in Wachenheim, Germany, and came to America in 1849. He owned a successful department store in Boston, and served in Congress from 1877-85. For further information, see: Ruetenik, *Berühmte deutsche Vorkämpfer*, pp. 471-72.

III. Editor's Conclusion

Conclusion

1. Statistical information as to the population size of the German element, the number of German societies, churches and newspapers is drawn from the German-American encyclopedia: Alexander Schem, ed., *Deutsch-Amerikanisches Conversations-Lexikon.*

2. Kaufmann, *Germans in the American Civil War*, p. 105.

3. Tolzmann, *The German-American Experience. A Revised and Expanded Edition of Theodore Huebener's The Germans in America*, p. 454.

4. Shirley J. Riemer, *The German Research Companion.* New revised edition. (Sacramento, California: Lorelei Press, 2000), p. 225.

5. Ibid, p. 221.

6. Ibid, p. 221.

IV. Appendices

1. Seidensticker, *Geschichte*, p. 18.

2. Here Koerner tries to grapple with how to come up with a usable formula to estimate the totality of the German-speaking immigration. Even today when one speaks of the German element as a whole, the U.S. Census statistics for the following ancestry groups have to be taken into consideration: German, Austrian, Swiss, Russian-German, Alsatian, Liechtenstein, Silesian, Pennsylvania-German, etc.

3. For von Löher's discussion of the Pittsburgh Conventions, see his: *Geschichte und Zustände der Deutschen in Amerika.* (Cincinnati: Verlag von Eggers und Wulkop, 1847), pp. 280-89.

Acknowledgements

One of the important manuscript sources that Koerner based his work on was the autobiography and diary of Johann Georg Wesselhöft (1805-59), who published the influential newspaper *Alte und Neue Welt* in Philadelphia, and was one of the founders of the German Settlement Society of Philadelphia, which established the town of Hermann, Missouri. Later in life, Wesselhöft moved from Philadelphia to St. Louis, and finally to Hermann. His manuscripts, which could not be located and are apparently lost, as well as his newspaper were important sources for Koerner's work on Pennsylvania. In tracking down information about him, I was assisted by a number of individuals. Many thanks to Lois Puchta, Director of the Archives and Research Center of the Gasconade County Historical Society in Hermann, for the information she provided about the burial site of Wesselhöft, as well as references to information about him. Also, thanks to Bruce Dean Ketchum of the Deutschheim State Histdoric Site in Hermann for the information that he provided as well. Helpful information was also provided by George Bocklage, President of Friends of the Deutschheim State Historical Site and Dorris Keeven-Franke, both of Washington, Missouri, as well as Adolf Schroeder, University of Missouri-Columbia.

Don Heinrich Tolzmann
Cincinnati, Ohio

About the Editor

Don Heinrich Tolzmann is the author and editor of numerous books on German-American history and culture. He has received many awards, including the Federal Cross of Merit from Germany, the Ohioana Book Award and the Outstanding Achievement Award of the Society for German-American Studies. Until retirement, he served as Curator of the German-Americana Collection and Director of German-American Studies at the University of Cincinnati, and has served on the board of many national and regional German-American societies and organizations. A frequent contributor to various publications, he serves on the board of journals, and is Book Review Editor of *German Life*.

Index

JAN 3 1 2013

9 780806 354989